Contents

D0288497

Introduction

Oxford Take Off In German is designed to help the beginner develop the basic language skills necessary to communicate in German in most everyday situations. It is intended for learners working by themselves, providing all the information and support necessary for successful language learning.

How to use the course

The book and the recording are closely integrated, as the emphasis is on speaking and listening. The recording contains step-by-step instructions on how to work through the units. The presenter will tell you when to use the recording on its own, when to use the book, and when and how to use the two together. The book provides support in the form of transcriptions of the recording material, translations of new vocabulary, and grammar explanations. You'll find this icon ⓐ in the book when you need to listen to the recording.

1 (recording/book) Read the unit objectives on the first page telling you what you will learn in the unit, and then begin by listening to the first **dialogue** on the recording. There are three of these sections. You may not understand everything the first time you hear it, but try to resist the temptation to look at the transcript in the book. The first

activity on the recording will help you develop your listening skills by suggesting things to concentrate on and listen out for. You'll be given the opportunity to repeat some of the key sentences and phrases from the dialogue before you hear it a second time. You may need to refer to the vocabulary list (book) before completing the second activity (book). Listen to the dialogue as many times as you like, but as far as possible try not to refer to the dialogue transcript (book).

2 (book) Once you have listened to all the new language, take some time to work through the **transcript, Vocabulary, Language Building,** and **activities** in the book to help you understand how it works.

3 (recording) Then it's time to practise speaking: first **Pronunciation practice** and then the **Your turn** activity. You will be given all the instructions and cues you need by the presenter on the recording. The first few times you do this you may need to refer back to the vocabulary and language building sections in the book, but aim to do it without the book after that.

4 (book) The fourth learning section, **Culture,** concentrates on reading practice. Try reading it

OXFORD

take off in

German

Heike Schommartz and Andrea Reitz

OXFORD
UNIVERSITY PRESS

OXFORD

UNIVERSITY PRESS

Great Clarendon Street, Oxford OX2 6DP

Oxford University Press is a department of the University of Oxford.
It furthers the University's objective of excellence in research, scholarship,
and education by publishing worldwide in

Oxford New York

Auckland Cape Town Dar es Salaam Hong Kong Karachi
Kuala Lumpur Madrid Melbourne Mexico City Nairobi
New Delhi Shanghai Taipei Toronto

With offices in

Argentina Austria Brazil Chile Czech Republic France Greece
Guatemala Hungary Italy Japan Poland Portugal Singapore
South Korea Switzerland Thailand Turkey Ukraine Vietnam

Oxford is a registered trade mark of Oxford University Press
in the UK and in certain other countries

Published in the United States
by Oxford University Press Inc., New York

© Oxford University Press 2000, 2008

British Library Cataloguing in Publication Data

Data available

Library of Congress Cataloging in Publication Data

Data available

ISBN 978-0-19-953439-5 (Book and CDs)
ISBN 978-0-19-860295-8 (Coursebook)

This coursebook is only available as a component of Take Off In German

2

Commissioning, development, and project management: Tracy Traynor
Audo production: Gerald Ramshaw, Richard Carrington
Music: David Stoll
Design: Keith Shaw
Editorial: Brigitte Lee
Teaching consultant: Jenny Ollerenshaw

Printed in China through Asia Pacific Offset

first without referring to the vocabulary list to see how much you can already understand, making guesses about any words or phrases you are not sure of. The activities which accompany the text will help you develop reading comprehension skills.

5 (recording/book) For the final learning section, return to the recording to listen to the **Story**. This section gives you the opportunity to have some fun with the language and hear the characters in the story use the language you have just learnt in different situations. The aim is to give you the confidence to cope with authentic German. There are activities in the book to help you.

6 (book) Return to the book, and work through the activities in the **Test** section to see how well you can remember and use the language you have covered in the unit. This is best done as a written exercise. Add up the final score and, if it is not as high as you had hoped, try going back and reviewing some of the sections.

7 (recording/book) As a final review, turn to the **Summary** on the last page of the unit. This will test your understanding of the new situations, vocabulary and grammar introduced in the unit. Use the book to prepare your answers, either by writing them down or speaking aloud, then return to the recording to

test yourself. You will be given prompts in English on the recording, so you can do this test without the book.

8 (book) At the very end of each unit you will find some suggestions for **revision** and ideas for further practice.

Each unit builds on the work of the preceding units, so it's very important to learn the vocabulary and structures from each unit before you move on. There are review sections after units 3, 7, 10, and 14 for you to test yourself on the material learnt so far.

Other support features
If you want a more detailed grammar explanation than those given in the Language Building sections, you will find a *Grammar Summary* at the end of the book. For a definition of the grammar terms used in the course, see the *Glossary of Grammatical Terms* on page 245.

The *Answers* section at the end of the book is designed not only to tell you if your responses were correct or not, but also to explain why, where possible. Some activities require you to give information about yourself, so you may also need to check some vocabulary in a dictionary.

At the end of the book you'll find a comprehensive German–English Vocabulary.

The German language

German is spoken by approximately 80 million people in Germany, and by several million in other European countries such as Austria (7 million), Luxemburg (*c.*300,000), Switzerland (3.4 million), and the region of Alsace-Lorraine in France (1.5 million). Other countries outside Europe where German is spoken are Canada (*c.*330,000), Brazil (*c.*550,000), and the United States (the Pennsylvania Dutch, who left Germany during the 18th century, speak a Rhine-Franconian dialect).

In the last few years there have been various attempts to change German spelling, which was consolidated at the end of the 19th century in the *Rechtschreibung der Deutschen Sprache* (*Orthography of the German Language*), by the German philologist Konrad Duden. After much controversy, all except one of the Bundesländer accepted the Rechtschreibreform ('spelling reform'). The Bundesland of Schleswig-Hollstein refused to accept the orthographical changes, and still upholds the former Duden dictionary as the authoritative guide to correct spelling, even though the overall changes are quite small. This course follows the new spelling rules.

To the English native speaker, the main difference between English and German is the use of grammatical genders and cases, which determine the endings of words. The structure of German and English sentences also differ in many instances. However, while at the beginning of the course things may look all too different to you, they will gradually begin to form a pattern. The vocabulary and grammatical structures covered in this course prepare you for everyday conversations in German.

Pronunciation

To achieve good pronunciation, there is no substitute for listening carefully to the recording and, if possible, to German native speakers, and trying to reproduce the sounds you hear. Here are a few guidelines for you to keep in mind when doing so. You will find this section most useful if you listen to the Pronunciation section on the recording as you read it.

Pronunciation

Vowels
Each vowel has a short and a long version. As a general rule, vowels are long when followed by a single consonant or by **h** and short when followed by two consonants. All double vowels are long.

		Phonetic symbol	English approximation	Example
a	short	/a/	*between* hat *and* hut	wann
	long	/a:/	barn	sagen
e	short	/e/	lesson	essen
	long	/e:/	gate	Regen
i	short	/i/	bit	immer
	long	/i:/	ease	Kino
o	short	/o/	hot	noch
	long	/o:/	post	wo
u	short	/ʊ/	put	und
	long	/u:/	moon	Fuß
ä	short	/ɛ/	left	Männer
	long	/ɛ:/	*between* pair *and* pace	spät
ö	short	/œ/	fur	können
	long	/ø:/	burn	mögen
ü	short	/ʏ/	short **ee** *with rounded lips*	müssen
	long	/y:/	longer **ee** *with rounded lips*	müde

Vowel combinations

au long	/au/	cow	Frau, Haus
äu long	/ɔy/	boy	Häuser, Bäume
ei long	/ai/	right	ein, mein
eu long	/ɔy/	boy	heute, Leute
ie long	/i:/	feel	die, Spiel

Consonants
Most consonants are pronounced as in English. The exceptions are:

	Phonetic symbol	English approximation	Example
b at end of word	/p/	bap	ab
d at end of word	/t/	bat	Kind
g at end of word	/k/	tick	Tag
h at end of syllable		*not pronounced, but makes the preceding vowel long*	nehmen, froh
j	/j/	young	ja, jung
s before a vowel	/z/	zoo	Samstag, Gemüse

Written as	Phonetic symbol	English approximation	Example
s otherwise	/s/	sat	lustig
z	/ts/	cats	zwei, ganz
v	/f/	fox	viel, vor
w	/v/	van	wie, wo
ß	/s/	sat	Fuß, Großmutter

Consonant combinations

ch after **a, o, u, au**	/x/	*Scottish* lo**ch**	To**ch**ter, Ku**ch**en
ch otherwise	/ç/	*similar to the first sound in* **h**uge	eu**ch**, mö**ch**ten
sch	/ʃ/	cra**sh**	Fla**sch**e, Ge**sch**enk
tsch	/ʧ/	la**tch**	Deu**tsch**
ig at end of word	/iç/	*similar to the first sound in* **h**uge	drei**ßig**, fert**ig**
sp *generally*	/ʃp/	**sh**p	**Sp**rache
st *generally*	/ʃt/	**sh**t	**St**unde

Starting out
Guten Tag

OBJECTIVES

In this unit you'll learn how to:

- ✓ greet people
- ✓ meet people and give your name
- ✓ order something to drink
- ✓ say please, thank you, and excuse me

And cover the following grammar and language:

- ✓ the present tense of regular verbs
- ✓ formal and informal ways of saying 'you'
- ✓ simple questions
- ✓ the definite article ('the') **der**, **die**, **das**
- ✓ the indefinite article ('a') **ein**, **eine**, **ein**

LEARNING GERMAN 1

Remember that you can go a long way with just a little language. Even if you feel unsure about your ability to form correct, complete sentences, you'll find that it is possible to communicate with just a few words. Above all, don't worry about getting things wrong: people will still be able to understand you.

Now start the recording for Unit 1.

Greetings

Guten Tag

ACTIVITY 1 is on the recording.

ACTIVITY 2

When did these three conversations take place? Pick the correct time of day (morning, afternoon, or evening) for each conversation.

DIALOGUE 1

○ Guten Tag, Frau Herbst.
■ Ah, Herr Müller, guten Tag.

○ Guten Abend, ich heiße Herbst, Peter Herbst. Und wie heißen Sie?
■ Ich heiße Müller, Johann Müller.

○ Guten Morgen, ich heiße Ingrid. Und wie heißt du?
■ Ich heiße Karin.

VOCABULARY	
guten Tag	hello [*literally* good day]
guten Abend	good evening
guten Morgen	good morning
Herr	Mr
Frau	Mrs
ich heiße	I'm called
wie heißen Sie?	what are you called?
Sie	you [*formal*]
und	and

✓ Capital letters

In German, all nouns are capitalized.

guten **Abend** good evening
guten **Morgen** good morning

✓ The letter ß

Note the use of the letter ß in the word **heißen**. This is an extra letter in the German alphabet, called **eszett**, or **scharfes s**. It sounds like 'ss'. You often find ß instead of **ss** after diphthongs (double vowels): **ei, au, ie, eu**.

✓ How to ask a question

In a statement, the subject ('I' / 'you' / 'he' / 'she', etc.) usually comes before the verb.

| Ich | heiße | Müller. | I'm called Müller. |
| *subject* | *verb* | | |

In a question the word order changes: the subject follows the verb.

| Wie | heißen | Sie? | What are you called? |
| | *verb* | *subject* | |

There is more on word order on pages 113 and 137.

✓ Formal and informal address

There are various ways of saying 'you' in German, depending on the level of formality.

Sie ('you') is used in formal situations. As a general rule, you should keep using this form until you are on first-name terms, which doesn't happen as readily as in Britain or the United States. It is often the case that people who have known each other for years still use the formal **Sie** form. Note that **Sie** is always written with a capital.

The informal **du** ('you') is used when you are talking to close friends or children. If you're not sure whether to use **Sie** or **du**, follow the lead of the German person you're talking to. Note that the verb endings for **Sie** and **du** are different: **Sie heißen**, but **du heißt**. For more on verb endings see page 5.

⊙ Now do activities 3 and 4 on the recording.

Kennenlernen

🔊 **ACTIVITY 5** is on the recording.

ACTIVITY 6

Where do they come from? Match each person with the correct city.

Ingrid Herbst   Munich
Frau Jung   Heidelberg
Michael Weiss   Frankfurt
Karl Schmidt   Berlin

DIALOGUE 2

○ Ich heiße Ingrid Herbst. Ich komme aus Berlin.
    Und woher kommen Sie?
■ Ich komme aus Frankfurt, mein Name ist Jung.

○ Ich heiße Michael Weiss. Und wer sind Sie?
■ Ich bin Karl Schmidt. Ich komme aus München.
    Woher kommen Sie?
○ Ich komme aus Heidelberg.

○ Guten Morgen, Frau Jung. Wie geht es Ihnen?
■ Gut, danke. Und Ihnen?
○ Ganz gut, danke.

VOCABULARY	
ich komme	I come
aus	from
woher?	where from?
Sie kommen	you come [*formal*]
mein Name ist	my name is
wer	who
Sie sind	you are [*formal*]
ich bin	I am
München	Munich
wie geht es Ihnen?	how are you? [*formal*]
gut	well
danke	thank you
und Ihnen?	and (how are) you?
ganz gut	fine

✅ Regular verbs

In German, verbs have different endings depending on the subject ('I' / 'you' / 'he' / 'she', etc.). This also happens in English, though to a lesser extent ('I come', 'he comes').

kommen ('to come') is a regular verb in the present tense. All verbs with a regular present tense have the same pattern of endings. Once you have mastered these, you will know the endings for the majority of German verbs. Note that you add the endings to the stem of the verb – the infinitive minus **-en: komm-, heiß-**.

ich komm**e**	I come	wir komm**en**	we come
du komm**st**	you come [*sing.*]	ihr komm**t**	you come [*pl.*]
er / sie / es	he / she / it	sie komm**en**	they come
komm**t**	comes	Sie komm**en**	you come [*formal*]

The verb **heißen** ('to be called') is slightly irregular. It has the same endings as **kommen**, with the exception of the informal **du** form – **du heißt**. On the use of **ihr** see page 49.

From now on, verbs will be given in the infinitive form in the vocabulary sections.

trinken to drink	**kaufen** to buy	**spielen** to play
gehen to go	**bezahlen** to pay	

✅ *Sie*

The formal **Sie** ('you') is used whether you're talking to one person or to several people.

Wie heißen **Sie**? What are you called?
Woher kommen **Sie**, Ingrid und Peter? Ingrid and Peter, where do you come from?

ACTIVITY 7

Put the words in the correct order to form a sentence, and then translate them.

1 heiße / Herbst / Johann / ich
2 Karin Müller / mein Name / ist
3 aus Berlin / ich / komme
4 heißen / wie / Sie
5 kommen / woher / Sie

🎧 Now do activities 8 and 9 on the recording.

🎧 **ACTIVITY 10** is on the recording.

ACTIVITY 11

What did Karin and Susanne order? Write your answer in English.

Susanne _____

Karin _____

DIALOGUE 3

○ Hallo Karin! Wie geht es dir?
■ Oh, hallo Susanne! Danke gut, und dir?
○ Sehr gut. Trinkst du auch eine Tasse Kaffee?
■ Nein, ich trinke eine Tasse Tee.
▼ Was darf es sein?
○ Eine Tasse Kaffee mit Milch und Zucker, bitte.
■ Und ich trinke eine Tasse Tee, bitte.

VOCABULARY	
wie geht es dir?	how are you? [*informal*]
und dir?	and (how are) you? [*informal*]
sehr	very
du	you [*informal*]
trinken	to drink
auch	also
die Tasse	cup
der Kaffee	coffee
nein	no
der Tee	tea
was darf es sein?	what would you like to order? [*literally* what is it to be?]
mit	with
die Milch	milk
der Zucker	sugar
bitte	please

✓ *der / die / das* and *ein / eine / ein*

All German nouns have a gender, and this determines the form of the definite article ('the') or indefinite article ('a') that goes with the noun. There are three genders in German: masculine, feminine, and neuter.

	the			a	
m	*f*	*n*	*m*	*f*	*n*
der	**die**	**das**	**ein**	**eine**	**ein**
der Wein	**die Milch**	**das Glas**	**ein Kaffee**	**eine Tasse**	**ein Bier**
the wine	the milk	the glass	a coffee	a cup	a beer

The best way to learn the gender of a noun is to memorize each new noun you learn with its article.

✓ *Ihnen / dir*

Ihnen is another form of the formal word for 'you' used in certain contexts, for example in the phrase **Wie geht es Ihnen?** ('How are you?'). The uses of **dir** and **Ihnen** are covered in more detail in Unit 8.

dir, another form of the word for 'you', is the informal equivalent of **Ihnen**. It's used in phrases such as **Wie geht es dir?** ('How are you?').

✓ *eine Tasse Kaffee*

Note that in the phrase **eine Tasse Kaffee** ('a cup of coffee'), there's no word in German for 'of'. Other expressions are:

eine Flasche Mineralwasser   a bottle of mineral water
ein Glas Orangensaft   a glass of orange juice
ein Glas Rotwein   a glass of red wine

ACTIVITY 12

You're in a café in Berlin. How would you order a cup of coffee with milk and sugar, a glass of orange juice, and a beer?

ACTIVITY 13

Match each German sentence with the correct English translation.

1 How are you?   a Was trinkst du?
2 What will you have to drink?   b Was darf es sein?
3 What would you like to order?   c Wie geht es dir?

⟪🎧⟫ Now do activities 14 and 15 on the recording.

1.4 Lake Constance
Der Bodensee

The shoreline of Lake Constance (**Bodensee**) is shared by the three main German-speaking countries: Switzerland, Austria, and Germany. Most of the lake belongs to Germany and it is one of the most popular German holiday resorts.

The 'Seehas' train is an interesting way to visit some of the smaller towns on the lake. (**Seehas** means 'lake hare' and is the traditional name for anyone who lives near the lake.) Cultural and historical points of interest round the lake include the cities of Konstanz, Friedrichshafen, and Lindau on the German side, Bregenz in Austria, and Rohrschach on the Swiss shore.

Konstanz, where the story you are going to hear next takes place, is located right on the Swiss border, and its university attracts students from all over Germany. Despite being a rather small city, Konstanz is a cultural centre of the region with a lively bar and restaurant scene.

Unfortunately, staying in Konstanz is costly! Have a look at this list of hotels and guesthouses in Konstanz. Can you find the German words for the following?

1 guest house
2 street
3 single room
4 double room
5 hotel
6 with shower
7 with en-suite bathroom

Pension Hänsel
Zollernstraße

Einzelzimmer	€ 25,50
Doppelzimmer	€ 48,50

Hotel Gertrud
Bodenstraße

Einzelzimmer mit Dusche	€ 31,70
Doppelzimmer mit Dusche	€ 59
Einzelzimmer mit Bad	€ 53,60
Doppelzimmer mit Bad	€ 86,90

(1A) HERZLICH WILLKOMMEN!
WELCOME!

It's a hot summer evening in Konstanz. Peter Ritter arrives at the reception of the Hotel Gertrud after a long drive from Hamburg. He is greeted by Susanne, the daughter of the hotel's owner, Frau Semmler.

Entschuldigung!	excuse me!
wie bitte?	I beg your pardon?
da sind Sie ja!	there you are!
herzlich	warm, kind
herzlich willkommen!	welcome!
aber	but
müde	tired
natürlich	of course
nichts	nothing
gerne!	certainly!
also gut ...	all right then ...
prost!	cheers!

ACTIVITY 17

Who says what? Is it Peter (P), Susanne (S), or Frau Semmler (FS)?

1	Entschuldigung!	P / S / FS
2	Wie heißen Sie bitte?	P / S / FS
3	Da sind Sie ja!	P / S / FS
4	Aber ich bin sehr müde.	P / S / FS
5	Trinken Sie eine Tasse Kaffee?	P / S / FS
6	Nichts, danke.	P / S / FS

ACTIVITY 18

One of the following things does not happen. Which is it?

___ Peter arrives at the Hotel.
___ Susanne greets Peter.
___ Frau Semmler welcomes Peter.
___ Peter declines a coffee.
___ Peter asks for a cup of tea.
___ Frau Semmler decides she will have a beer.

Peter	Puhh! Guten Tag!
Susanne	Guten Abend!
Peter	Ach, Entschuldigung! Guten Abend!
Susanne	Wie heißen Sie, bitte?
Peter	Peter Ritter.
Susanne	Wie bitte?
Peter	Peter Ritter.
Frau Semmler	Da sind Sie ja, Herr Ritter! Herzlich willkommen!
Peter	Hallo, Frau Semmler! Vielen Dank!
Frau Semmler	Wie geht es Ihnen denn, Herr Ritter?
Peter	Danke, ganz gut. Aber ich bin sehr müde.
Frau Semmler	Ja, natürlich. Trinken Sie eine Tasse Kaffee?
Peter	Nein, danke. Aber ein Bier!
Frau Semmler	Gerne! Ich trinke auch ein Bier! Susanne, was trinkst du?
Susanne	Nichts, danke.
Frau Semmler	Also gut.
	Prost, Herr Ritter!
Peter	Prost, Frau Semmler!

Test

Now it's time to test your progress in Unit 1.

1 Match these words and phrases to their German translations. Watch out: there is one German phrase too many!

1	Good morning!	a	Danke
2	How are you? (formal)	b	Mein Name ist …
3	I come from …	c	Guten Morgen!
4	My name is …	d	Wie gehts?
5	I am …	e	Ich komme aus …
6	You are …	f	Wie geht es Ihnen?
7	Thank you	g	Ich bin …
		h	Sie sind …

`7`

2 Add the correct endings for the verbs (**-e**, **-st**, **-t**, or **-en**).

1 Ich heiß___ Ingrid Herbst.
2 Wie heiß__ Sie?
3 Woher komm__ Sie?
4 Ich komm__ aus Frankfurt.
5 Ich trink__ ein Glas Cola.

`5`

3 **Der**, **die**, or **das**? Choose the correct form of the article.

1 Glas   _____
2 Flasche   _____
3 Tasse   _____

`3`

4 Can you sort these phrases into a dialogue?

1 Guten Morgen, Frau Müller!
2 Sehr gut, und Ihnen?
3 Ah, guten Morgen, Frau Herbst!
4 Auch gut, danke.
5 Wie geht es Ihnen?

`5`

5 How would you say the following in German? (2 points for each correct answer, 1 point if you make one error.)

1 I am called …
2 A bottle of mineral water, please.
3 A glass of orange juice, please.
4 A cup of tea with milk, please.
5 Good evening.

10

6 Two friends, Susanne and Karin, meet at a bar in Konstanz. Using the outline of their conversation in 1–5, can you complete the dialogue below?

1 The two friends greet each other.
2 They ask 'How are you?'.
3 Karin asks Susanne what she will have to drink.
4 Susanne says she will have a beer.
5 Karin orders a beer and a glass of red wine.

Susanne: Hallo Karin! _____ ?
Karin: _____ gut, und ____?
Susanne: Auch _____, danke.
Karin: Was trinkst ___?
Susanne: Ich _____ ein _____.
Karin: _____ Bier und _____ Glas _____, bitte.

10

TOTAL SCORE **40**

If you scored less than 30, go through the dialogues and the Language Building sections again before completing the Summary on page 14.

Summary 1

 Now try this final test summarizing the main points covered in this unit. You can check your answers on the recording.

How would you:
1 greet someone in the morning? in the afternoon? in the evening?
2 ask for someone's name?
3 give your own name?
4 ask someone you don't know very well how she is?
5 ask where she comes from?
6 say that you come from England?
7 ask a friend what he'll have to drink?
8 order a coffee with milk and sugar?
9 say 'thank you'?

REVISION

Before moving on to Unit 2, play Unit 1 through again and compare what you can say and understand now with what you knew when you started. Make a note of any vocabulary you still feel unsure of. It might also be a good idea to go through the verb endings again, since you will have to use these all the time.

If you feel you still haven't got to grips with what has been taught in Unit 1, do go through it slowly again. It is better to do the unit a couple of times and be really sure of what you have learned than to rush ahead when you've not fully mastered new material.

Remember that it will also be useful revision to come back and listen to Unit 1 again after working through the next few units, in order to reinforce what you have learned here.

2

Telling the time
Wie spät ist es?

OBJECTIVES

In this unit you'll learn how to:

- ✓ count from 0 to 20
- ✓ ask and tell the time
- ✓ say and understand when events start and finish
- ✓ ask about opening and closing times
- ✓ ask for something to be repeated

And cover the following grammar and language:

- ✓ the subject pronoun 'it' – **er, sie, es**
- ✓ the verb **sein** ('to be')
- ✓ negatives with **nicht** ('not')
- ✓ the prepositions **um, von … bis** in time phrases
- ✓ the modal verb **können** ('can', 'be able')

LEARNING GERMAN 2

Don't try to do too much at once. You will find you can learn more effectively if you study for half an hour or so at regular intervals, rather than try to do a whole unit at one sitting.

It also helps if you can learn with someone else. If you can persuade a friend or family member to study with you, it will give you an extra impetus to keep working. Agree times to meet and goals for the week, and test each other regularly.

Now start the recording for Unit 2.

Wie spät ist es?

ACTIVITY 1 is on the recording.

ACTIVITY 2

1 What are Sabine and Christine planning to do?
2 When does the film begin?
3 Why does Sabine decide not to have a coke?
4 Where does she decide to buy her drink?

DIALOGUE 1

○ Hallo Sabine.
■ Hallo Christine. Puh, es ist so heiß! Ich trinke eine Cola.
○ Tut mir Leid, aber wir sind schon spät.
■ Warum? Wann beginnt der Film?
○ Der Film beginnt um neun Uhr.
■ Wie spät ist es jetzt?
○ Es ist zehn vor neun. Wir sind spät.
　 Du kannst im Kino eine Cola kaufen.
■ Gut, ich kaufe im Kino eine Cola.

VOCABULARY

es ist	it is
so	so
heiß	hot
tut mir Leid	I'm sorry
wir sind	we are
schon	already
spät	late
warum	why
wann	when
beginnen	to start
der Film	film, movie
um neun Uhr	at nine o'clock
wie spät ist es?	what time is it?
jetzt	now
vor	before
können	to be able
im Kino	at the cinema, at the movie theatre
kaufen	to buy

✓ The numbers from 0 to 20

0 null			
1 eins	6 sechs	11 elf	16 sechzehn
2 zwei	7 sieben	12 zwölf	17 siebzehn
3 drei	8 acht	13 dreizehn	18 achtzehn
4 vier	9 neun	14 vierzehn	19 neunzehn
5 fünf	10 zehn	15 fünfzehn	20 zwanzig

✓ Telling the time

Es ist **fünf Uhr**. It's five o'clock.
Um fünf Uhr. At five o'clock.

Es ist **Viertel vor** fünf. It's quarter to five.
Es ist **Viertel nach** fünf. It's quarter past five.

zwanzig **nach** acht twenty past eight
zwanzig **vor** neun twenty to nine

Minuten is added in more formal contexts, such as on radio or television.

zwanzig **Minuten** nach acht twenty (minutes) past eight

✓ Sentences with *können* ('to be able')

ich kann	I can	wir können	we can
du kannst	you can	ihr könnt	you can
er / sie / es kann	he / she / it can	sie können	they can
		Sie können	you can [*formal*]

können is a modal verb (verbs such as 'can', 'should', and 'must' in English). In German, modal verbs are always accompanied by an infinitive (such as **kaufen**, 'to buy', or **trinken**, 'to drink'), which has to be placed at the end of the sentence.

Ich **kann** eine Cola **kaufen**. [*literally* I can a coke buy.]
I can buy a coke.

Du **kannst** das Mineralwasser **trinken**. You can drink the mineral water.

ACTIVITY 3

Rearrange the following elements to make sentences.

1 der Film / wann / beginnt
2 wie viel / es / Uhr / ist
3 spät / sind / wir
4 du / eine Cola / kannst / trinken
5 eine Tasse Kaffee / kannst / trinken / du

Now do activities 4 and 5 on the recording.

2.2 Opening and closing times
Öffnungszeiten

 ACTIVITY 6 is on the recording.

ACTIVITY 7

1	The post office closes at	16.00	17.00	18.00
2	What time is it in the dialogue?	4.30 p.m.	4.45 p.m.	5 p.m.
3	The bank closes at	14.00	14.30	15.00

DIALOGUE 2

○ Entschuldigung, wo kann ich hier Briefmarken kaufen?

■ Briefmarken? Die Post verkauft Briefmarken. Aber sie schließt um siebzehn Uhr.

○ Wie viel Uhr ist es?

■ Es ist Viertel vor fünf.

▼ Oh, und wo können wir Geld wechseln?

■ Die Bank und die Touristeninformation wechseln Geld. Die Bank schließt leider schon um vierzehn Uhr.

▼ Wann hat die Touristeninformation geöffnet?

■ Sie hat von neun bis neunzehn Uhr geöffnet.

○ Vielen Dank. Auf Wiedersehen.

VOCABULARY

die Öffnungszeiten	opening times
wo	where
hier	here
die Briefmarken	stamps
die Post	post office
verkaufen	to sell
schließen	to close
wie viel Uhr ist es?	what time is it?
das Geld	money
wechseln	to exchange
die Bank	bank
die Touristeninformation	tourist information office
leider	unfortunately
wann hat ... geöffnet?	when is ... open? [*literally* when has ... opened?]
von ... bis	from ... until
hat ... geöffnet	is open
vielen Dank	thank you very much
auf Wiedersehen	goodbye

✓ Subject pronoun 'it' – er, sie, es

The German word for 'it' (as the subject of a sentence) has three different forms, depending on the gender of the word it is replacing.

der → er **Der Wein** ist ziemlich teuer, aber **er** schmeckt gut.
The wine is quite expensive, but it tastes good.

die → sie **Die Post** verkauft Briefmarken. **Sie** hat bis fünf Uhr geöffnet.
The post office sells stamps. It's open until five o'clock.

das → es **Das Brot** schmeckt gut. **Es** ist aus Frankreich.
The bread tastes good. It's from France.

✓ The verb sein ('to be') – irregular

ich bin	I am	wir sind	we are
du bist	you are	ihr seid	you are
er / sie / es ist	he / she / it is	sie sind	they are
		Sie sind	you are [formal]

✓ More on time

In English, 'half past nine' means 9.30 – you are saying how much time has passed since the full hour. However, in German, **halb neun** means 8.30, or literally, 'half an hour to nine'. You say how much time is left to the full hour. So **halb zehn** is 9.30, **halb elf** 10.30, and so on.

Germans often use the 24-hour clock especially in broadcasting and in official statements.

✓ Questions with a modal verb and a question word

In questions with a modal verb and a question word (such as **wo**, 'where', **wann**, 'when'), the modal verb appears after the question word and the infinitive goes to the end.

Wo kann ich hier Postkarten **kaufen**? Where can I buy postcards here?

ACTIVITY 8

What time is it?

1 halb fünf   2 halb sieben   3 halb acht   4 halb zwölf
a 7.30   b 11.30   c 4.30   d 6.30

ACTIVITY 9

er, sie, or **es**? Fill in the correct subject pronoun.

die Post / das Geld / das Kino / die Briefmarke / der Film / der Tee

🎧 Now do activities 10 and 11 on the recording.

19

2.3 Going to the cinema
Ins Kino gehen

ACTIVITY 12 is on the recording.

ACTIVITY 13

When do the films begin and how much are the tickets?

a *Golden Eye*   b *Das Piano*   c *Dr Dolittle*

DIALOGUE 3

○ Hallo, ist dort das Capitol?

■ Nein, hier ist nicht das Capitol. Hier ist das Princess. Sie haben die falsche Telefonnummer.

○ Haben Sie die richtige Nummer?

■ Ja, natürlich. Sie ist 7-4-8-5-3-7.

○ Können Sie das bitte wiederholen?

■ Ja, 7-4-8-5-3-7.

○ Vielen Dank. Auf Wiederhören.

○ Beginnt der James Bond Film heute Abend um acht Uhr?

▼ *Golden Eye* beginnt nicht um acht Uhr. Er beginnt um 9.30. *Das Piano* beginnt um 8.00 Uhr und um 6.00 Uhr zeigen wir *Dr Dolittle*.

○ Wie viel kostet die Eintrittskarte?

▼ *Golden Eye* und *Das Piano* kosten €8. *Dr Dolittle* kostet €6 für Kinder und €8 für Erwachsene.

VOCABULARY

ist dort	is this [*on the phone*]
nicht	not
haben	to have
die falsche Telefonnummer	the wrong telephone number
die richtige Nummer	the right number
wiederholen	to repeat
auf Wiederhören	goodbye [*on the phone*]
heute Abend	this evening
zeigen	to show
wie viel	how much
kosten	to cost
die Eintrittskarte	ticket
für	for
die Kinder	children
der Erwachsene	adult

✓ Negatives with *nicht*

nicht, meaning 'not', is used with names (**Herr Müller**), time phrases (**um sieben Uhr**), and nouns preceded by a definite article (**das Kino**).

Das ist **nicht Herr Müller**. This is not Herr Müller.
Der Film beginnt **nicht um acht Uhr**. The film doesn't begin at eight o'clock.
Das ist **nicht das Kino**. This is not the cinema.

In these examples **nicht** always comes before the noun or phrase it negates.

You will learn more about negatives in Unit 4.

✓ Asking questions without a question word

In questions without a question word, the verb comes at the beginning of the sentence, followed by the subject.

Trinken Sie eine Tasse Tee? [*literally* Drink you a cup of tea?]
Will you have a cup of tea?

Kann ich Briefmarken kaufen?
Can I buy stamps?

Hast du die Eintrittskarte?
Do you have the ticket?

ACTIVITY 14

Put the following sentences into the negative.

Example: Der Wein ist teuer. Der Wein ist nicht teuer.

1 Der Mann heißt Müller.
2 Der Film beginnt um 9.30.
3 Das ist der James Bond Film.
4 Das ist das Hotel Gertrud.

ACTIVITY 15

These questions are muddled up. Correct the word order.

1 Sie / trinken / eine Tasse Tee
2 haben / Sie / eine Briefmarke
3 wechseln / Sie / können / Geld
4 eine Cola / du / kaufen / kannst
5 der Film / um acht Uhr / beginnt

Now do activities 16 and 17 on the recording.

2.4 Opening times
Öffnungszeiten

The following passage will tell you about some of the peculiarities of German shop opening hours. You may find some of the regulations quite surprising!

ACTIVITY 18

Which of the following statements about the text are true, and which are false?

1	Many supermarkets are open all night.	T / F
2	Some bakeries open at six o'clock on Saturdays.	T / F
3	Many hairdressers are closed on Mondays.	T / F
4	On Sundays only service stations are open.	T / F
5	You can buy some groceries at service stations.	T / F

Viele Geschäfte in Deutschland haben nur von 9.00 bis 18.30 geöffnet. Große Supermärkte öffnen von 9.00 bis 20.00 Uhr. Manche Bäckereien öffnen am Samstag schon um 6 Uhr und schließen um 14 Uhr. Viele Friseure haben montags geschlossen. Sonntags haben nur Tankstellen und ein paar Bäckereien geöffnet. Dort können Sie auch ein paar Lebensmittel kaufen.

viele Geschäfte	many shops, many stores
in Deutschland	in Germany
nur	only
der Supermarkt	supermarket
große Supermärkte	large supermarkets
öffnen	to open
manche	some
die Bäckereien	bakeries
am Samstag	on Saturday
die Friseure	hairdressers
haben … geschlossen	… are closed [*literally* … have closed]
montags	on Mondays
sonntags	on Sundays
die Tankstellen	service stations, gas stations
ein paar	a few
die Lebensmittel	groceries

CULTURE

22

 **ACTIVITY 19**

A supermarket is offering discounts on certain items, but unfortunately the flyer with all the special offers written on it is torn. Listen to the supermarket announcement on the recording. Can you write down the correct prices for each item?

1 Pfund Spagetti
6 Baguettebrötchen
1 kg Bananen
5 Flaschen Bier
5 Kilo-Packung Waschmittel
1 Flasche Wein

€7
€0,79
€2,10
€0,60
€0,80
€4

unsere Angebote	our offers
das Pfund	pound
die Bananen	bananas
das Waschmittel	washing powder, detergent
die fünf Kilo-Packung	five-kilo pack
die Baguettebrötchen	bread rolls

PETERS PLÄNE
PETER'S PLANS

Back to the Hotel Gertrud. Frau Semmler and Susanne are busy clearing the breakfast tables in the dining hall.
Everybody except Peter Ritter has left. He's lingering over his breakfast, and Susanne asks him about his plans for the day.

noch eine Tasse	another cup [*literally* yet a cup]
Herrn	to Mr, for Mr [*dative of* **Herr**; *see Unit 8*]
bringen	to bring
die Pläne	plans
heute	today
heute Morgen	this morning
schwimmen gehen	to go swimming
heute Abend	this evening
ins Kino gehen	to go to the cinema, to go to the movies
was machen Sie heute?	what are you going to do today?
machen	to do, make
heute Nachmittag	this afternoon
zum Friseur	to the hairdresser's
bleiben	to stay
die Lebensmittellieferung	grocery delivery
der Friseurtermin	hairdresser's appointment
schade!	what a pity!

ACTIVITY 20

Who said what? Listen again to the dialogue. Decide whether Peter (P), Susanne (S), or Frau Semmler (FS) said the following. Then put the sentences in the order you hear them.

1 Was? Kannst du heute nicht im Hotel bleiben? P / S / FS
2 Haben Sie schon Pläne für heute? P / S / FS
3 Die Lebensmittellieferung kommt heute Nachmittag. P / S / FS
4 Ich gehe heute Nachmittag zum Friseur. P / S / FS
5 Trinken Sie noch eine Tasse Kaffee? P / S / FS

ACTIVITY 21

Decide whether the following statements are true or false.

1 Peter has another cup of coffee.	T / F
2 Peter is going to play tennis this morning.	T / F
3 Peter is going to the cinema this evening.	T / F
4 Susan has a hairdresser's appointment this morning.	T / F
5 Frau Semmler is expecting a grocery delivery in the afternoon.	T / F

ACTIVITY 22

Write down in English what Peter and Susanne are doing today.

PETER	SUSANNE
1 Heute Morgen:	1 Heute Nachmittag:
_____	_____
2 Heute Abend:	
_____	

STORY TRANSCRIPT

Frau Semmler	Trinken Sie noch eine Tasse Kaffee, Herr Ritter?
Peter	Ja, sehr gerne.
Frau Semmler	Susanne, kannst du Herrn Ritter noch eine Tasse Kaffee bringen?
Susanne	Ja, naturlich.
	Hier ist der Kaffee.
Peter	Vielen Dank, Susanne.
Susanne	Haben Sie schon Pläne für heute, Herr Ritter?
Peter	Ja, heute Morgen gehe ich schwimmen, und heute Abend gehe ich ins Kino. Und was machen Sie heute?
Susanne	Ich gehe heute Nachmittag zum Friseur.
Frau Semmler	Was? Kannst du heute nicht im Hotel bleiben?
	Die Lebensmittellieferung kommt heute Nachmittag.
Susanne	Nein, tut mir Leid. Der Friseurtermin ist um drei Uhr.
Frau Semmler	Ach, schade!

Test

Now it's time to test your progress in Unit 2.

1 Rearrange the following elements to ask questions.

Wo	kostet	Sie
Woher	beginnt	die Bank
Wann	ist	der Kaffee
Wie viel	kommen	der Film

4

2 Fill the blanks using the correct form of **sein**.

1 Der Wein ___ aus Deutschland.
2 Die Kinder ___ in England.
3 ___ Sie aus Hamburg?
4 Wir ___ spät.
5 Wie viel Uhr ___ es?
6 Hier ___ nicht das Princess, Sie haben die falsche Nummer.

6

3 **Der, die**, or **das**? Choose the correct article.

1 _____ Film
2 _____ Kino
3 _____ Minute
4 _____ Kind
5 _____ Telefonnummer

5

4 In the following sentences replace the underlined noun by a subject pronoun (**er**, **sie**, or **es**).

1 <u>Der Mann</u> trinkt ein Bier.
2 <u>Das Kind</u> kauft eine Cola.
3 <u>Die Telefonnummer</u> ist falsch.
4 <u>Die Bank</u> schließt um 14 Uhr.
5 <u>Der Film</u> beginnt um 21 Uhr.

5

5 What is the German for the following phrases? (2 points for each correct answer, 1 if you make one error.)

    1 Can I buy a cup of coffee?
    2 Can I pay for a coke and a mineral water?
    3 When does the film start?
    4 How much is a ticket?
    5 Do you have the right telephone number?

10

6 Claire and Susanne meet in a café. Read the outline of their conversation in 1–4, then complete the dialogue below.

    1 They greet each other, asking 'How are you?'.
    2 Susanne asks if the film starts at eight o'clock.
    3 Claire tells her that it starts at 8.30.
    4 Susanne says they can have a cup of tea.

Susanne: Hallo Claire. _____?
Claire: Danke_____und _____?
Susanne: Auch gut. _____ der Film um acht Uhr?
Claire: Nein, ____beginnt nicht um acht Uhr. _____beginnt um 8.30.
Susanne: Oh wir _____ noch eine Tasse Tee
_____.

10

TOTAL SCORE **40**

If you scored less than 30 go through the dialogues and the Language Building sections again before completing the Summary on page 28.

Summary 2

 Now try this final test summarizing the main points covered in the unit. You can check your answers on the recording.

How would you:
1 count to 10?
2 ask what time it is?
3 say it's 3.30?
4 ask when the bank is open?
5 ask if you can buy stamps here?
6 ask for someone to repeat something?
7 say goodbye at the end of a phone call?
8 ask how much a cup of coffee costs?
9 ask where you can change money?

REVISION

Before moving on to Unit 3, which covers shopping and money and introduces more numbers, make sure you're familiar with the numbers up to 20. To review them, ask a friend to say some numbers in English, then see if you can give the German straightaway.

3

Money, Money, Money
Geld, Geld, Geld

OBJECTIVES

In this unit you'll learn how to:

- ✔ count from 20 to 100
- ✔ get by at the post office
- ✔ say what you have to do and what you would like to do
- ✔ ask for items and prices
- ✔ ask for the right size when trying on clothes in a clothes shop

And cover the following grammar and language:

- ✔ plurals of nouns
- ✔ the modal verb **müssen** ('must', 'have to')
- ✔ the modal verb form **ich möchte** ('I'd like')
- ✔ verbs with stems ending in **-t**
- ✔ the accusative case of definite and indefinite articles

LEARNING GERMAN 3

Learning vocabulary is very important when you are learning a new language. Write down new words in a notebook or on index cards. In the beginning, it will be helpful to write down whole phrases as well as single words. You may want to organize your vocabulary according to topics. For instance, you could start collecting words and phrases that have to do with food, clothes, the post office, and so on. In this way, you will have key words and phrases to hand when you're actually out shopping in Germany.

Now start the recording for Unit 3.

3.1 At the post office
Wie viel kostet die Briefmarke?

 ACTIVITY 1 is on the recording.

ACTIVITY 2

Who says what – the post office clerk (C) or Frau Specht (S)?

1 Ich möchte einen Brief nach England schicken.   _ C _ S
2 Es tut mir Leid. Wir haben geschlossen.   _ C _ S
3 Ich muss einen Brief nach England schicken.   _ C _ S
4 Wie viel kostet die Briefmarke?   _ C _ S
5 Ein Brief nach England kostet 70 Cent.   _ C _ S

DIALOGUE 1

○ Guten Tag, ich möchte einen Brief nach England schicken.
■ Es tut mir Leid, aber es ist 12 Uhr. Wir haben geschlossen.
○ Nein, es ist erst fünf vor zwölf.
■ Also gut. Was möchten Sie?
○ Ich muss einen Brief nach England schicken. Wie viel kostet die Briefmarke?
■ Ein Brief nach England kostet 70 Cent.
○ 70 Cent! Das ist aber teuer!
  Vielen Dank. Auf Wiedersehen.
■ Auf Wiedersehen.

VOCABULARY	
ich möchte	I would like
der Brief(e)	letter
nach	to
schicken	to send
erst	only
ich muss	I must, I have to
das	that
das ist aber teuer!	that's quite expensive!

✓ Saying what you have to do and what you would like to do

You use the modal verb **müssen** to say what you have to do. Remember to place the infinitive at the end of the sentence:

Ich **muss** einen Brief nach England **schicken**.
I have to send a letter to England.

To express what you would like or want to do, you use the modal verb form **ich möchte** ('I'd like'):

Ich **möchte** einen Brief nach England **schicken**.
I would like to send a letter to England.

✓ Plurals of nouns

From now on, vocabulary lists will give plural endings of nouns, and any vowel changes in the plural, in brackets after the noun. For example: **der Brief(-e)**, plural form Briefe. Note that the definite article for all plural nouns is **die: die Briefe**. A full explanation of how plurals are formed and how they are shown is given on pages 225–6.

✓ The direct object

The subject (S) of a sentence performs the action expressed by the verb (V), while the direct object (DO) of a sentence receives the action expressed by the verb (V).

Der Mann	schlägt	→	**den** Hund.	**Der** Hund	beißt	→	**den** Mann.
The man	hits		the dog.	The dog	bites		the man.
S	V		DO	S	V		DO

	Ich	schicke	→	**einen** Brief	nach England.
	I	am sending		a letter	to England.
	S	V		DO	

The form of the article changes according to gender and whether it is the subject (in the nominative case) or the object (in the accusative case).

	m	*f*	*n*	*m*	*f*	*n*
Nominative case	der	die	das	ein	eine	ein
Accusative case	**den**	die	das	**einen**	eine	ein

ACTIVITY 3

Of the words printed in **bold**, circle the direct objects and underline the subjects.

1 Ich brauche **einen Tee**.
2 **Der Tee** schmeckt gut.
3 **Die Briefmarke** ist rot.
4 Ich kaufe **eine Cola**.
5 **Der Pullover** ist teuer.
6 **Ich** möchte eine Briefmarke.

Now do activities 4 and 5 on the recording.

3.2 Shopping for food
Einen Apfelkuchen, bitte

 ACTIVITY 6 is on the recording.

ACTIVITY 7

Match the quantities with the appropriate items.

1	dreißig	a	Apfelkuchen
2	zwanzig	b	Vollkornbrot
3	einen	c	Brezeln
4	ein	d	Brötchen

DIALOGUE 2

○ Guten Morgen, Frau Specht. Was darf es sein?

■ Dreißig Brötchen, zwanzig Brezeln und einen Apfelkuchen, bitte.

○ Gerne. Noch etwas?

■ Ja, ich brauche auch ein Vollkornbrot.

○ Hier ist das Vollkornbrot. Möchten Sie noch etwas?

■ Nein danke, das ist alles. Was macht das?

○ Das macht einunddreißig Euro, bitte.

VOCABULARY	
das Brötchen(-)	roll
die Brezel(-n)	pretzel
der Apfelkuchen(-)	apple cake
noch etwas?	anything else?
brauchen	to need
das Vollkornbrot(-e)	wholewheat bread
Sie möchten	you would like
alles	all
was macht das?	what does that come to?
das macht ...	that comes to ...

✅ Tens from 20 to 100

20	zwanzig	50	fünfzig	80	achtzig
30	dreißig	60	sechzig	90	neunzig
40	vierzig	70	siebzig	100	hundert

Note that the final **s** of sechs and the **en** of sieben are omitted in sech**zig** and sieb**zig**, and that drei**ßig** ends in **-ßig** rather than **-zig**.

✅ Numbers from 20 to 100

When counting in English, you say the tens first and then the units: twenty-one, twenty-two, and so on. In German, you do it the other way around: one and twenty, two and twenty, and so on. Note also that German numbers are written as one word.

21	einund**zwanzig**	26	sechsund**zwanzig**
22	zweiund**zwanzig**	27	siebenund**zwanzig**
23	dreiund**zwanzig**	28	achtund**zwanzig**
24	vierund**zwanzig**	29	neunund**zwanzig**
25	fünfund**zwanzig**	31	einund**dreißig**

Note that the **s** of eins is omitted in **ein**undzwanzig, **ein**unddreißig, **ein**undvierzig, and so on.

✅ Asking for things which are masculine in gender

When asking for things which are masculine in gender (e.g. **der Apfelkuchen**), you change the indefinite article from **ein** to **einen**, and the definite article from **der** to **den**.

Einen Apfelkuchen, bitte. An apple cake, please.
Den Apfelkuchen, bitte. The apple cake, please.

This is because in the full sentence – **Ich möchte einen Apfelkuchen** – **Apfelkuchen** is the direct object of the sentence, and **Ich** is the subject.

ACTIVITY 8

Write down the German words for these numbers:

a 23　　b 35　　c 76　　d 69　　e 91

ACTIVITY 9

Order these items in German:

1 A red wine, please.　　3 A wholewheat bread, please.
2 A coffee, please.　　4 A cup of tea, please.

🔊 Now do activities 10 and 11 on the recording.

3.3 Shopping for clothes
Ich suche einen Pullover

ACTIVITY 12 is on the recording.

ACTIVITY 13

1 When does Hilde Specht enter the shop?   a.m. / p.m.
2 Which size does Hilde Specht try first?   42 / 44
3 Which size does she decide on?   46 / 44

DIALOGUE 3

○ Guten Tag. Ich suche einen Pullover in Größe 42.
■ Ja, hier haben wir einen in Größe 42.
○ Kann ich den Pullover gleich anprobieren?
■ Ja, natürlich. Hier sind die Umkleideräume.

■ Passt er?
○ Nein, er ist zu klein.
■ Wir haben das Modell leider nur noch in Größe 46.
○ Schade, Größe 46 ist zu groß.
■ Ach, hier ist er auch in Größe 44!
○ Ja, der Pullover passt. Und er gefällt mir. Wie viel kostet er?
■ Er kostet neunundvierzig Euro.
○ Gut, ich nehme den Pullover in Größe 44.

VOCABULARY

suchen	to look for
der Pullover(-)	jumper, sweater
die Größe(-n)	size
gleich	[*here=*] now
anprobieren	to try on
der Umkleideraum(-ˈ-e)	changing room, dressing room
passen	to fit
passt er?	does it fit?
klein	small
zu klein	too small
das Modell(-e)	style, model
nur noch	only
groß	big
zu groß	too big
er gefällt mir	I like it [*literally* it is pleasing to me]
nehmen	to take

34

✓ *haben* ('to have')

haben has the same endings in the present tense as **kommen**. However, in the forms **du hast** and **er / sie / es hat**, the **b** of the stem is omitted.

ich habe	I have	wir haben	we have
du hast	you have	ihr habt	you have [*informal*]
er / sie / es hat	he / she / it has	sie haben	they have
		Sie haben	you have [*formal*]

✓ Verbs with a stem ending in *-t*

kosten is an example of a verb with a stem ending in -t (**kost-**). These verbs are regular, but add an extra **-e** in the **du**, **er / sie / es**, and **ihr** forms. Other verbs in this category: **arbeiten** ('to work') and **warten** ('to wait').

ich arbeite	wir arbeiten
du arbeitest	ihr arbeitet
er / sie / es arbeitet	sie arbeiten
	Sie arbeiten

✓ *ich möchte* ('I'd like')

The verb form **ich möchte**, etc., has the same endings as **arbeiten**. However, the **er / sie / es** form is identical to the **ich** form:

ich möchte	wir möchten
du möchtest	ihr möchtet
er / sie / es möchte	sie möchten
	Sie möchten

✓ *müssen*

Note that there is no umlaut (¨ over the **u**) in the **ich**, **du**, and **er / sie / es** forms, and no ending for the **ich** and **er / sie / es** forms:

ich muss	wir müssen
du musst	ihr müsst
er / sie / es muss	sie müssen
	Sie müssen

ACTIVITY 14

Fill in the missing endings.

1 Sie möcht___ Rotwein?
2 Eine Flasche Rotwein kost___ heute nur 2,10 Euro!
3 Sie müss___ Vollkornbrot kaufen! Es kost___ nur 50 Cent.
4 Wir hab___ alles!
5 Das Supermarkt-Team arbeit___ für Sie!

🎧 Now do activities 15 and 16 on the recording.

3.4 Shopping
Einkaufen

From fashion to food and wine, you should find something to your taste in the big department stores or smaller boutiques many German cities have to offer.

ACTIVITY 17

A huge delivery of clothing items has just arrived at **Kaufhaus Sommer**. Sort the deliveries below into their appropriate departments.

Die Lieferung

ANZÜGE	STIEFEL	HERRENSOCKEN
RÖCKE	KINDERSCHUHE	BLUSEN
DAMENHOSEN		HEMDEN
DAMENJACKEN		PULLOVER
HERRENMÄNTEL	KLEIDER	SCHUHE

Die Abteilungen

Schuhabteilung	Damenbekleidung	Herrenbekleidung

das Kaufhaus(-̈-er)	department store
die Lieferung(-en)	delivery
der Anzug(-̈-e)	suit
die Socke(-n)	sock
die Hose(-n)	(pair of) trousers, pants
die Jacke(-n)	jacket
der Mantel(-̈-)	coat
der Stiefel(-)	boot
der Rock(-̈-e)	skirt
die Bluse(-n)	blouse
das Hemd(-en)	shirt
das Kleid(-er)	dress
der Schuh(-e)	shoe
die Abteilung(-en)	department
Damen-	ladies'
Herren-	men's
die Bekleidung	clothing

CULTURE

Germany has much more to offer wine lovers than the often ubiquitous Liebfraumilch. Read the following advertisement and answer these questions.

1 What does the wine merchant offer its customers when it says: 'Sie können zuerst probieren und dann kaufen'?
2 Which wine is sold for each of the following prices?
   a acht Euro zehn   c fünfundzwanzig Euro fünfundneunzig
   b neun Euro zwanzig   d sieben Euro sechzig

WEINHANDLUNG SCHMITT
Aachen

Diese Woche haben wir deutsche Spitzenweine im Angebot:
Sie können zuerst probieren und dann kaufen!

1 1997er FORSTER UNGEHEUER
   Riesling Spätlese trocken (Pfalz)   0,75 l € 9,20
2 1997er WÜRZBURGER KÄMMERLEIN
   Kerner Kabinett trocken (Franken)   0,75 l € 8,10
3 1997er BERNKASTELER WITWE
   Müller Thurgau Auslese (Mosel)   0,75 l € 25,95
4 1996er RIESLING WINZERSEKT
   halbtrocken (Rheingau)   0,75 l € 7,60

---

die Weinhandlung(-en)	wine merchant's
die Woche(-n)	week
diese Woche	this week
der Spitzenwein(-e)	top wine
im Angebot	on offer
zuerst	(at) first
probieren	to try
dann	then
die Spätlese(-n)	*wine not as sweet as Auslese*
trocken	dry
halbtrocken	medium dry [*literally* half-dry]
der Kabinett(-e)	*lighter wine, less sweet and less expensive than Auslese*
die Auslese(-n)	*very sweet wine*
der Winzersekt(-e)	*sparkling wine*
der Sekt(-e)	sparkling wine
der Euro	euro

DIE LIEFERUNG
THE DELIVERY

While Susanne is at the hairdresser's, Frau Semmler unpacks deliveries from the baker and the supermarket, and checks them against the delivery notes. How many times do you hear her complain about how expensive things are?

in Ordnung	all right, ok
mein Gott!	my God! [*exclamation*]
pro	per
der Bäcker(-)	baker
einen anderen Bäcker	another baker
finden	to find
der Pflaumenkuchen(-)	plumcake
doch	[*here* =] but
na	well [*colloquial*]
mal sehen	let's see, we'll see
bringen	to bring
das Glas(-¨-er)	jar
das Würstchen(-)	sausage, hotdog
wirklich	really
weißt du was?	you know what? [*colloquial*]
schick	chic, stylish
die Frisur(-en)	hairdo
wie teuer?	how expensive?
mehr	more
Mensch!	heavens! [*exclamation – literally* man!]

ACTIVITY 19

How many of these items does Frau Semmler actually receive? Fill in the missing numbers.

BÄCKEREI HUBER

Rheinstraße 44, Konstanz

___	Brötchen, pro Brötchen €0.60	€18
___	Brote	€15,50
___	Brezeln	€12
___	Pflaumenkuche	€17

ACTIVITY 20

True or false? Circle the correct answers and correct the false ones.

1 The baker delivered everything in the required amounts. T / F
2 Frau Semmler decides to look for another baker. T / F
3 Frau Semmler likes Susanne's new haircut. T / F
4 Susanne's new hairdo cost DM 67,50. T / F
5 Frau Semmler thinks that Susanne paid a reasonable price at the hairdresser's. T / F

STORY TRANSCRIPT

Frau Semmler Dreißig Brötchen, fünf Brote, zwanzig Brezeln – das ist in Ordnung. Mein Gott, 1 Mark zwanzig pro Brötchen! Das ist aber teuer! Ich muss einen anderen Bäcker finden! Und nur zwei Pflaumenkuchen! Wir brauchen doch drei! Na, mal sehen, was der Supermarkt bringt ... Zehn Gläser Würstchen – in Ordnung. Was, 3 Mark pro Glas? Das ist aber wirklich zu teuer!

Susanne Hallo Mama.

Frau Semmler Hallo! Weißt du was? Wir müssen einen anderen Bäcker finden! Oh, schick! Eine schicke Frisur hast du da!

Susanne Danke!

Frau Semmler Und wie teuer?

Susanne Och, nicht so teuer.

Frau Semmler Sechzig Mark?

Susanne Mehr. Neunzig Mark und fünfzig Pfennig.

Frau Semmler Neunzig Mark und fünfzig Pfennig! Mensch, ist das teuer ...

Test

Now it's time to test your progress in Unit 3.

1 Combine the numbers using **und** to form the amounts in each of the price tags. The first one is done for you. (2 points for a correct answer, 1 point if you make one mistake.)

1	zwanzig ✓	a	ein	75	
2	dreißig	b	drei ✓	92	
3	neunzig	und	c	zwei	66
4	sechzig		d	fünf	31
5	siebzig		e	sechs	23 ✓ = dreiundzwanzig

8

2 Which is the odd one out in each group?

1 das Brötchen / der Kuchen / das Würstchen / das Vollkornbrot
2 die Briefmarke / der Brief / die Post / der Bäcker
3 der Rock / der Supermarkt / die Größe / die Umkleideräume
4 zu klein / zu groß / zu teuer / suchen

4

3 Fill in the missing endings.

1 Ich muss ein___ Brief nach England schicken.
2 Ich suche ein___ Rock in Größe 38.
3 Ich nehme d___ Apfelkuchen und d___ Brot.
4 Ein__ Brief nach England kostet seibzig Cent.
5 Ich nehme d___ Rock in Größe 42.

5

4 What is the German for: (2 points for each correct answer, 1 point if you make one mistake.)

1 Five rolls, one loaf of bread, and one apple cake, please.
2 I need a skirt.
3 Excuse me, I am looking for the wine.
4 How much is a letter to England?
5 The skirt is too small / too large.

10

5 Tick the pronouns that can go with these verbs.

1	musst	__du	__sie	__ich
2	kostet	__es	__du	__sie
3	arbeite	__ich	__er	__du
4	arbeitest	__es	__du	__ich
5	muss	ich	__du	__er
6	möchten	__du	__Sie	__er
7	habe	__er	__Sie	__ich

```
9
```

6 Sort sentences a–f into a dialogue between a salesperson and a customer:

Die Kundin (customer)
a Kann ich den Rock gleich anprobieren?
b Guten Tag, ich suche einen Rock in Größe 42.
c Ja, er passt und er gefällt mir. Ich nehme den Rock!

Die Verkäuferin (salesperson)
e Also gut. Wir haben hier einen Rock in Größe 42.
f Ja, natürlich. Hier sind die Umkleideräume.
h Passt er?

```
6
```

7 These sentences are muddled up. Correct the word order.

1 ein Brot / kaufen / ich / muss
2 schicken / einen Brief / ich / nach England / möchte
3 einen Kaffee / ich / trinken / muss
4 kaufen / ich / eine Flasche Wein / möchte
5 anprobieren / den Rock / möchte / ich

```
5
```

TOTAL SCORE `47`

If you scored less than 37, go through the dialogues and the Language Building sections again before working through the Summary on page 42.

Summary 3

Now try this final test summarizing the main points covered in the unit. You can check your answers on the recording.

How would you:
1 count from 30 to 35?
2 order 15 rolls and a loaf of bread?
3 say that you are looking for a coat?
4 ask whether you can try the coat on?
5 ask where the fitting rooms are?
6 ask how much the coat costs?
7 ask how much a letter to England costs?

REVISION

Before moving on to the Review, you may find it useful to work through the Language Building section on direct objects again. If you still feel uncertain about this, you may find the explanations in the answer key for activity 3 and for exercise 3 in the Test section helpful.

Review 1

VOCABULARY

1 Which is the odd one out in each group?

1 beginnen / bestellen / heißen / heiß
2 der Kaffee / der Tee / das Brötchen /
   das Mineralwasser
3 Guten Tag / Auf Wiederhören / Guten Morgen /
   Auf Wiedersehen
4 teuer / falsch / richtig / brauche
5 können / kommen / suchen / einen

2 Match each English sentence with the correct sentence in German.

1	I have to buy a skirt.	a	Kann ich den Rock
2	I would like to pay for		bezahlen?
	the skirt.	b	Ich nehme den Rock.
3	Can I pay for the skirt?	c	Ich muss einen Rock kaufen.
4	How much is the skirt?	d	Wie viel kostet der Rock?
5	I'll take the skirt.	e	Ich möchte den Rock
			bezahlen.

GRAMMAR AND USAGE

3 Fill the blanks with the correct form of the pronoun: **er, sie,** or **es.**

1 Wie viel kostet der Rock?_____ kostet € 25,50.
2 Wann beginnt der Film? _____ beginnt um 9 Uhr.
3 Hat die Touristeninformation heute geöffnet? Ja, _____ hat heute geöffnet.
4 Wie viel kosten die Brötchen? _____ kosten € 1.
5 Wie viel kostet das Brötchen? _____ kostet 25 Cent.
6 Wie viel kostet der Apfelkuchen? _____ kostet € 4,10.
7 Schmeckt der Wein gut? Ja, _____ schmeckt sehr gut.

4 Fill the blanks with the correct form of the article: **ein**, **eine**, or **einen**.

1 Der Mann trinkt _____ Tee.
2 Die Frau bestellt _____ Tasse Kaffee.
3 Kann ich _____ Kaffee bestellen?
4 Ich suche _____ Rock in Größe 42.
5 Die Kinder trinken _____ Mineralwasser.
6 Ich möchte _____ Briefmarke kaufen.

5 Fill the blanks with the correct form of the relevant verb:

anprobieren / kosten / möchte / können / heißen / sein / schicken / können / wiederholen

1 Guten Tag, ich _____ Johann Müller.
2 _____ das Herr Herbst?
3 Wie viel _____ die Brötchen?
4 _____ ich den Rock _____?
5 Ich _____ einen Brief nach England _____ .
6 _____ Sie das bitte _____?

6 Fill the blanks with the most appropriate question word: **wie viel**, **wie**, **woher**, **wo**, or **wann**.

1 _____ kommen Sie?
2 _____ heißen Sie?
3 _____ kosten die Brötchen?
4 _____ beginnt der Film?
5 _____ Uhr ist es?
6 _____ ist die Touristeninformation?

7 Form questions by putting the words/phrases in the correct order.

1 trinken / möchten / eine Tasse Kaffee / Sie?
2 eine Cola / kaufst / du?
3 kaufst / die Brötchen / du / wann?
4 kosten / wie viel / die Hemden?
5 Sie / sind / Herr Meier?

8 Someone has left this message on an answering machine. Listen to the message on the recording and answer the questions.

1 Who called?
2 How many tickets does she have?
3 What's the name of the film she wants to see?
4 What time does it start?
5 What time will they meet?
6 Where will they meet?
7 What will they do there?

bis später!   see you later! [*literally* until later]

9 Sabine and Ralf are expecting some friends for the evening. Listen to their conversation and answer these questions.

1 What do they have to buy?
2 Why can't Sabine go shopping this morning?
3 Why can't Ralf go?
4 At what time does Sabine's friend Katrin want to visit?
5 Who is finally going to shop?
6 What besides the two items mentioned first is that person going to buy?
7 How much money does (s)he take along?

10 You're going to supply the correct question for each of the following answers. First of all, write the questions down; then try to do the activity using only the recording, without looking at your notes.

1 Die Briefmarken kosten 2 Euro.
2 Nein, hier ist nicht das Capitol.
3 Nein, wir haben den Rock nicht in Größe 40.
4 Ich heiße Hans Merkel.
5 Der Film beginnt um 8 Uhr.
6 Ich komme aus Hamburg.
7 Einen Apfelkuchen und 10 Brötchen, bitte.

11 Now it's time to give some information about yourself. Listen to the questions on the recording. The questions will be about the following topics, but in a different order. You'll be asked:

– your name
– where you come from
– if you drink coffee or tea
– if you have children
– how you are
– if you're going to the cinema today

Eating out
Essen gehen

LEARNING GERMAN 4

At this point you may feel a bit confused about the different endings of definite and indefinite articles. But don't worry: throughout this course you'll have plenty of practice using the articles correctly. In spontaneous speech don't worry too much about the endings at this stage. Above all, don't let it stop you speaking German, because people will understand what you mean even if you get some of the endings wrong. The more German you listen to, the more you will get them right. Practise key phrases in each unit as often as you can, if possible with a study partner. You may also want to consider recording yourself while practising key phrases. You can then listen to the phrases that are most important to you again and again and check on your pronunciation.

Now start the recording for Unit 4.

Wir möchten bestellen, bitte!

ACTIVITY 1 is on the recording.

ACTIVITY 2

Tick each of the following words every time you hear it.

1 Rinderbraten   _____   3 Schweinefilet   _____
2 Forelle   _____   4 Vorspeise   _____

DIALOGUE 1

○ Mensch, ich habe Hunger! Ich esse den Rinderbraten. Was nimmst du?

▼ Vielleicht nehme ich die Forelle. Hallo Angela, da bist du ja. Wir haben schon Hunger!

■ Gut, dann bestellen wir gleich. Ich nehme das Schweinefilet. Was esst ihr?

○ Ich nehme den Rinderbraten und Sabine isst die Forelle.

■ Also gut. Herr Ober, wir möchten bestellen, bitte!

△ Bitte schön, was darf es sein?

■ Einen Rinderbraten, ein Schweinefilet und eine Forelle, bitte.

△ Gerne. Möchten Sie auch eine Vorspeise?

■ Nein danke, wir machen Diät!

VOCABULARY

der Hunger	hunger
Hunger haben	to be hungry
essen	to eat
der Rinderbraten(-)	roast beef
nehmen	to have
was nimmst du?	what will you have?
ich nehme ...	I'll have ...
vielleicht	perhaps
die Forelle	trout
bestellen	to order
das Schweinefilet(-s)	pork fillet
die Vorspeise	starter, appetizer
die Diät(-en)	diet
wir machen Diät!	we're on a diet!

✓ Using the subject pronouns *wir* ('we') and *ihr* ('you')

wir means 'we' and is used in the same way as in English. **ihr** ('you', informal plural) is used whenever you are addressing two or more people informally. As with **du**, this means children or others who address you using **du**. Otherwise you use **Sie** ('you', formal) to address one or more people.

✓ Irregular verbs with a vowel change

The verb **essen** is irregular: ich esse, Sabine isst. Some irregular verbs such as **essen** and **nehmen** take the regular present tense endings, but change their vowel in the **du** and **er / sie / es** forms:

ich esse	wir essen	ich nehme	wir nehmen
du isst	ihr esst	du nimmst	ihr nehmt
er / sie / es isst	sie essen	er / sie / es nimmt	sie nehmen
	Sie essen		Sie nehmen

Other common verbs in this category:

fahren to drive (du fährst, er fährt)
sehen to see (du siehst, er sieht)
lesen to read (du liest, er liest)

From now on, any vowel change in the present tense will be shown in the vocabulary section, for example:

laufen (er läuft)   to run

Note: **essen** is an example of a verb whose stem ends in **-s** (**ess-**). Another example is **reisen**, 'to travel'. To create the **du** form of these verbs, you simply add a **-t** instead of **-st: er isst, du reist**. The same rule applies to verbs whose stems end in **-ß**, **-z**, and **-x**: grüßen, 'to greet', heißen, 'to be called', **tanzen**, 'to dance', **sitzen**, 'to sit', **mixen**, 'to mix'.

ACTIVITY 3

Sie or **ihr**? Fill in the appropriate pronoun.

1 Sabine und Elfie, was esst _____?
2 Frau Meier, was nehmen ____?
3 Meine Herren, möchten _____ bestellen?
4 Hallo Lisa, hallo Rolf. Möchtet ____ etwas Fisch?
5 Heiko und Anna, fahrt _____ nach Hamburg?

ACTIVITY 4

Following the example of **essen** above, write down the present tense of **lesen** and **fahren**.

 Now do activities 5 and 6 on the recording.

4.2 Saying what you don't like
Das mag ich nicht!

(4 A) **ACTIVITY 7** is on the recording.

ACTIVITY 8

1 Herr Schleier knows right away what to order.   T / F
2 He likes most items on the menu.   T / F
3 Herr Schleier is a vegetarian.   T / F
4 He finally decides on a soup and a salad.   T / F

DIALOGUE 2

○ Meine Herren, was möchten Sie bestellen?

▼ Ich nehme das Hähnchen mit Reis. Was nehmen Sie, Herr Schleier?

■ Hmm, ich weiß noch nicht. Können Sie etwas empfehlen?

○ Der Rehbraten ist sehr gut.

■ Nein danke! Ich mag keinen Rehbraten. Ich mag überhaupt kein Fleisch.

○ Mögen Sie Fisch?

■ Nein, ich mag auch keinen Fisch. Ich bin Vegetarier.

○ Dann kann ich leider nur eine Gemüsesuppe empfehlen.

■ Also gut, ich nehme die Gemüsesuppe und einen Salat.

○ Gerne. Möchten Sie auch die Getränkekarte?

▼ Ja bitte.

VOCABULARY	
das mag ich nicht!	I don't like that!
das Hähnchen(-)	chicken
der Reis	rice
wissen (er weiß)	to know
noch nicht	not yet
empfehlen (er empfiehlt)	to recommend
der Rehbraten(-)	roast venison
überhaupt	[*here* =] at all
kein ...	not a ..., not any ..., no ...
das Fleisch [*sing.*]	meat
der Fisch(-e)	fish
der Vegetarier(-)	vegetarian
die Gemüsesuppe(-n)	vegetable soup
der Salat(-e)	salad
die Getränkekarte(-n)	drinks list

⊘ Saying what you like to eat using *mögen*

mögen is a modal verb which is used with a noun rather than an infinitive. Note the vowel change.

Ich **mag** Sahnetorte. I like gâteau.

ich mag	wir mög-en
du mag-st	ihr mög-t
er / sie / es mag	sie mög-en
	Sie mög-en

⊘ Expressing the negative using *kein*

kein translates as 'not a ...', 'not any ...', 'no ...'. You use it with nouns to change the indefinite article **ein** into the negative. **kein** takes the same endings as **ein** (see page 7).

With masculine and neuter nouns: **kein**

Da ist ein Haus. There is a house.
Da ist **kein** Haus. There is no house.

Das ist ein Mantel. That is a coat.
Das ist **kein** Mantel. That isn't a coat.

With feminine nouns and nouns in the plural: **keine**

Ich mag Forelle. I like trout.
Ich mag **keine** Forelle. I don't like (any) trout.

Da sind Kinder. There are children.
Da sind **keine** Kinder. There are no children.

With masculine direct objects: **keinen**

Du brauchst einen Mantel. You need a coat.
Du brauchst **keinen** Mantel. You don't need a coat.

ACTIVITY 9

-e, -en, or no ending? Fill in the gaps.

1 Er hat kein__ Mantel.
2 Ich mag kein__ Fisch.
3 Ich mag kein__ Fleisch.
4 Das ist kein__ Vorspeise, das ist ein Hauptgericht.
5 Er braucht kein__ Jacke.

ACTIVITY 10

Translate the sentences in activity 9 into English.

⊕ Now do activities 11 and 12 on the recording.

4.3 Asking for the bill
Die Rechnung, bitte!

 ACTIVITY 13 is on the recording.

ACTIVITY 14

1 Do the friends order dessert (**Nachspeise**)?
2 What does one of them have as a drink after dinner?
3 What kinds of meat did they have?
4 How much is the bill?

DIALOGUE 3

○ Möchtet ihr noch eine Nachspeise?
▼ Nein danke, ich bin satt.
■ Ich habe auch genug.
○ Möchtet ihr vielleicht noch einen Kaffee?
▼ Hm, ich trinke lieber Tee. Ich nehme noch einen Tee.
■ Ich möchte nichts mehr, danke.
○ Also gut. Herr Ober! Einen Tee und die Rechnung, bitte.
△ Ja, natürlich. Zahlen Sie getrennt oder zusammen?
● Zusammen, bitte. Ich zahle das Schweinefilet, die
   gebackene Forelle und den gerösteten Rinderbraten.
△ Das macht genau achtundfünfzig Euro, bitte.

VOCABULARY

die Nachspeise(-n)	dessert
satt	full
ich habe genug	I've had enough
ich trinke lieber Tee	I prefer tea
nichts mehr	nothing more
die Rechnung(-en)	bill, check
zahlen	to pay (for)
getrennt	separate(ly)
oder	or
zusammen	together
gebacken	baked
geröstet	sautéed
genau	exactly

⊘ The meanings of *noch*

noch can have many meanings. The meaning is usually clear from the context.

> Möchten Sie **noch etwas** Tee?   Would you like **some more** tea?
> Er ist **noch nicht** da.   He is **not** here **yet**.
> Ich habe **nur noch** fünf Euro.   I have **only** five euros left.

⊘ Expressing a preference using *lieber*

To express a preference add **lieber** ('preferably') after the verb:

> Ich trinke keinen Kaffee. Ich trinke **lieber** Tee.
> I don't drink coffee. I prefer (drinking) tea.

> Ich trinke keinen Alkohol. Ich trinke **lieber** Orangensaft.
> I don't drink alcohol. I prefer (drinking) orange juice.

⊘ Adjective endings after *der, die, das,* and *den*

When adjectives come before a noun the ending changes. If **der, die** [*sing.*], or **das** precede the adjective, the ending is always **-e**.

> Das ist **der** geröstete Schweinebraten. That's the sautéed pork.
> Hier ist **die** grüne Jacke. Here is the green jacket.
> Ich nehme **das** graue Hemd. I'll take the grey shirt.

If **den** or the plural **die** precede the adjective, the ending is **-en**.

> Ich nehme **den** blauen Rock. I'll take the blue skirt.
> Ich nehme **den** roten Mantel. I'll take the red coat.
> Hier sind **die** gelben Blusen. Here are the yellow blouses.
> Da sind **die** grauen Anzüge. There are the grey suits.

ACTIVITY 15

Shop till you drop! Here's what you're buying. Choose a colour for each item and then complete the sentences, writing the colour adjective you've chosen in the gap. Don't forget to put the correct ending on each adjective.

grau	grün	gelb	rot	blau

1 Ich kaufe die _____ Bluse.
2 Ich kaufe die _____ Schuhe.
3 Ich kaufe den _____ Anzug.
4 Ich kaufe die _____ Hose.
5 Ich kaufe den _____ Rock.

🎧 Now do activities 16 and 17 on the recording.

4.4 Eating out
Essen gehen

ACTIVITY 18

If you want to know how to get by in a German restaurant, read the following passage and answer the questions.

1 What, according to the article, happens quite often when you are in a restaurant?
2 How can you attract a waiter's / waitress's attention if you want to order?
3 How else can you call for a waiter?
4 Why shouldn't you call a waitress **Fräulein**?
5 How can you attract her attention instead?

Das passiert oft: Sie sind im Restaurant. Sie warten und warten, aber die Bedienung kommt nicht. Was können Sie tun?

1 Sie können winken und rufen: 'Entschuldigung!'.
2 Sie können winken und sagen: 'Die Speisekarte, bitte!' oder 'Wir möchten bestellen, bitte!'.
3 Sie können einen Kellner auch so rufen: 'Herr Ober!'.

4 Früher rief man eine Kellnerin 'Fräulein!'. Das ist heute veraltet. Sie können stattdessen 'Entschuldigung!' rufen und winken.

---

passieren	to happen
oft	often
das Restaurant(-s)	restaurant
im Restaurant	in a / the restaurant
warten	to wait
die Bedienung(-en)	service
kommen	to come
tun (er tat)	to do
winken	to wave
rufen	to call
sagen	to say
die Speisekarte(-n)	menu
der Kellner(-)	waiter
so	like this
früher	in the past [*literally* earlier]

rief	called
man	one [*impersonal*]
die Kellnerin(-nen)	waitress
das Fräulein(-)	Miss
veraltet	obsolete, outdated
stattdessen instead	

ACTIVITY 19

For a fast snack you will find regional specialities as well as ethnic foods in Germany. To find out more about them, study the menu below and answer the questions in the following fast-food quiz.

1 Which typically Italian dishes do you find on the menu?
2 Which dish is mostly provided by Turkish fast-food restaurants in Germany?
3 This rissole is typically associated with Berlin. What is it called?
4 What are 'french fries' called in Germany?
5 This sausage in a red sauce with curry powder on top can be found all over Germany. What is its name?

SCHNELLIMBISS KOCHLÖFFEL

Kurfürstendamm 103, Berlin
geöffnet: Montag – Sonntag, 9–19 Uhr

Kebab	€ 3,50
Pizza, pro Stück	€ 2,45
Spaghetti Bolognese	€ 4,60
Currywurst	€ 2,30
Pommes frites mit Ketchup / Mayonnaise	€ 3,30
Bulette	€ 2,55

---

pro Stück   per slice

ACTIVITY 20

Write out the prices of the items on the menu above in words.

EIN ABENDESSEN ZU ZWEIT
A DINNER FOR TWO

Peter Ritter trifft Hubert für ein Abendessen im Hotel. Hubert ist ein Freund aus seiner Konstanzer Studienzeit. Er is sehr gesundheitsbewusst. Deshalb kann er viele Gerichte nicht essen.

Peter Ritter meets Hubert for dinner at the hotel. Hubert is a friend from his student days in Konstanz. He is very health-conscious, which is why he cannot eat many dishes.

als Vorspeise	as a starter, as an appetizer
die Spargelcremesuppe(-n)	cream of asparagus soup
die Schlachtplatte(-n)	platter of assorted sausages and meats
fett	fat
viel zu fett	much too fat
was anderes	something else
die Rahmsauce(-n)	sauce made with cream
das Rinderfilet(-s)	fillet of beef
das Rindfleisch	beef
mit BSE	with BSE [*mad cow disease*]
empfindlich	sensitive
gesundheitsbewusst	health conscious
als Hauptgericht	as a main course
die Salatplatte(-n)	platter of mixed salad and raw vegetables
dazu	[*here* =] with that

ACTIVITY 21

Look at this menu from the Hotel Gertrud. Write 'P' next to what Peter has, and 'H' next to what Hubert has.

Speisekarte Hotel-Restaurant Gertrud

Vorspeisen

(*der*) Krabbencocktail

(*der*) Tomatensalat

(*die*) Spargelcremesuppe

Hauptgerichte

(*die*) Schlachtplatte

(*das*) Wiener Schnitzel

(*das*) Schweinefilet in Rahmsauce

(*das*) Rinderfilet

(*die*) Salatplatte 'Gärtnerin'

Nachspeisen

(*die*) Mousse au chocolat

(*der*) Apfelkuchen mit Schlagsahne

(*das*) Vanilleeis mit Erdbeeren (strawberries)

ACTIVITY 22

You and a friend are in a restaurant. You want to order from the menu above. Write down your orders (as given below).

1 A prawn cocktail and a cream of asparagus soup as a starter, please.
2 A Wiener schnitzel and a fillet of beef as a main course, please.
3 We'd like a mousse au chocolat and applecake with whipped cream for dessert (**als Nachspeise**), please.

STORY TRANSCRIPT

Peter	Mensch Hubert, wie geht es dir?
Hubert	Danke gut, und dir?
Peter	Auch sehr gut.
	…
Peter	Komm, wir bestellen gleich. Ich habe schon Hunger. Als Vorspeise nehme ich die Spargelcremesuppe und dann die Schlachtplatte.
Hubert	Schlachtplatte? Mensch, das ist doch viel zu fett. Also ich nehme was anderes.
Peter	Also, ich empfehle das Schweinefilet in Rahmsauce.
Hubert	Ich esse keine Rahmsauce. Das ist doch auch viel zu fett!
Peter	Hmm, magst du Rinderfilet?
Hubert	Rindfleisch? Mit BSE? Nein, also danke.
Peter	Du bist aber empfindlich!
Hubert	Ich bin nicht empfindlich. Ich bin gesundheitsbewusst! Also, ich nehme keine Vorspeise. Als Hauptgericht nehme ich die Salatplatte – und dazu ein Mineralwasser!
Peter	Also gut. Susanne!

Test

Now it's time to test your progress in Unit 4.

1 Match each German dish with the correct English translation.

1	der Apfelkuchen mit Schlagsahne	a	prawn cocktail
		b	roast venison
2	das Hähnchen	c	fish
3	der Rinderbraten	d	rice
4	das Schweinefilet	e	meat
5	die Forelle	f	soup
6	der Reis	g	salad
7	der Rehbraten	h	chicken
8	der Fisch	j	roast beef
9	das Fleisch	k	trout
10	die Suppe	l	pork fillet
11	der Salat	m	apple cake with whipped
12	der Krabbencocktail		cream

12

2 Choose from a–f as many ways as possible of politely refusing the offers 1–4.

1 Möchten Sie etwas Rinderbraten?
2 Möchten Sie ein Bier?
3 Möchten Sie noch eine Nachspeise?
4 Möchten Sie etwas Rotwein?

a Nein danke, ich habe genug.
b Nein danke, ich trinke keinen Alkohol.
c Nein danke, ich bin Vegetarier.
d Nein, ich esse lieber Fisch.
e Nein danke, ich bin satt.
f Nein danke, ich trinke lieber Weißwein.

9

3 A **Suppenkasper** is a fictional character that doesn't like to eat his soup, or anything else for that matter. Fill the appropriate form of **kein** into Suppenkasper's refusals.

1 Ich mag _____ Suppe!
2 Ich mag _____ Vorspeise!

3 Ich esse _____ Rinderbraten!
4 Ich esse _____ Apfelkuchen!
5 Ich esse _____ Nachspeise!

4 Tick the verb that can go with each pronoun. Watch out: once again, more than one option is possible!

Sie: ___essen ___isst ___esse
er: ___nehmt ___nehmen ___ nimmt
du: ___laufen ___laufe ___läufst
sie: ___empfiehlt ___empfehlen ___empfiehlst
ich: ___siehst ___sehe ___seht

5 A fashion magazine gives some tips for matching (**kombinieren**) items of clothing. Fill in the endings.

1 Sie können die blau__ Bluse und den rot__ Rock kombinieren.
2 Sie können die gelb__ Hose und den braun__ Mantel kombinieren.
3 Sie können den grau__ Anzug und das blau__ Hemd kombinieren.
4 Sie können auch die blau___ Schuhe und das grün__ Kleid kombinieren.

6 Rewrite the following conversation so that people address each other with **ihr** or **du**.

Ober: Meine Herren, **Sie** möchten bestellen?
Herr A: Ja, ich nehme den Rinderbraten. Was ess**en Sie**, Herr B?
Herr B: Ich nehme das Schweinefilet in Rahmsauce.
Herr A: Und was **nehmen Sie**, Herr C?
Herr C: Ich nehme den Rehbraten.
Ober: Möch**ten Sie** auch eine Vorspeise, meine Herren?
Herr A: Nein, danke.

TOTAL SCORE 44

If you scored less than 34, go through the dialogues and the Language Building sections before working through the Summary on page 60.

Summary 4

 Now try this final test summarizing the main points covered in the unit. You can check your answers on the recording.

How would you:
1 say you'd like to order?
2 say you'll have the pork fillet and a soup, please?
3 say you won't have a starter?
4 say you don't like fish – you prefer (eating) meat?
5 say you're a vegetarian?
6 say thank you, you're full?
7 ask for the bill?

REVISION

So far, you have come across these irregular verbs: (1) **haben**, (2) **sein**, (3) verbs that change their vowel (e.g. **essen**), and (4) the modal verbs **können**, **mögen**, and **müssen** and the modal verb form **ich möchte**. You may find it worth writing down **haben**, **sein**, and the modal verbs with their endings on an extra sheet, which you can then use as a reference for the remainder of the course. You may also find it helpful to start a list of those verbs that change their vowel. By systematizing your approach to the irregular verbs in this way, you will soon become familiar with them.

Meeting people
Leute treffen

OBJECTIVES

In this unit you will learn how to:

- ✓ introduce yourself
- ✓ say what your occupation is and what nationality you are
- ✓ talk about your family

And cover the following grammar and language:

- ✓ the possessive adjectives ('my', 'his', 'your', etc.)
- ✓ nouns of nationality
- ✓ **sie** ('they')
- ✓ the modal verb **wollen** ('to want to')

LEARNING GERMAN 5

Try not to feel discouraged if you can't get an activity right straight away. Have a first go at it and write down your answers. For the activities following the Language Building sections, have another look at the grammar explanations to check whether you followed the rules outlined there. After that, look at the answer key to find out why a specific answer is correct and what you had to look out for. If you didn't get the answers right, go back to the activity after a while and try it again. You'll see that this time you'll do much better!

🎧 Now start the recording for Unit 5.

Introducing yourself

Darf ich mich vorstellen?

ACTIVITY 1 is on the recording.

ACTIVITY 2

1 Where do Walter März and Monika Spree come from?
2 How are Klaus and Monika Spree related to each other?
3 Where does Klaus Spree live now?
4 What does Walter ask for at the end of the dialogue?

DIALOGUE 1

○ Hallo! Darf ich mich vorstellen? Ich bin Walter März.
■ Hallo, Herr März. Ich bin Monika Spree.
○ Was sind Sie denn von Beruf, Frau Spree?
■ Ich bin Ingenieurin. Und Sie?
○ Ich bin auch Ingenieur! Und woher kommen Sie?
■ Ich komme aus Lüneburg.
○ So ein Zufall! Ich komme auch aus Lüneburg! Ich kenne
  Ihre Eltern und Ihren Bruder Klaus! Wohnt Klaus noch in
  Lüneburg?
■ Nein, in England. Er ist dort Programmierer bei Siemens.
○ Ach, wirklich? Haben Sie seine Telefonnummer?
■ Ja, natürlich. Hier ist sie …

VOCABULARY	
treffen	to meet
darf ich mich vorstellen?	may I introduce myself?
denn	then
was sind Sie von Beruf?	what is your occupation?
der Beruf(-e)	occupation
die Ingenieurin(-nen)	(female) engineer
der Ingenieur(-e)	(male) engineer
Lüneburg	*small town in northern Germany*
so ein Zufall!	what a coincidence!
kennen	to know (a place, situation, person)
die Eltern	parents
der Bruder(-̈-)	brother
wohnen	to live
der Programmierer(-)	(male) programmer
bei Siemens	at Siemens

✓ Talking about occupations

A male engineer is an **Ingenieur**, but a female engineer is an **Ingeneurin**. You add the ending -in to occupations when referring to a woman. Some female job titles also add an umlaut (ä, ü, ö).

der **Arzt**	die **Ärztin**	doctor
der **Lehrer**	die **Lehrerin**	teacher
der **Sekretär**	die **Sekretärin**	secretary

✓ Possessive adjectives *mein, sein,* and *Ihr*

Words such as **mein** ('my'), **sein** ('his'), and **Ihr** ('your') are called possessive adjectives.

mein my	**unser** our
dein your	**euer** your
sein his	**ihr** your
ihr hers	**Ihr** your [*formal*]
sein its	

All possessive adjectives add the same endings as **ein** and **kein**. So:
– no ending before masculine or neuter nouns as subjects (nominative)
– + -e before a feminine noun or a noun in the plural
– + -en before a masculine direct object (accusative)

Das ist meine Hose. Those are my trousers.
Hast du deine Jacke? Do you have your jacket?
Das sind seine Hosen. Those are his trousers.
Wir brauchen unsere Jacken. We need our jackets.
Kennen Sie meinen Bruder? Do you know my brother?
Ja, ich kenne Ihren Bruder. Yes, I know your brother.
Er sucht seinen Anzug. He is looking for his suit.

	m	f	n	pl
Nominative	mein Anzug	meine Hose	mein Haus	meine Hosen
Accusative	meinen Anzug	meine Hose	mein Haus	meine Hosen

ACTIVITY 3

-e, -en, or no ending at all? Complete the possessive adjectives.

1 Er sucht sein__ Bruder. Sein__ Bruder ist hier.
2 Ich suche mein__ Eltern. Ihr__ Eltern sind hier.
3 Ich suche sein__ Schuhe. Sein__ Schuhe sind hier.
4 Ich suche Ihr__ Anzug. Mein__ Anzug ist hier.

(4A) Now do activities 4 and 5 on the recording.

ACTIVITY 6 is on the recording.

ACTIVITY 7

Correct the statements which are false.

1 The young couple have been in Berlin for two days.   T / F
2 One of them is from Spain, the other from the US.   T / F
3 They want to stay for four more days.   T / F
4 They have two children.   T / F
5 Their children are three and five years old.   T / F

DIALOGUE 2

○ Seid ihr schon lange in Berlin?
■ Nein, erst drei Tage.
○ Woher kommt ihr denn?
■ Ich bin Spanierin und Ben kommt aus den USA.
○ Und wie lange wollt ihr noch bleiben?
▼ Noch fünf Tage. Dann wollen wir unsere Kinder wieder sehen.
○ Ach, habt ihr schon Kinder? Wie alt sind eure Kinder denn?
▼ Unsere Tochter ist zwei und unser Sohn ist drei Jahre alt. Hast du auch Kinder?
○ Nein, noch nicht – zum Glück!

VOCABULARY

seid ihr schon lange in ... ?	have you been in ... for long?
schon lange	for long
der Tag(-e)	day
die Spanierin(-nen)	Spaniard [*female*]
wie lange?	(for) how long?
wollen	to want to
das Kind(-er)	child
wieder sehen	to see again
wie alt?	how old?
die Tochter(-¨-)	daughter
der Sohn(-¨-e)	son
das Jahr(-e)	year
zum Glück	luckily! [*colloquial*]

✓ Stating your nationality

You can state your nationality in two ways.

Ich komme aus ... I am from ... [*literally* I come from ...]

England	England	**Frankreich**	France
Italien	Italy	**Deutschland**	Germany
Großbritannien	Great Britain	**Schottland**	Scotland

but: **aus den** USA (from the US)

Or you can use **Ich bin** ... (I am ...) and the appropriate noun of nationality. For example:

Ich bin **Engländer**. I am English.

If you're female, you add the ending **-in**, and sometimes an umlaut (ä, ö, ü), to the masculine noun of nationality.

der Engländer	die Engländer**in**	der Brite	die Brit**in**
der Franzose	die Französ**in**	der Schotte	die Schott**in**
der Italiener	die Italiener**in**	but:	
der Amerikaner	die Amerikaner**in**	der Deutsche	die Deutsche

Note that in German these words are nouns, but in English they are adjectives.

✓ Possessive adjective *euer* ('your')

You use the possessive adjective **euer** for 'your' when talking to people you address with **ihr**. Note that in **eure** and **euren** the e in the middle is omitted.

Habt ihr **euer** Geld? Do you have your money?
Ist das **eure** Katze? Is that your cat?
Habt ihr **eure** Jacken? Do you have your jackets?
Habt ihr **euren** Schlüssel? Do you have your key?

ACTIVITY 8

In a youth hostel, some young people have to sort out which item of clothing belongs to whom. Translate these sentences into German, using **euer** for 'your':

1 Are these your shirts? No, these aren't our shirts.
2 Are these your shoes? No, these aren't our shoes.
3 Are these your coats? Yes, those are our coats.
4 Where are your socks? Our socks are here.
5 Are these your trousers? Yes, those (**das**) are our trousers.

 Now do activities 9 and 10 on the recording.

Das ist meine Familie!

🔊 **ACTIVITY 11** is on the recording.

ACTIVITY 12

1 Christoph's father is from _____.
2 His mother's parents are from _____.
3 His sister's husband is from _____.
4 His wife is from _____.

DIALOGUE 3

○ Also, das ist mein Vater. Er kommt aus Spanien.
■ Aha. Und das ist deine Mutter?
○ Ja, und hier sind ihre Eltern. Sie sind Amerikaner.
■ Puh, deine Familie ist ja ganz schön international!
○ Ja klar! Hier ist übrigens meine Schwester. Ihr Mann ist Italiener. Sie wollen bald nach Italien ziehen.
■ Und deine Frau ist aus Frankreich?
○ Ja, sie ist Französin.
■ Und diese drei, sind das deine Kinder?
○ Genau. Das sind meine drei Kinder und ihre Haustiere. Jetzt kennst du die ganze Familie!

VOCABULARY	
Spanien	Spain
der Vater(-¨-)	father
die Mutter(-¨-)	mother
ganz schön	quite [*colloquial*]
international	international
ja klar!	of course! [*colloquial*]
übrigens	by the way
die Schwester(-n)	sister
der Mann(-¨-er)	husband, man
bald	soon
nach Italien	to Italy
ziehen	to move
die Frau(-en)	wife, woman
diese	[*here* =] those
das Haustier(-e)	pet
ganz	whole
die Familie(-n)	family

✓ Using the possessive adjectives *ihr* and *Ihr*

The possessive adjective **ihr** can mean 'her' or 'their'. The context will make it clear which one is meant:

> Hier ist meine Mutter, und das ist **ihr** Auto.
> Here is my mother, and this is her car.

> Hier sind meine Kinder. Und das sind **ihre** Haustiere.
> Here are my children. And these are their pets.

Ihr with a capital means 'your' in a formal context.

> Herr Meiser, ist das **Ihr** Auto? Mr Meiser, is this your car?

✓ When to use *dein* for 'your'

You use the possessive adjective **dein** for 'your' when you address someone with **du**:

> Ralf, hast du **deine** Eintrittskarte? Ralf, have you got your ticket?

✓ The modal verb *wollen* ('to want to')

The present tense of the modal verb **wollen**:

ich will	wir wollen
du willst	ihr wollt
er / sie / es will	sie wollen
	Sie wollen

Like the other modal verbs, **wollen** always goes with an infinitive, which appears at the end of the sentence or question.

> Ralf **will** ein Steak **essen**. Ralf wants to eat a steak.
> Warum **wollen** Sie schon **gehen**? Why do you want to leave already?
> **Wollt** ihr nach Bremen **fahren**? Do you want to go to Bremen?

ACTIVITY 13

Add the appropriate endings to the possessive adjectives.

1 Ist das Ihr___ Tochter?
2 Das sind mein__ Eltern.
3 Das ist dein__ Hose.
4 Ich sehe dein___ Vater.
5 Sie suchen ihr__ Schuhe.

🎧 Now do activites 14 and 15 on the recording.

5.4 Coffee, cake, and a chat

Kaffeeklatsch!

Drinking a cup of coffee with friends is an important part of German social life. Cafés are popular places for people to meet and have a **Kaffeeklatsch**: coffee, cake, and a chat. Many cafés open early for breakfast and may stay open until late at night. As well as coffee, cakes, and light refreshments, cafés often provide other entertainments, too.

ACTIVITY 16

Read this menu of a café in Heidelberg. Choosing from the words listed below, fill in the blanks to find out what this café can offer.

a geöffnet	b Speisekarte	c Torten
d Live-Auftritte	e Cocktailbar	f Ausstellungen

Kaffeehaus Schriesmann
– am Markt, Heidelberg

Café – Bistro – Restaurant

täglich _____: von 9– 1 Uhr

Frühstück: täglich von 9 – 14 Uhr

_____ und Kuchen, täglich
frisch aus unserer Konditorei

_____ mit Snacks, täglich
wechselnd

große Sonnenterrasse

Klassische Cocktails an unserer

_____

_____ lokaler Soul – und
Jazzkünstler

_____ namhafter
Künstler

das Frühstück(-e)	breakfast
täglich	daily
die Torte(-n)	gâteau, cake
der Auftritt(-e)	appearance, gig
die Ausstellung(-en)	exhibition
frisch	fresh
die Konditorei(-en)	cake shop and confectioner's
wechselnd	changing
die Sonnenterrasse(-n)	patio
klassisch	classic
an	at
lokaler Künstler	of local artists
der Künstler(-)	artist
namhafter Künstler	of well-known artists

ACTIVITY 17

Read these descriptions by Stefanie Wagner and Norbert
Wichtig of themselves and their families. Why would you
recommend the **Kaffeehaus Schriesmann** to them?

Stefanie Wagner:
Hallo, ich heiße Stefanie Wagner. Ich bin
33 Jahre alt und habe einen Sohn und
eine Tochter. Meine Familie und ich
wohnen in Heidelberg. Die Kinder
mögen Kuchen und Torte, und ich
trinke gerne mal einen Cocktail. Mein
Mann und ich mögen Musik, und ganz
besonders Jazz!

Norbert Wichtig:
Mein Name ist Norbert Wichtig. Ich bin
52 Jahre alt. Meine Frau und ich wohnen
in Heidelberg. Wir haben eine Tochter
und zwei Söhne. Unsere Tochter ist 19
Jahre alt, unsere Söhne sind 23 und 25
Jahre. Hans, mein ältester Sohn, ist
Künstler. Meine Tochter spielt in einer
Band. Meine Frau mag Kuchen und eine
Tasse Kaffee, ich esse lieber eine Suppe
oder einen Salat.

gerne	with pleasure
mal	[*here* =] once in a while
ganz besonders	particularly
mein ältester Sohn	my eldest son
in einer Band spielen	to play in a band

69

**EIN ABENDESSEN ZU ZWEIT
A DINNER FOR TWO (CONTINUED)**

Peter Ritter und sein Freund Hubert sind immer noch im
Hotel Gertrud und trinken eine Tasse Kaffee. Susanne kommt
dazu, und alle drei unterhalten sich.

Peter Ritter and his friend Hubert are still at the Hotel Gertrud
and are having a cup of coffee. Susanne joins in and all three
have a chat.

wie gefällt dir ... ?	how do you like ... ? [*literally* how is ... pleasing to you?]
vermissen	to miss
verstehen	to understand
arbeiten	to work
sagen	to say
noch nicht so lange	not too long yet
du kannst ruhig 'du' sagen	you can go ahead and address me with '**du**'
der Monat(-e)	month
seit	since
geschieden	divorced
seitdem	since then
der Kleine	the little one
verheiratet	married
noch nicht!	not yet!
na dann!	well, then! [*colloquial*]
ein bisschen	a bit
aufräumen	to tidy up
bis morgen!	see you tomorrow [*literally* until tomorrow]
bis	until
tschüss!	bye!

ACTIVITY 18

Listen to the conversation of Hubert (H), Peter (P), and Susanne (S) again. Tick who says what.

1 Aber ich vermisse Konstanz.   __H __P __S
2 Du kannst ruhig 'du' sagen.   __H __P __S
3 Wie lange arbeitest du schon hier?   __H __P __S
4 Du bist geschieden?   __H __P __S
5 Seid ihr verheiratet – oder geschieden?   __H __P __S
6 Nein, ich bin nicht verheiratet. Noch nicht!   __H __P __S

ACTIVITY 19

Match the sentences in Activity 18 with the translations below.

a Are you married – or divorced?   ____
b No, I'm not married. Not yet!   ___
c But I miss Konstanz.   ____
d How long have you been working here?   ____
e You are divorced?   ____
f You can go ahead and address me with 'du'. ____

STORY TRANSCRIPT

Hubert	Wie gefällt dir denn Hamburg?
Peter	Ach, ganz gut. Aber ich vermisse Konstanz.
Susanne	Ja, das verstehe ich! So, hier ist noch ein Tee!
Peter	Danke schön. Wie lange arbeiten Sie denn schon hier im Hotel?
Susanne	Noch nicht so lange, aber du kannst ruhig 'du' sagen!
Peter	Oh, ok. Also: wie lange arbeitest du denn schon hier, Susanne?
Susanne	Erst drei Monate, seit ich geschieden bin.
Hubert	Du bist geschieden?
Susanne	Ja. Seitdem wohnen mein Sohn und ich hier im Hotel.
Peter	Ach, der Kleine hier im Hotel ist dein Sohn!
Susanne	Hmmm. Er ist fünf Jahre alt. Und ihr? Seid ihr verheiratet – oder geschieden?
Peter	Nein, ich bin nicht verheiratet. **Noch** nicht!
Hubert	Und ich bin auch nicht verheiratet.
Susanne	Na dann! So, ich muss jetzt noch ein bisschen aufräumen. Bis morgen, Peter! Tschüs, Hubert!
Hubert	Ja, tschüss!
Peter	Bis morgen, Susanne!

Now it's time to test your progress in Unit 5.

1 Write the missing possessive adjectives on the lines. The last two have been done for you:

my _____   our _____
your [*informal*] _____   your [*informal*, pl.] _____
his _____   their _____
her _____   your [*formal*] **Ihr**
its **sein**

_____ **7**

2 A German friend wants you to talk about your family. Can you translate the expressions in this family-tree into German?

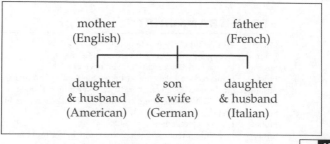

_____ **13**

3 Fill in the appropriate endings for these possessive adjectives:

1 Das ist mein___ Mutter.
2 Sind das Ihr___ Kinder?
3 Da sind eu___ Eltern.
4 Das sind unser___ Mäntel.
5 Ich sehe sein___ Bruder.

_____ **5**

4 Two young women meet in a youth hostel. Translate the English sentences into German to complete the conversation they have.

A: Hallo, woher kommst du?
B: (I am American). Und du?
A: (I am French). Wie lange bist du schon hier?
B: (Three days). Und du?
A: Auch erst drei Tage. (What's your occupation)?
B: (I am a secretary).
A: Interessant! Und wie lange willst du bleiben?
B: (I would like to stay for five days).
A: Ach, (is that your jacket)?
B: Ja, vielen Dank!

| | 7 |

5 Rewrite the following conversation so that people address each other with **Sie**. Remember to change the verb if necessary.

Example: A: Wie heißt **du**? A: Wie heiß**en Sie**?

A: Woher kommt **ihr**?
B: Wir kommen aus den USA.
A: Und wie lange bleibt **ihr**?
B: Wir bleiben fünf Tage. Und **du**?
A: Ich bleibe noch eine Woche. Ach, sind das **eure** Socken?
C: Nein, das sind nicht unsere Socken. Aber ist das **deine** Jacke?
A: Ja, danke! Wisst **ihr** auch, wo mein Mantel ist?
C: Ich glaube, er ist dort. Ja, hier ist **dein** Mantel!

| | 7 |

TOTAL SCORE 39

If you scored less than 29 go through the dialogues and the Language Building sections again, before completing the Summary on page 74.

Summary 5

 Now try this final test summarizing the main points covered in the unit. You can check your answers on the recording.

How would you:
1 ask someone her occupation?
2 say that you're an engineer?
3 ask how long someone has been here?
4 say you want to stay for five days?
5 say you're American?
6 say you're British?
7 say that you have a son and a daughter?
8 say that you're married?
9 say that you're divorced?

REVISION

Before going on to Unit 6, you may find it worthwhile to work through the explanations on possessive adjectives again. Pay particular attention to the possessive adjectives **dein** ('your'), **euer** ('your', *informal plural*), **ihr** ('her'), and **Ihr** ('your', *formal*), and when to use them.

Think of simple sentences and how you would change them if talking to someone you'd address as **du** and someone you'd address as **Sie**, for example:

Mögt **ihr** Tee?   Magst **du** Tee?   Mögen **Sie** Tee?

You may also find it helpful to review the pronouns that have been introduced up to now: **ich** ('I'), **du** ('you', *informal singular*), **er** ('he'), **sie** ('she'), **es** ('it'), **wir** ('we'), **ihr** ('you', *informal plural*), **sie** ('they'), and **Sie** ('you', *formal*).

6

Out and about

Unterwegs

OBJECTIVES

In this unit you'll learn how to:

- ✓ ask where places are
- ✓ understand simple directions
- ✓ tell a taxi driver where you want to go
- ✓ talk about how you travel to work

And cover the following grammar and language:

- ✓ the dative case
- ✓ prepositions followed by the dative case
- ✓ the imperative

LEARNING GERMAN 6

To help you remember vocabulary, use a small notebook or index cards to organize the vocabulary by topic. A particularly good way of learning prepositions is to illustrate them with a simple sketch. Get into the habit of taking your notebook with you, and whenever you've got some spare time read through and test yourself on some vocabulary.

Now start the recording for Unit 6.

ACTIVITY 1 is on the recording.

ACTIVITY 2

Correct the statements which are false.

1 Kurt muss an der Ampel rechts gehen.	T / F
2 Die Theaterkasse hat jetzt geöffnet.	T / F
3 In der Elbestraße können Sie Konzertkarten kaufen.	T / F
4 Der Marktplatz ist gleich neben der Elbestraße.	T / F

DIALOGUE 1

○ Entschuldigung, wo ist das Theater?

■ Das Theater ist am Marktplatz.

○ Und wie komme ich dorthin?

■ Gehen Sie hier immer geradeaus bis zur Ampel. An der Ampel gehen Sie links und die zweite Straße rechts.

○ Vielen Dank. Kann ich dort auch Konzertkarten kaufen?

■ Ja, die Theaterkasse hat aber erst um halb sechs geöffnet. In der Elbestraße können Sie jetzt Karten kaufen.

○ Und wie komme ich zur Elbestraße?

■ Oh, die Elbestraße ist neben dem Marktplatz.

○ Vielen Dank, auf Wiedersehen.

VOCABULARY

das Theater(-)	theatre
der Marktplatz(-¨-e)	market place
dorthin	there
gehen	to go
geradeaus	straight
immer geradeaus	straight on, straight ahead
die Ampel(-n)	traffic light
links	left
die Straße(-n)	street
zweite	second
rechts	right
die Konzertkarte(-n)	concert ticket
die Theaterkasse(-n)	box office
jetzt	now
neben	next to

✓ Describing where things are

When describing where something is located using the following prepositions, the noun that follows must be in the dative case.

an at, next to, on	**auf** on (top of)	**in** in
neben beside, next to	**vor** in front of	**unter** under
hinter behind	**zwischen** between	**über** over, above

The dative is indicated by a change in the article.

	m	*f*	*n*
Nominative	der Marktplatz	die Ampel	das Theater
Dative	**dem** Marktplatz	**der** Ampel	**dem** Theater

For nouns in the plural the dative article is **den**. Plural nouns in the dative always take the ending **-n**, unless their plural already ends in **-n**: **das Kind, die Kinder**, but **den Kindern**.

	m	*f*	*n*
Nominative	die Männer	die Frauen	die Autos
Dative	**den** Männern	**den** Frauen	**den** Autos

Some prepositions are contracted with the article into a single word:

an + dem → am	am Marktplatz
in + dem → im	im Theater

ACTIVITY 3

Add the correct article in the dative.

1 Das Theater ist an ____ Marktplatz.
2 Das Café ist in ____ Elbestraße.
3 Die Kinder sind vor ____ Kino.
4 Die Hauptstraße ist neben ____ Marktplatz.
5 Die Kinder spielen auf ____ Straße.

🎧 Now do activities 4 and 5 on the recording.

Fahren Sie zum Hotel, bitte

ACTIVITY 6 is on the recording.

ACTIVITY 7

1 Where does Frank tell the taxi driver to go to?
2 Does the taxi driver know the hotel?
3 What is next to the hotel?
4 What is the name of the street?
5 How much does Frank have to pay?
6 How much does he give the driver?

DIALOGUE 2

○ Fahren Sie zum Hotel Adler, bitte.

■ Das Hotel Adler kenne ich nicht. Wie heißt die Straße?

○ Das weiß ich leider nicht. Aber fahren Sie zur Post, das Hotel ist neben der Post.

■ Ah, jetzt weiß ich, wo es ist. Das Hotel muss in der Herderstraße sein.

○ Halten Sie bitte hier. Das Hotel ist auf der linken Seite. Vielen Dank, wie viel kostet das?

■ Das macht €7,20.

○ Hier sind €8. Der Rest ist für Sie.

■ Vielen Dank. Auf Wiedersehen.

VOCABULARY	
fahren (er fährt)	to go (in a vehicle)
kennen	to know, be acquainted with
wissen (er weiß)	to know (a fact)
leider	unfortunately
die Seite(-n)	side
auf der linken Seite	on the left-hand side
der Rest	the change [*literally* the rest]

✓ Telling somebody to do something

When giving a command or instruction, you use the imperative form of the verb. In the formal imperative form, the verb (e.g. **gehen**) comes first, and the pronoun **Sie** comes immediately after. The formal imperative is identical to the **Sie** form of the present tense, with the exception of **sein**.

Fahren Sie nach rechts. Turn right.
Gehen Sie an der Metzgerei vorbei. Go past the butcher's.
Seien Sie bitte ruhig! Be quiet, please!

✓ Giving directions with *zu* ('to')

When giving directions with the preposition **zu**, the noun that follows is in the dative. **zu** + the definite article is usually contracted.

zu + dem → zum (in front of masculine / neuter nouns)
zu + der → zur (in front of feminine nouns)

Ich fahre **zum** Supermarkt. I'm going to the supermarket.
Ich gehe **zur** Bäckerei. I'm going to the bakery.

✓ *wissen* and *kennen*

The verbs **wissen** and **kennen** both mean 'to know'. **kennen** is used when talking about a person, a place, or something one is acquainted with; **wissen** means to know something as a fact.

Ich **weiß**, wo er arbeitet, aber ich **kenne** den Mann nicht.
I know where he works, but I don't know the man.
Ich **kenne** Frankfurt gut. I know Frankfurt well.
Ich **weiß** nicht, wer das ist. I don't know who that is.

wissen is irregular:

ich **weiß**	wir **wissen**
du **weißt**	ihr **wisst**
er / sie / es **weiß**	sie **wissen**
	Sie **wissen**

ACTIVITY 8

wissen or **kennen**? Supply the correct form.

1 ____ Sie, wo der Bahnhof ist?
2 ____ Sie den Mann?
3 Nein, aber ich ____, wo er wohnt.
4 ____ Sie Hamburg?
5 ____ Sie, wo die Universität dort ist?

Now do activities 9 and 10 on the recording.

6.3 Going to work
Der Weg zur Arbeit

ACTIVITY 11 is on the recording.

ACTIVITY 12

1 Was ist Rita von Beruf?
2 Wann beginnt ihre Arbeit?
3 Bis wann arbeitet Rita?
4 Hat Rita ein Auto?
5 Was macht Rita in der Mittagspause?

DIALOGUE 3

○ Mein Name ist Rita Henkel. Ich bin Sekretärin in einem
Büro in Frankfurt. Meine Arbeit beginnt um halb acht und
ich arbeite bis halb fünf.
Ich habe kein Auto. Deshalb fahre ich immer mit dem Bus
und mit dem Zug zur Arbeit. Mit dem Bus fahre ich zum
Bahnhof. Dort nehme ich einen Zug nach Frankfurt.
In der Mittagspause gehe ich mit einer Kollegin in die
Kantine. Freitags gehen wir oft zum Italiener.

VOCABULARY	
das Büro(-s)	office
die Arbeit(-en)	work
das Auto(-s)	car
deshalb	therefore
der Bus(-se)	bus
mit dem Bus fahren	to go by bus
der Zug(-̈-e)	train
der Bahnhof(-̈-e)	station
die Mittagspause(-n)	lunch break
die Kollegin(-nen)	female colleague
die Kantine(-n)	canteen
freitags	on Fridays
der Italiener(-)	Italian (restaurant) [*colloquial*]

⊘ More prepositions with the dative

Like **zu** ('to'), these prepositions are followed by the dative. Note that **bei** + **dem** is commonly contracted to **beim**, **von** + **dem** to **vom**.

mit with, by (transport)	**bei** at, by
aus from, out of	**nach** to, after
von from	**seit** since

Das Kind geht **mit dem** Vater. The child goes with the father.
Die Kinder kommen **aus dem** Kino. The children are coming out of the cinema.
Ich wohne fünf Minuten **vom** Bahnhof. I live five minutes from the station.
Er ist **beim** Fußball. He's playing football [*literally* He's at football].

When it is used without an article, **nach** means 'to'. **nach** followed by the dative means 'after'. **seit** ('since') is used in time phrases.

Ich fahre **nach** Hamburg. I'm going to Hamburg.
Nach der Ampel gehen Sie links. After the traffic light turn left.
Seit dem Sommer wohnt er in Bremen. Since the summer he's been living [*literally* he's living] in Bremen.

⊘ Indefinite article in the dative

	m	*f*	*n*
Nominative	ein	eine	ein
Dative	einem	einer	einem

Remember that the possessive adjectives (**mein**, **dein**, etc.) and **kein** are **ein** words. Their endings in the dative are identical to those of **ein**.

⊘ *Fahren mit*

Whenever you want to say 'to go by' you use **fahren mit**. Note that **fahren** is used only with vehicles.

Rita **fährt mit** dem Bus zum Bahnhof. Rita goes by bus to the station.
Dann **fährt** sie **mit** dem Fahrrad. Then she goes by bike.

ACTIVITY 13

Add the correct form of the indefinite article.

1 Ich fahre mit ___ Kollegin.
2 Er fährt mit ___ Bus.
3 Sie arbeitet in ___ Büro.
4 Der Mann wohnt in ___ Hotel.
5 Die Frau geht zu ___ Konzert.

🎧 Now do activities 14 and 15 on the recording.

6.4 Hiking
Wandern

Hiking is a favourite pastime for many Germans. This excerpt from a travel brochure describes a three-day hiking trip to Switzerland.

CULTURE

3-tägige Wandertour

DAVOS–LENZERHEIDE

Am ersten Tag:

Ankunft mit dem Zug in Davos. Sie können die Stadt besichtigen.

Am zweiten Tag:

6 Stunden wandern bis Arosa. In Arosa können Sie in Ihrem Hotel zu Abend essen.

Am dritten Tag:

4 Stunden wandern bis nach Lenzerheide. In Lenzerheide haben Sie ein Zimmer in einem 5-Sterne Hotel. Es gibt dort ein Schwimmbad und eine Sauna. Zum Abendessen gibt es Schweizer Spezialitäten.

Preise: 2 Übernachtungen:
(a) Doppelzimmer pro Person € 205
(b) Einzelzimmer pro Person € 230

---

besichtigen	to go sightseeing, look round
wandern	to hike
am zweiten Tag / Abend	on the second day / evening
am dritten Tag	on the third day
die Übernachtung(-en)	overnight stay
die Person(-en)	person
die 3-tägige Wandertour	three-day hiking trip
die Wandertour(-en)	hiking trip
am ersten Tag	on the first day
die Ankunft(-˜-e)	arrival
die Stadt(-˜-e)	town
die Stunde(-n)	hour
zu Abend essen	to have dinner
das 5-Sterne Hotel(-s)	five-star hotel
es gibt dort	there is, there are
	[*literally* it gives there]
das Schwimmbad(-˜-er)	swimming pool
die Sauna(-s)	sauna
zum Abendessen	for dinner
die Schweizer Spezialität(-en)	Swiss speciality
der Preis(-e)	price
pro Person	per person

ACTIVITY 16

Imagine you're planning a hiking trip for yourself and a friend. Your friend has lots of questions. To answer her queries, read the article from the travel brochure below.

1 Wie fahren wir nach Davos?
2 Können wir Davos besichtigen?
3 Wie lange wandern wir am zweiten Tag?
4 Wo essen wir am zweiten Abend?
5 Wie lange wandern wir am dritten Tag?
6 Was essen wir im Hotel in Lenzerheide?
7 Wie viel kosten zwei Übernachtungen für zwei Personen im Doppelzimmer?
8 Wie viel kosten zwei Übernachtungen im Einzelzimmer?

6.5 Hotel Gertrud

 EIN BESUCH IN DER GALERIE
A VISIT TO THE GALLERY

Peter möchte heute Abend eine neue Kunstgalerie in Konstanz besuchen.

Peter plans to go out this evening to visit a new art gallery in Konstanz.

der Besuch(-e)	visit
die Kunstgalerie(-n)	art gallery
besuchen	to visit
der Kollege(-n)	male colleague
die Fotoausstellung(-en)	photo exhibition
mein alter Freund	my old friend
in welcher	in which
glauben	to believe
der Moment(-e)	moment
von hier aus	here [*literally* starting from here]
über	over
die Kreuzung(-en)	crossroads

ACTIVITY 17

Answer the following questions about the dialogue.

1 Was macht Peter heute Abend?
2 Wie heißt Peters Freund?
3 Was gibt es in der neuen Galerie?
4 Kennt Frau Semmler die neue Kunstgalerie?
5 Warum kennt Frau Semmler die Kurfürstenstraße?

ACTIVITY 18

Listen to Frau Semmler's description on the recording and try to find the gallery on the map. Mark the building with a cross.

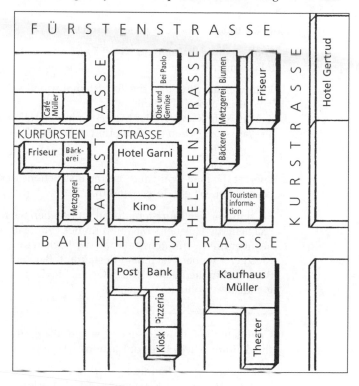

STORY TRANSCRIPT

Frau Semmler Hallo, Herr Ritter. Wie geht es Ihnen?

Peter Oh, danke, sehr gut. Und wie geht es Ihnen?

Frau Semmler Auch gut. Und, haben Sie schon Pläne für heute?

Peter Ja, heute Mittag besuche ich einen Kollegen und heute Abend möchte ich in die neue Kunstgalerie gehen. Es gibt dort eine Fotoausstellung von meinem alten Freund Michael. Wissen Sie, wie ich zur Galerie Gallo komme?

Frau Semmler Die neue Galerie kenne ich leider nicht. Wissen Sie, in welcher Straße sie ist?

Peter Ich glaube sie ist in der Kurfürstenstraße.

Frau Semmler Ach, in der Kurfürstenstraße. Mein Friseur ist auch in der Kurfürstenstraße. Ja, also, gehen Sie von hier aus links, immer geradeaus bis zur Ampel. An der Ampel gehen Sie rechts in die Bahnhofstraße. Gehen Sie über die Kreuzung, und dann rechts in die Karlstraße. In der Karlstraße immer geradeaus. Nach der Bäckerei gehen Sie links, das ist die Kurfürstenstraße. Die Galerie muss neben dem Café Müller sein.

Peter Vielen Dank Frau Semmler. Jetzt finde ich den Weg.

Test

Now it's time to test your progress in Unit 6.

1 Look again at the map on page 85 and answer the following questions.

Look again at the map on page 85

   1 In welcher Straße ist die Touristeninformation?
   2 Was ist neben der Bank?
   3 Was ist links neben der Metzgerei in der Helenenstraße?
   4 Was ist zwischen der Bank und dem Kiosk?

      4

2 Look at the map again and use the instructions that you've been given. Where do you end up?

Sie sind vor der Touristeninformation. Gehen Sie nach rechts in die Helenenstraße und immer geradeaus. Gehen Sie über die Kurfürstenstraße, an der Bäckerei und an der Metzgerei vorbei. Nach dem Restaurant 'Bei Paolo' gehen Sie rechts in die Fürstenstraße. Gehen Sie dann immer geradeaus. Wohin kommen sie?

      5

3 Complete the following sentences with the correct form of the definite article. Use contractions where possible.

   1 Er geht zu _____ Bahnhof.
   2 Wir essen in _____ Restaurant.
   3 Das Café ist neben _____ Marktplatz.
   4 Das Kind kommt aus _____ Haus.
   5 Sie arbeitet in _____ Büro.

      5

4 Reorder the words below to form statements. Remember to change the article where appropriate. (2 points for a correct answer, 1 point if you make one mistake.)

   1 die Elbestraße / kaufen / Sie / können / in / eine Theaterkarte
   2 ich / kenne / das Hotel Adler / nicht
   3 Herr Maier / das Hotel / ist / in
   4 die Kinder / neben / das Kino / warten

      8

5 Answer the following questions using the words in brackets. (2 points for a correct answer, 1 point if you make one mistake.)

1 Wo warten die Kinder? (das Haus / vor)
2 Wo kauft Frau Meier den Rock? (das Kaufhaus / in)
3 Wo kauft Inga die Theaterkarten? (die Elbestraße / in)
4 Wo ist Petras Suppe? (der Tisch / auf)
5 Wo gibt es den James Bond Film? (das Kino / in)

| 10 |

6 Answer the following questions about yourself.

1 Wie fahren Sie zur Arbeit?
2 Von wann bis wann arbeiten Sie?
3 Wo essen Sie in der Mittagspause?
4 Was essen Sie gerne?
5 Gehen Sie oft ins Restaurant?

| 10 |

7 Fill in the missing endings.

1 Ich muss zu____ Supermarkt.
2 Kommst du zu____ Kino?
3 Ich fahre morgen zu____ Arbeit.
4 Ich komme zu____ Café Neubauer.
5 Gehen Sie bis zu____ Marktplatz.

| 5 |

TOTAL SCORE | 47 |

If you scored less than 37, go through the dialogues and the Language Building sections again before completing the Summary on page 88.

Summary 6

Now try this final test summarizing the main points covered in the unit. You can check your answers on the recording.

How would you:
1   tell a taxi driver to take you to the theatre?
2   ask someone how to get to the market place?
3   ask where you can buy tickets for the cinema?
4   tell someone that the hotel is on the right?
5   tell someone that the bakery is next to the tourist information office?
6   tell a taxi driver to keep the change?

REVISION

Before going on to the next unit you might find it helpful to revise and practise the prepositions you've learnt so far. You could take a dictionary and collect the words for various items in your room. Then you could form simple sentences to say where things are, for example:

> **Das Bild ist an der Wand.** The picture is on the wall.
> **Die Lampe ist an der Decke.** The lamp is on the ceiling.
> **Die Tasse ist auf dem Tisch.** The cup is on the desk.
> **Das Buch ist im Regal.** The book is on the shelf.

Remember: **an, auf, in, neben, vor, unter, hinter, zwischen,** and **über** must be followed by the dative when you're describing where something is located. In the next unit, you'll learn that these prepositions can also be followed by the accusative, which is why they're called 'two-way' prepositions. However, **mit, von, zu, bei, nach, seit,** and **aus** are always followed by the dative.

Travelling
Reisen

OBJECTIVES

In this unit you'll learn how to:

✓ ask about arrival and departure times

✓ ask which platform a train leaves from

✓ buy a bus or train ticket

✓ ask whether you can pay by cash, cheque, or credit card

✓ make a seat reservation on a train

✓ book a room in a hotel or guest house

And cover the following grammar and language:

✓ verbs with a separable prefix (e.g. **ankommen**, **umsteigen**, **abfahren**)

✓ direct object pronouns (**mich**, **dich**, **ihn**, **sie**, **es**, **uns**, **euch**, **sie**, **Sie**)

✓ ordinal numbers (e.g. **erste**, **zweite**, **dritte**)

✓ prepositions followed by the accusative case

LEARNING GERMAN 7

A good way to practise speaking German is to talk to yourself about things you have to do, or things you are doing at the moment (**ich trinke den Kaffee, ich esse den Kuchen**, etc.). Start with simple sentences and you will realize how much you can already express. Then you can start to change these simple sentences into more complicated ones – for example, try to make them negative (**ich trinke den Kaffee nicht, ich esse den Kuchen nicht**).

Now start the recording for Unit 7.

Arrival and departure times
Ankunfts- und Abfahrtszeiten

ACTIVITY 1 is on the recording.

ACTIVITY 2

Correct the statements which are false.

1	The next train leaves at 1.30.	T / F
2	The train arrives at 3.45.	T / F
3	He has to change trains.	T / F
4	The ticket costs €87,30.	T / F

DIALOGUE 1

○ Wann fährt der nächste Zug nach Hamburg?

■ Der nächste Zug nach Hamburg fährt um 12.30 Uhr.

○ Und wann kommt er in Hamburg an?

■ Er kommt um 15.45 Uhr an.

○ Muss ich umsteigen?

■ Nein, es ist ein Intercity, er fährt direkt nach Hamburg.

○ Wie viel kostet die Fahrkarte?

■ Wollen Sie eine einfache Fahrkarte oder eine Hin-und Rückfahrkarte?

○ Eine einfache Fahrkarte.

■ Das kostet 79,30 Euro plus 8 Euro IC-Zuschlag.

○ Von wo fährt der Zug ab?

■ Von Gleis 5.

VOCABULARY

die Ankunftszeit(-en)	arrival time
die Abfahrtszeit(-en)	departure time
fahren(er fährt)	to run [of a train]
nächste	next
ankommen	to arrive
umsteigen	to change trains
der Intercity(-s)	Intercity
direkt	direct
die einfache Fahrkarte(-n)	single ticket, one way ticket
die Hin-und Rückfahrkarte(-n)	return ticket, round trip ticket
IC-Zuschlag(-¨-e)	Intercity supplement
abfahren	to depart
das Gleis(-e)	platform [*literally* track]

✅ Verbs with separable prefixes

Separable prefix verbs function to some extent like certain English verbs that are made up of two parts (e.g. to get up, to get out). In statements, questions, and the imperative, the prefix is separated from the main verb and is put at the end of the sentence.

ankommen	Der Zug **kommt** um 7 Uhr **an**.
	The train arrives at 7 o'clock.
abfahren	**Fährt** der Zug um 8 Uhr **ab**?
	Does the train leave at 8 o'clock?
umsteigen	**Steigen** Sie in Frankfurt **um**.
	Change trains in Frankfurt.

Note that **fahren** is irregular in the **du** and **er/sie/es** forms. An umlaut is added to the a: **du fährst, er/sie/es fährt**.

When a verb with a separable prefix is used with a modal verb, the prefix is not separated and the verb in the infinitive form comes at the end of the sentence.

Wo muss ich **umsteigen**? Where do I have to change trains?

From now on, verbs with a separable prefix will be shown in vocabulary lists as follows: **ab/fahren**. Some common separable prefixes:

ab-	abfahren	to depart
an-	ankommen	to arrive
auf-	aufmachen	to open
aus-	ausgehen	to go out
ein-	eingießen	to pour
her-	herkommen	to come here
mit-	mitbringen	to bring along

ACTIVITY 3

Reorder the words to form statements. Watch out: you'll have to separate the verbs and add the correct verb endings in four of the five sentences!

1 ausgehen / heute Abend / ich
2 Peter / eine Flasche Wein / mitbringen
3 um 3 Uhr / abfahren / der Zug
4 um 13 Uhr / ankommen / Sabine
5 eingießen / ich / kann / den Tee

🔊 Now do activities 4 and 5 on the recording.

7.2 Buying a ticket
Eine Fahrkarte kaufen

 ACTIVITY 6 is on the recording.

ACTIVITY 7

1 Where does Franziska want to go?
2 When does her train leave?
3 When does it arrive?
4 Does she want a smoking compartment?
5 How does she pay?

DIALOGUE 2

○ Können Sie mich mit dem Fahrkartenschalter verbinden?
▼ Ja, warten Sie einen Moment, bitte.
■ Guten Tag, was kann ich für Sie tun?
○ Ich möchte am Montagmorgen nach Freiburg fahren. Gibt es eine direkte Zugverbindung?
■ Ja, es gibt einen Zug um 9.37 Uhr. Er kommt um 11.30 Uhr in Freiburg an.
○ Gut, muss ich für den Zug einen Sitzplatz reservieren?
■ Ja, es ist besser, Sie reservieren ihn gleich. Raucher oder Nichtraucher?
○ Nichtraucher.
■ Das macht 60 Euro, der IC-Zuschlag 8 Euro und die Platzreservierung 1,50 Euro. Alles zusammen 69,50 Euro.
○ Kann ich mit Kreditkarte bezahlen?
■ Ja, natürlich.

VOCABULARY

---

der Fahrkartenschalter(-)	ticket office
verbinden	to connect
der Montagmorgen	Monday morning
die Zugverbindung(-en)	rail connection (link)
der Sitzplatz(-̈-e)	seat
reservieren	to reserve, book
besser	better
Raucher oder Nichtraucher?	smoking or non-smoking?
die Platzreservierung(-en)	seat reservation
die Kreditkarte(-n)	credit card
mit Kreditkarte bezahlen	to pay by credit card

✓ Accusative of personal pronouns

When you use a pronoun as a direct object, it changes form.

	s		pl
Nominative	Accusative	Nominative	Accusative
ich	mich (me)	wir	uns (us)
du	dich (you)	ihr	euch (you)
er	ihn (him)	sie, Sie	sie, Sie (them, you)
sie	sie (her)		
es	es (it)		

Er fragt mich. Ich frage ihn. He asks me. I ask him.

✓ Using 'it'

Remember, you have three words for 'it' when replacing a noun in the nominative – er, sie, es.

In the nominative you replace a der word with er.

Der Kaffee ist heiß. Er ist heiß. The coffee is hot. It is hot.

In the accusative you replace a den word with ihn.

Ich trinke den Kaffee. Ich trinke ihn. I drink the coffee. I drink it.

To replace female and neuter words in the accusative, you use sie and es, respectively. In the plural you use sie.

Ich suche die Tasse. Ich suche sie. I'm looking for the cup. I'm looking for it.
Ich suche das Kleid. Ich suche es. I'm looking for the dress. I'm looking for it.
Ich suche die Kleider. Ich suche sie. I'm looking for the dresses. I'm looking for them.

ACTIVITY 8

Replace the underlined word by a pronoun.

1 Wann fährt der Zug ab?
2 Er trinkt den Wein nicht.
3 Wie viel kostet die Fahrkarte?
4 Woher kommt Franz?
5 Woher kommt die Frau?

🎧 Now do activities 9 and 10 on the recording.

Booking a room
Ein Zimmer reservieren

🔊 **ACTIVITY 11** is on the recording.

ACTIVITY 12

Which of the following statements is wrong?

1 In der Woche vom 28. Januar sind noch Zimmer frei.
2 Hans reserviert ein Einzelzimmer mit Bad.
3 Die Pension ist in der Büchnerstraße.
4 Die Pension ist auf der linken Seite.

DIALOGUE 3

■ Haben Sie in der Woche vom 28. Januar ein Zimmer frei?
○ Wie lange wollen Sie denn bleiben?
■ Bis zum zehnten Februar.
○ Ja, da ist noch etwas frei.
■ Sehr gut. Kann ich bitte gleich ein Doppelzimmer reservieren?
○ Ja, natürlich. Mit oder ohne Bad?
■ Mit Bad, bitte. Wie viel kostet das?
○ Das macht 55 Euro pro Nacht. Und wie ist Ihr Name, bitte?
■ Hans Meyer. Sagen Sie, wie komme ich denn vom Bahnhof zur Pension?
○ Vom Bahnhof gehen Sie links, an den Parkplätzen vorbei. Gehen Sie bis zur Ampel. Dann in die Büchnerstraße. Die Pension ist auf der linken Seite.
■ Vielen Dank. Auf Wiederhören.

VOCABULARY	
die Woche(-n)	week
in der Woche vom ...	in the week beginning ...
der Januar	January
der Februar	February
bis zum zehnten Februar	until the tenth of February
frei	vacant
mit / ohne Bad	with / without bathroom
die Pension(-en)	guest house
vorbei	past
der Parkplatz(-̈-e)	car park, parking lot

✅ Ordinal numbers

You've already come across the words for 1st, 2nd, and 3rd: **erste**, **zweite**, **dritte**. Ordinal numbers from 4th to 19th add **-te** to the number, and ordinal numbers from 20th add **-ste** to the number:

4th **vierte**	20th **zwanzigste**
19th **neunzehnte**	29th **neunundzwanzigste**

Ordinal numbers take the same endings as adjectives. After **der, die**, and **das** the adjective ending is **-e**; after **den** and the plural **die** it is **-en**:

✅ Dates

To give a date you can say: **Heute ist der fünfte Mai** ('Today is the 5th of May'). To say 'on the 5th of May', etc. use the preposition **am**. The ordinal number takes the ending **-en**.

am Montag, den **2**. Dezember / am **zweiten** Dezember
on Monday the 2nd of December / on 2nd December
Ich komme **am** siebzehnten Juni. I'm coming on the 17th of June.

der Januar	der April	der Juli	der Oktober
der Februar	der Mai	der August	der November
der März	der Juni	der September	der Dezember

✅ The dative with location and the accusative with movement

The prepositions **an, auf, in, neben, über, vor, unter, hinter**, and **zwischen** are used with the dative when saying where something is located (answering the question **wo?**, 'where?'):

Wir sind **im** Bahnhof. We are in the station.
Wir sind **auf dem** Marktplatz. We are in the market place.

When used with a verb indicating movement from one place to another (a verb of motion), these prepositions are used with the accusative (answering the question **wohin?**, 'where to?'):

Wir fahren **in den** Bahnhof. We are driving to the station.
Wir gehen **vor das** Museum. We are going to the front of the museum.

ACTIVITY 13

Supply the correct form of the definite article.

1 Die Kinder spielen vor ____ Museum.
2 Herr Müller geht in ____ Museum.
3 Er stellt das Glas auf ____ Tisch. (**stellen**, to put)
4 Das Glas ist auf ____ Tisch.

🎧 Now do activities 14 and 15 on the recording.

7.4 Go by train!

Fahren Sie mit der Bahn!

In Germany going by train is quite comfortable. Services are mostly reliable and convenient. However, getting a ticket from a ticket machine and dealing with the typical jargon involved needs some practice, as you'll see below.

ACTIVITY 16

Where can you get a ticket at various times of the day? Read the text and answer the questions below.

1 Es ist 10 Uhr. Wo können Sie eine Fahrkarte kaufen?
2 Es ist 24 Uhr. Wo können Sie jetzt eine Fahrkarte kaufen?

Sie wollen mit dem Bus oder mit dem Zug fahren? Dann müssen Sie einen Fahrschein kaufen. Sie können ihn von 7 bis 22 Uhr im Bahnhof am Schalter kaufen. Am Fahrscheinautomaten können Sie immer einen Fahrschein ziehen.

---

der Fahrschein(-e)	ticket
der Schalter(-)	ticket office
der Fahrscheinautomat(-en)	ticket vending machine
ziehen	to get [*literally* to pull]

ACTIVITY 17

A non-German-speaking friend of yours wrote down these instructions from a ticket machine, but got them mixed up. Can you sort them into the right order?

1 Lesen Sie die Geldanzeige: wie viel müssen Sie bezahlen?

2 Entnehmen Sie Ihr Ticket und das Wechselgeld.

3 Wählen Sie zuerst Ihr Fahrtziel.

4 Werfen Sie das Geld ein.

5 Dann drücken Sie: Erwachsener oder Kind?

die Geldanzeige(-n)	display [*literally* money display]
entnehmen (er entnimmt)	to take out (of the ticket machine)
das Wechselgeld(-er)	change
wählen	to choose
das Fahrtziel(-e)	destination
ein / werfen	to insert
das Geld(-er)	money
drücken	to push (a button)
der Geldschein(-e)	bank note
die Zahl(-en)	number

ACTIVITY 18

You are at the railway information desk in Zurich and want to find out the following things. Translate your questions into German.

1 How much is a return ticket to Frankfurt?
2 When does the train depart?
3 When does the train arrive in Frankfurt?
4 Do I have to change trains?
5 Do I have to make reservations?
6 From where does the train depart?

(1A) **SUSANNE KAUFT EINE FAHRKARTE**
SUSANNE BUYS A TICKET

Susanne ist am Bahnhof und möchte eine Zugfahrkarte
kaufen. Die Frau am Schalter ist eine Freundin von Susannes
Mutter.

Susanne is at the station and wants to buy a train ticket. The
woman at the ticket office is a friend of Susanne's mother.

verreisen	to go away
Urlaub machen	to go on holiday, to go on vacation
der Urlaub(-e)	holiday, vacation
morgens	in the morning
gegen 9 Uhr	around nine o'clock
nicht so spät	not too late
am Abend	in the evening
heutzutage	nowadays
der Scheck(-s)	cheque
bar	cash
ich muss nach Hause	I have to go home [*colloquial*]
nach Hause	home [*literally* to house, to home]
der Gast(-¨-e)	guest
das Mittagessen(-)	lunch
der Gruß(-¨-e)	greetings

ACTIVITY 19

Listen for these sentences in the dialogue and number them in
the order they occur.

So, du rauchst also nicht.   _____

Möchtest du morgens fahren?   _____

Ja, am Montag.   _____

Machst du Urlaub in Berlin?   _____

Ich möchte eine Fahrkarte nach Berlin kaufen.   _____

ACTIVITY 20

Say if these statements are true, false, or you don't know because the information wasn't given.

1	Susanne wants to buy a ticket to Berlin.	T / F / DK
2	She wants to go there on holiday.	T / F / DK
3	She wants to stay in Berlin for five days.	T / F / DK
4	There is a train at 8.34.	T / F / DK
5	Susanne reserves a seat in a smoking compartment.	T / F / DK
6	She pays by cheque.	T / F / DK
7	Frau Weinheimer asks Susanne to greet Frau Semmler.	T / F / DK

STORY TRANSCRIPT

Susanne	Guten Tag, Frau Weinheimer.
Frau W.	Oh, guten Tag, Susanne, was kann ich für dich tun?
Susanne	Ich möchte eine Fahrkarte nach Berlin kaufen.
Frau W.	Nach Berlin möchtest du verreisen?
Susanne	Ja, am Montag.
Frau W.	Machst du Urlaub in Berlin?
Susanne	Nein, ich bleibe nur 3 Tage.
Frau W.	Möchtest du morgens fahren?
Susanne	Ja, ich möchte gerne so gegen 9 Uhr abfahren. Ich möchte nicht so spät am Abend in Berlin ankommen.
Frau W.	Also, da gibt es eine Zugverbindung nach Berlin um 8.34 Uhr.
Susanne	Sehr gut, ich reserviere gleich einen Platz in einem Nichtraucherabteil.
Frau W.	So, du rauchst also nicht. Das ist sehr gut. Heutzutage …
Susanne	Kann ich die Fahrkarte mit einem Scheck bezahlen?
Frau W.	Natürlich, du kannst mit Kreditkarte, mit Scheck oder bar bezahlen.
Susanne	Gut, Frau Weinheimer, ich muss gleich nach Hause. Die Gäste warten auf das Mittagessen. Auf Wiedersehen und vielen Dank.
Frau W.	Und viele Grüße an deine Mutter!

Test

Now it's time to test your progress in Unit 7.

1 Reorder the words to form statements. Watch out: in all sentences except one, you'll have to change the verbs. (2 points for a correct answer, 1 point if you make one mistake.)

   1 ankommen / der Zug / um 7 Uhr
   2 er / umsteigen / nicht / muss
   3 aufmachen / ich / die Flasche Wein
   4 Petra / Inga / und / heute Abend / ausgehen
   5 abfahren / der Zug / auf Gleis 5

   10

2 Replace the underlined noun with a pronoun.

   1 Ich treffe <u>den Mann</u> heute Abend.
   2 Ich mag <u>die Kinder</u>.
   3 Susanne trinkt <u>den Kaffee</u>.
   4 Sie kauft <u>den Rock</u> im Kaufhaus.
   5 Er isst <u>den Apfelkuchen</u> später.

   5

3 Translate the sentences into German. (2 points for a correct answer, 1 point if you make one mistake.)

   1 He sees me.
   2 We see her in the cinema.
   3 She sees him in the café.
   4 We see you [*pl., informal*] in the theatre.
   5 We see you [*sing., informal*] in the bakery.

   10

4 Work out the questions for the following answers. (2 points for a correct answer, 1 point if you make one mistake.)

1 Q:
  A: Eine Hin-und Rückfahrkarte kostet 55 Euro.
2 Q:
  A: Nein, Sie müssen nicht umsteigen.
3 Q:
  A: Der Zug fährt um 11.20 Uhr.
4 Q:
  A: Von Gleis 3.
5 Q:
  A: Nein, sie müssen nicht reservieren.

| 10

5 Complete each sentence with the correct form of the definite article.

1 Das Theater ist neben ____ Polizei.
2 Er geht in____ Theater.
3 Wir warten vor ____ Kino.
4 Der Kaffee ist in ____ Tasse.
5 Sie gehen heute in ____ James Bond Film.

| 5

6 Answer the questions by saying ja, 'yes', and replacing the underlined noun with a pronoun.

Example: Sehen Sie das Auto? Ja, ich sehe es.

1 Nehmen Sie den Rock?
2 Bezahlen Sie die Cola?
3 Kaufen Sie die Fahrkarte jetzt?
4 Sehen Sie die Kinder?
5 Essen Sie den Apfelkuchen mit Sahne?

| 5

TOTAL SCORE | 45

If you scored less than 35, go through the dialogues and the Language Building sections again before completing the Summary on page 102.

Summary 7

Now try this final test summarizing the main points covered in the unit. You can check your answers on the recording.

How would you:
1 ask when the next train to Mannheim departs?
2 ask if the train goes to Frankfurt?
3 say that you want to buy a return ticket?
4 ask if you can pay by credit card?
5 say you'd like to reserve a seat in a non-smoking compartment?
6 ask how much a double room with a bathroom costs?
7 reserve a single room for Tuesday, the 2nd of January?
8 ask how you get from the tourist information office to the station?

REVISION

Before going on to the second Review, you may find it useful to practise prepositions with the accusative and dative again. You could begin by using a dictionary to look up the words for the rooms in your house: bathroom, kitchen, bedroom, study, dining room, living room, hall. Write them down with their article in the nominative, accusative, and dative case: **die Küche**, **die Küche**, **der Küche** (see page 77 for the dative case of the definite article). Then imagine going from room to room. **Ich gehe in die Küche** ('I'm going into the kitchen'). **Ich bin in der Küche** ('I'm in the kitchen'), and so on.

You could also look up the words for things on your desk and talk about them, saying where they are – **Der Stift is auf dem Tisch** – or where you're putting them – **Ich lege den Stift auf den Tisch**.

Review 2

VOCABULARY

1 Which sentence matches which picture?

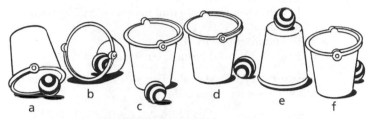

b a c d e f

1 Der Ball ist im Eimer.
2 Der Ball ist neben dem Eimer.
3 Der Ball ist vor dem Eimer.
4 Der Ball ist auf dem Eimer.
5 Der Ball ist unter dem Eimer.
6 Der Ball ist hinter dem Eimer.

2 Which is the odd one out in each group?

1 Schlachtplatte / Schweinebraten / Fisch / Rinderfilet
2 Sohn / Tochter / Kind / Engländerin
3 verheiratet / gesundheitsbewusst / geschieden
4 Hauptgericht / Vorspeise / Kellnerin / Nachspeise
5 Post / Bahnhof / Deutschland / Theater / Restaurant
6 Bus / Zug / Arbeit / Auto

3 Match the following questions with the correct answer from a–f below.

1 Wohin möchten Sie fahren?
2 Wie kann ich bezahlen?
3 Von wo fährt der Zug ab?
4 Wo kann man hier Fahrkarten kaufen?
5 Wollen Sie eine einfache Fahrt?
6 Muss ich umsteigen?

a Nein, das ist eine Direktverbindung.
b Ja, bitte.
c Am Fahrkartenschalter.
d Mit Kreditkarte oder in bar.
e Von Gleis sieben.
f Nach Hamburg.

4 A day in the life of a train conductor. To find out all about it, fill the following prefixes into the gaps: **an, aus, ab, mit, um**.

1 Um sieben Uhr fährt er aus Hamburg ____ .
2 Er nimmt einen Zug nach Berlin. Seine Frau kommt

____.

3 In Berlin steigt er ____ und nimmt einen Zug nach München.
4 Er kommt müde in München ____ .
5 Er geht ____ und besucht ein Restaurant.

5 **Sie** (formal 'you'), **sie** ('she'), or **sie** ('they')? Translate the following sentences into English.

1 Wann kommen Sie in New York an?
2 Wann fährt sie nach Hamburg ab?
3 Ich glaube, sie fährt morgen nach Berlin.
4 Kommen sie am dreiundzwanzigsten März nach Hannover?
5 Ich glaube, sie fahren um fünfzehn Uhr ab.

6 Replace the underlined words with the appropriate pronoun. Write the pronouns on the lines provided.

1 <u>Der Zug</u> fährt um sieben Uhr ab. ____
2 Kann ich <u>einen Platz</u> reservieren? ____
3 Ich nehme <u>den Mantel</u> mit. ____
4 <u>Der Mann</u> geht in die Elbestraße. ____
5 <u>Das Restaurant</u> ist am Marktplatz. ____
6 <u>Barbara</u> ist fünfzehn Jahre alt. ____

7 A busy day in Frau Specht's life. Here's where she went. First fill in the missing definite articles. Then fill these times into the appropriate gaps: **zehn vor zehn, zwanzig Uhr, halb zehn, Viertel nach neun**.

1 Neun Uhr: Sie geht auf ____ Bahnhof.
2 _____: Sie ist auf ____ Bahnhof.
3 _____: Sie geht zu____ Marktplatz.
4 _____: Sie ist auf ____ Marktplatz.
5 _____: Sie geht in____ Theater.
6 Zwanzig Uhr dreißig: Sie ist in____ Theater.

8 **nicht** or **kein / keine / keinen**? Put the appropriate word in the gaps.

1 Ich mag _____ Fisch.
2 Ich gehe heute _____ ins Kino.
3 Es gibt hier _____ Wein.
4 Er ist _____ geschieden.
5 Wir haben heute leider _____ Apfelkuchen.
6 Ich mag ihn _____ .

🔊 LISTENING

9 Listen to people giving directions on the recording and follow them on the map below. Which places do you get to?

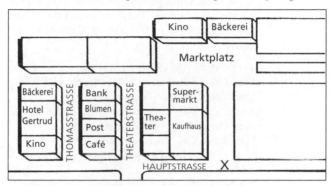

10 Listen to the conversation on the recording between Maria and Rudolf. Answer the questions below.

1 Wo sind Maria und Rudolf? Sie sind im

_____ .

2 Wie will sie nach Berlin fahren? Mit _____ .
3 Wohin möchte Maria? Sie will in_____ .
4 Wohin will Rudolf gehen? Er möchte in

_____ .

5 Wie ist Maria von Beruf? Sie ist _____ .
6 Wie fährt sie zur Arbeit? Sie fährt mit

_____ .

7 Was ist Rudolf von Beruf? Er ist _____ .
8 Wer hat eine Tochter?_____ .
9 Wer hat einen Sohn? _____ .

11 At a New Year's Eve party, Frau Meier lost the most unlikely items. Complete the conversation she had with the party's host by writing in the correct possessive adjectives. Then listen to the recording to check your answers.

- Guten Morgen. Entschuldigung, Herr Winn, ich suche _____(my) Mantel.
- Hallo, Frau Meier. _____ (your) Mantel ist da.
- Ach, vielen Dank. Haben Sie auch _____ (my) Schuhe?
- Ja, natürlich. _____ (Your) Schuhe sind hier.
- Ich suche auch noch _____ (my) Pullover.
- Kein Problem. Er ist hier.

⟨🔊⟩ SPEAKING

12 You're in a restaurant with a client. Read through this conversation and write out what you would say according to the cues. Once you've prepared your part, read through it a couple of times. Then switch on the recording and see if you can respond in the pauses, without looking at your notes.

Your client: Was nehmen Sie?
You: 1 ask 'What can you recommend?'
Your client: Mögen Sie Fleisch?
You: 2 say 'No, I don't like meat. I prefer fish.'
Your client: Die Forelle ist sehr gut.
You: 3 say 'OK, I'll have the trout.'
Your client: Herr Ober, die Speisekarte bitte. Möchten Sie auch etwas Wein?
You: 4 say 'I can't drink alcohol. I'm driving.'
Your client: Ach so, natürlich.

Your client: Möchten Sie noch eine Nachspeise?
You: 5 answer 'No thank you. I'm full.'
You: 6 call the waiter and say 'We'd like to pay please.'

13 Listen to the recording. You're being interviewed by a market researcher, who is going to ask you some questions about yourself. You'll be asked:

– how old you are
– your occupation
– whether you are married
– whether you have children
– how you get to work

Prepare your answers (the questions will appear in a different order on the recording), then listen to the recording and respond in the pauses.

Free time
Freizeit

OBJECTIVES
In this unit you'll learn how to:
✓ make suggestions and express preferences
✓ make arrangements to meet
✓ express likes and dislikes
And cover the following grammar and language:
✓ adjective endings after an indefinite article
✓ the dative of personal pronouns
✓ prepositions with the dative
✓ word order of direct and indirect objects

LEARNING GERMAN 8

If you're studying with a friend, why not meet on a regular basis and try to talk German for at least 15 minutes? Choose a topic from one of the units and try a little conversation, using the vocabulary given. For Unit 8 you could talk about things you like to do and things you don't like. Ask your friend about his or her hobbies. If there's a word you don't know, look it up in the dictionary, but try to stick to words you can remember.

Now start the recording for Unit 8.

Informationen erfragen

🔊 **ACTIVITY 1** is on the recording.

ACTIVITY 2

1 Who is coming next week?
2 Does Sandra's father eat meat?
3 What restaurant does Sandra's colleague recommend?
4 Why does he recommend it?
5 Why does she want to know what's on at the theatre?

DIALOGUE 1

■ Meine Eltern kommen nächste Woche. Kennen Sie vielleicht ein gutes Restaurant? Mein Vater ist Vegetarier.

○ Ja, das Parasol ist sehr gut. Es gibt dort ein großes Büffet. Da gibt es etwas für jeden Geschmack. Wie lange bleiben ihre Eltern in Hamburg?

■ Nur drei Tage. Was läuft denn im Theater? Meine Eltern gehen sehr oft ins Theater.

○ Das weiß ich leider nicht, aber ich habe hier einen sehr guten Veranstaltungskalender. Sie finden dort alle Informationen über kulturelle Ereignisse.

■ Ah, das ist eine gute Idee. Vielen Dank für Ihre Hilfe.

VOCABULARY	
das Büfett(-s)	buffet
jeder	every
der Geschmack(-¨-er)	taste
laufen* (er läuft)	to walk, to run, [*here =*] to be on
der Veranstaltungskalender (-)	calendar of events
das Ereignis(-se)	event
die Idee(-n)	idea

✅ Adjective endings after an indefinite article

When adjectives come after an indefinite article, they take the following forms in the singular:

	Nominative	Accusative	English
m	ein schoner Abend	einen schönen Abend	a nice evening
f	eine schöne Ausstellung	eine schöne Ausstellung	a nice exhibition
n	ein schönes Auto	ein schönes Auto	a nice car

Nominative

Das ist ein guter Veranstaltungskalender! That's a good calendar of events!
Das ist eine gute Idee. That's a good idea.
Das ist ein gutes Restaurant. That's a good restaurant.

Accusative

Es gibt einen guten Veranstaltungskalender. There's a good calendar of events.
Ich habe eine gute Idee! I've got a good idea!
Kennen Sie ein gutes Restaurant? Do you know a good restaurant?

Note the similarity between these endings and the endings for the definite article in the nominative case (**der, die, das**) and accusative case (**den, die, das**).

After **kein** and the possessive adjectives (**mein, dein, sein,** etc.), the adjectives take the same endings. In the plural the adjective ending is **-n**.

meine kleinen Kinder my little children
keine guten Filme no good films

ACTIVITY 3

Add the correct ending to the adjective.

1 Er fährt ein neu___ Auto.
2 Ich suche einen rot_____ Rock.
3 Er kennt ein gut_____ Restaurant.
4 Meine Kollegin hat eine schick_____ Frisur.

🔊 Now do activities 4 and 5 on the recording.

Making suggestions

Vorschläge machen

🔊 **ACTIVITY 6** is on the recording.

ACTIVITY 7

1 What does Michael order first?
2 Why does he finally order a vegetable soup?
3 What does Anna prefer to watching an action film?
4 What does Anna say about the new art gallery?

DIALOGUE 2

○ Ich nehme den Rinderbraten und ein Bier.

■ Du isst Fleisch? Ich esse kein Fleisch. Ich esse lieber Gemüse.

○ Ach so, hmm, dann nehme ich eine Gemüsesuppe. Möchtest du später in den neuen James Bond-Film gehen?

■ Nein, lieber nicht. Actionfilme gefallen mir nicht. Ich gehe lieber ins Theater.

○ Kennst du schon die neue Kunstgalerie?

■ Ja, die kenne ich, die Bilder dort gefallen mir sehr gut.

○ Ich kenne den Künstler.

■ Oh, das ist interessant. Kannst du mich dem Künstler vielleicht vorstellen?

○ Natürlich. ... Er sitzt vor dir.

| VOCABULARY |

der Actionfilm(-e) action film, action movie
vor/stellen to introduce
sitzen to sit

✓ Using the dative case for the indirect object

As well as being used after certain prepositions – **bei, nach, von, aus, zu, mit, seit** (see page 81) – the dative case is used for the indirect object of a sentence. The indirect object is the person (or thing) to whom or for whom the action of the verb is being done. To identify the indirect object in English, you often need to rephrase the sentence.

> Ich stelle dich **dem Künstler** vor. I'll introduce you to the artist.
> Ich bringe **ihm** einen Kaffee. I'll get him a coffee. (I'll take the coffee to him.)

In the dative case, the personal pronouns (**ich, du,** etc.) take the following forms:

Nominative	Dative	Nominative	Dative
ich	**mir**	wir	**uns**
du	**dir**	ihr	**euch**
er	**ihm**	sie	**ihnen**
sie	**ihr**	Sie	**Ihnen**
es	**ihm**		

✓ Verbs taking the dative case

A number of verbs in German must be followed by an indirect object in the dative case, for example:

danken to thank   **gehören** to belong to   **folgen** to follow
gefallen to please   **helfen** to help   **passen** to fit

> Ich helfe **dir**. I'll help you.
> Der Mantel gehört **mir**. The coat belongs to me.
> Sie danken **ihm**. They thank him.

ACTIVITY 8

Supply the correct pronoun in the dative case.

1 Er kommt mit _____ (me) ins Kino.
2 Sie gibt _____ (you *sing.*) die Eintrittskarten.
3 Ich gehe mit _____ (them) in die Galerie.
4 Sie spielt mit _____ (him) Tennis.
5 Er gibt _____ (her) seine Telefonnummer.

Now do activities 9 and 10 on the recording.

8.3 Talking about hobbies
Über Hobbies reden

 ACTIVITY 11 is on the recording.

ACTIVITY 12

Correct the statements which are false.

1 Sandra doesn't like Hamburg.	T/F
2 She doesn't know a lot of people.	T/F
3 She likes swimming.	T/F
4 She plays tennis and badminton.	T/F
5 Petra and Sandra decide to play tennis on Friday.	T/F

DIALOGUE 3

○ Na, wie gefällt es dir hier in Hamburg?

■ Oh, Hamburg gefällt mir sehr gut. Leider kenne ich noch nicht so viele Leute.

○ Im Sportverein kannst du leicht Leute kennen lernen. Schwimmst du gerne?

■ Nein, ich schwimme nicht so gerne, ich spiele lieber Tennis oder Badminton.

○ Ich spiele nächste Woche mit zwei Freunden Tennis. Ich kann dich ihnen vorstellen. Hast du am Freitagabend Zeit?

■ Ja, Freitag habe ich Zeit.

○ Gut. Kannst du um 7 Uhr zu mir kommen?

■ Ja, gibst du mir noch deine Adresse und Telefonnummer?

○ Natürlich, ich schreibe sie dir nach der Mittagspause auf.

VOCABULARY

die Leute	people
der Sportverein(-e)	sports club
leicht	[*here* =] easily
kennen lernen	to get to know
schwimmen	to swim
Zeit haben	to have time
geben (er gibt)	to give
schreiben	to write

✓ Word order of indirect and direct objects

In general, the direct object (DO) follows the indirect object (IO):

Sie	gibt	**dem Mann**	**den Kaffee.**
		IO	DO

She gives the coffee to the man (gives the man the coffee).

Sie	gibt	**ihm**	**den Kaffee.**
		IO	DO

She gives the coffee to him (gives him the coffee).

However, when the direct object is a personal pronoun, it comes before the indirect object:

Sie	gibt	**ihn**	**dem Mann.**
		DO	IO

She gives it to the man.

Sie	gibt	**ihn**	**ihm.**
		DO	IO

She gives it to him.

✓ Expressing likes and dislikes

To say that you like doing something, you use **gern** or **gerne** after the verb. To say that you don't like doing something, add **nicht** before **gern** or **gerne**:

Ich fahre **(nicht) gern** Ski. I (don't) like skiing.
Ich spiele **(nicht) gerne** Tennis. I (don't) like playing tennis.

In a question, **gern** or **gerne** follows the subject:

Gehst du gerne ins Kino? Do you like going to the cinema?

ACTIVITY 13

Underline the indirect object and replace it with the correct pronoun.

Example: Sie danken dem Mann. Sie danken **ihm**.

1 Ich helfe der Frau.
2 Die Hose gefällt dem Mann.
3 Wir danken den Musikern (musicians) für das Konzert.
4 Er gibt den Kindern die Schokolade.
5 Er gibt dem Taxifahrer das Geld.

Now do activities 14 and 15 on the recording.

Visit Hamburg
Besuchen Sie Hamburg

CULTURE

ACTIVITY 16

1 Wie viele Leute wohnen in Hamburg?
2 Wo können Sie schon um 6 Uhr einkaufen?
3 Können Sie auf dem Fischmarkt nur Fisch kaufen?
4 Wo gibt es viele Kaufhäuser und Cafés?
5 Wie heißt ein sehr interessantes Museum?

Die 1,7 Millionen-Stadt Hamburg bietet etwas für jeden Geschmack. Essen Sie gerne Fisch? Dann können Sie schon um 6 Uhr morgens auf dem Fischmarkt Fisch und viele andere Dinge kaufen. Danach können Sie in einem Café am Jungfernstieg frühstücken und dann in den vielen Kaufhäusern einkaufen.

Und was können Sie sonst noch tun? Im Sommer können Sie eine Hafenrundfahrt machen. Im Winter besuchen Sie vielleicht gerne ein Museum. Sehr interessant ist zum Beispiel das Hot Spice Museum, ein Gewürzmuseum. Sie können natürlich auch ins Theater gehen, zum Beispiel in das Deutsche Schauspielhaus oder in das Thalia Theater.

die Million(-en)	million
der Fischmarkt (-¨-e)	fish market
das Ding(-e)	thing
danach	after that
der Jungfernstieg	*shopping street in Hamburg*
frühstücken	to have breakfast
ein/kaufen	to shop (for something)
was ... sonst noch?	what else ... ?
der Sommer(-)	summer
die Hafenrundfahrt(-en)	harbour cruise
der Winter(-)	winter
interessant	interesting
zum Beispiel	for instance
das Gewürz(-e)	spice
das Deutsche Schauspielhaus	*theatre in Hamburg*
das Thalia Theater	*theatre in Hamburg*

ACTIVITY 17

Lisa and Jannick have just arrived in Hamburg. Using the information in the chart, say what they like to do and what they don't like to do.

Example: Lisa geht gerne ins Theater.

Lisa

ins Theater gehen	[✓]
einkaufen gehen	[✓]
essen gehen	[✗]
ins Museum gehen	[✗]
ins Café gehen	[✓]

Jannick

ins Theater gehen	[✗]
einkaufen gehen	[✗]
essen gehen	[✓]
ins Museum gehen	[✓]
ins Café gehen	[✗]

ACTIVITY 18

Now look at the charts again and list two things each of them could do in Hamburg, e.g.:

Lisa, du kannst ins Thalia Theater gehen.
Du kannst am Jungfernstieg ...

Jannick, du kannst ...

EINE EINLADUNG ZUM WANDERN
AN INVITATION TO GO HIKING

Peter trifft Susanne im Speisezimmer. Sie deckt gerade den Tisch.

die Einladung(-en)	invitation
treffen (er trifft)	to meet
wie immer	as always
ja klar, ich mache ja auch Urlaub!	why, of course, I'm on holiday!
frei haben	to have the day off
warum (nicht)	why (not)
los/gehen	to set off
mit/kommen	to come too
na	[*here* =] why [*exclamation*]
der Wanderverein(-e)	hiking club
bestimmt	certainly, definitely
lustig	amusing, funny
es wird bestimmt lustig	it will certainly be great fun
nett	nice, kind
Bescheid sagen	to let (someone) know
in Ordnung	all right

ACTIVITY 19

Listen to the conversation and say if these statements are true, false, or you don't know because the information isn't mentioned.

1 Peter doesn't have any plans for today. T/F/DK
2 Susanne has to work on Saturday morning. T/F/DK
3 Peter asks Susanne to go hiking with him
  on Sunday. T/F/DK
4 They all meet at 10 o'clock. T/F/DK
5 Susanne doesn't know if she will come. T/F/DK
6 Hubert is going as well. T/F/DK
7 Susanne will let Peter know on Saturday
  afternoon. T/F/DK

ACTIVITY 20

Put these sentences from the dialogue in the right order.

1 Möchtest du vielleicht mit mir wandern gehen?
2 Ich wandere nicht so gerne mit vielen Leuten.
3 Ist das in Ordnung?
4 Was machst du denn heute?
5 Wann möchtest du denn losgehen?
6 Ja klar, ich mache ja auch Urlaub.

STORY TRANSCRIPT

Peter	Hallo Susanne, du arbeitest, wie immer.
Susanne	Hallo Peter, und du arbeitest **nicht**, auch wie immer?
Peter	Ja klar, ich mache ja auch Urlaub! Arbeitest du im Urlaub?
Susanne	Nein, natürlich nicht. Was machst du denn heute?
Peter	Was machst **du** denn am Samstag? Hast du frei?
Susanne	Am Samstag morgen muss ich arbeiten. Aber dann habe ich frei.
Peter	Möchtest du vielleicht mit mir wandern gehen?
Susanne	Wandern – ja gerne, warum nicht? Wann möchtest du denn losgehen?
Peter	Ich treffe die anderen Leute um halb zehn.
Susanne	Die anderen Leute? Wer kommt denn noch mit?
Peter	Na, die Leute aus dem Wanderverein! Es wird bestimmt sehr lustig. Du kannst viele nette Leute kennen lernen.
Susanne	Ich kenne aber schon viele nette Leute. Ich wandere nicht so gerne mit vielen Leuten.
Peter	Aber die Leute sind alle sehr nett! Und Hubert kommt auch.
Susanne	Ich weiß noch nicht. Ich kann dir ja am Samstag Bescheid sagen. Ist das in Ordnung?
Peter	Natürlich. Ich sehe dich ja beim Frühstück.

Test

Now it's time to test your progress in Unit 8.

1 Translate the following sentences into German. (It is easier if you underline the indirect object first, and then translate.) (2 points for a correct answer, 1 point if you make one mistake.)

1 He gives me the menu
2 Can you help me?(*formal*)
3 I'll play tennis with him next week.
4 The shoes belong to her.
5 He gives us his tickets.

10

2 Match the German phrases 1–4 with the correct translation a–d.

1 wir schwimmen gerne   a   we are on holiday
2 wir danken ihm   b   we help him
3 wir machen Urlaub   c   we thank him
4 wir helfen ihm   d   we like swimming

4

3 Supply the correct adjective endings.

1 Ich möchte einen lustig___ Film sehen.
2 Das ist aber ein schick___ Kleid.
3 Sie kauft ihrem Mann einen neu___ Mantel.
4 Sie bestellt eine gebacken___ Forelle.
5 Kennen Sie schon meine neu___ Telefonnummer?

5

4 Replace the indirect object with the correct pronoun.

1 Die Bedienung gibt dem Mann den Kaffee.
2 Sie kauft ihren Kindern ein Eis.
3 Er bestellt seiner Frau eine Gemüsesuppe.
4 Ich gebe Hans die Briefmarken.

4

5 Now replace both the direct object and the indirect object with the correct pronouns. Watch out for the word order!

1 Die Bedienung gibt dem Mann den Kaffee.
2 Sie kauft ihren Kindern ein Eis.
3 Er bestellt seiner Frau eine Gemüsesuppe.
4 Ich gebe Hans die Briefmarken.

4

6 Choose the correct adjective to complete the sentences.

rote/alte/schöner/neues/blauen

1 Sie kauft einen _____ Rock.
2 Ich nehme die _____ Hose.
3 Hans fährt ein _____ Auto.
4 Das ist ein _____ Urlaub.
5 Ich treffe meine _____ Freundin.

5

7 Rewrite the sentences replacing the nouns with the correct pronouns.

Example: Ich helfe der Frau. Ich helfe **ihr**.

1 Er hilft Sabine.
2 Sie hilft den Kindern.
3 Wir helfen dem Mann.
4 Er hilft der alten Frau.
5 Ich helfe dem kleinen Kind.

5

TOTAL SCORE **37**

If you scored less than 27, go through the dialogues and the Language Building sections again before completing the Summary on page 120.

Summary 8

Now try this final test summarizing the main points covered in the unit. You can check your answers on the recording. Use the informal **du** where necessary.

How would you:
1 tell someone that you have to work on Saturday?
2 ask your friend if she knows a good restaurant?
3 say you like Munich very much? (use **gefallen**)
4 say you don't like his new jacket? (use **gefallen**)
5 tell your brother that you can introduce him to your friends?
6 ask your friend 'Can you give me his telephone number?'
7 say that on Saturday you're playing tennis with him?

REVISION

A good way to remember the different personal pronouns is to write each one in a sentence. It would be a good idea to create your own sentences using, for example, the phrase **Ich gebe es dem Mann** and then replacing **dem Mann** with **ihm**. Now take another sentence: **Ich gebe es den Kindern** and replace **den Kindern** with **ihnen**. Use the Language Building sections to help you get the sentences right. Once you have written the sentences down, read them aloud as often as possible. In this way, they will start to sound familiar to you.

All in the past
Alles in der Vergangenheit

OBJECTIVES

In this unit you'll learn how to:

- ✓ talk about what you did on holiday
- ✓ talk about what you did at the weekend
- ✓ ask questions about events in the past

And cover the following grammar and language:

- ✓ the perfect tense with **haben**
- ✓ the past participles of regular and irregular verbs
- ✓ the simple past tense of **sein**

LEARNING GERMAN 9

If you have access to the Internet, you may find it interesting to have a look at the web pages of German magazines and newspapers. Magazines that offer easier as well as more challenging articles are *Stern* (www.stern.de) and the women's magazine *elle* (www.elle.de). The magazine *Der Spiegel* (www.spiegel.de) is a leading political magazine in Germany, but you may want to save its web pages until you reach a more advanced level of German. Daily newspapers of interest are the conservative *Die Welt* (www. welt.de) and the leftist *tageszeitung* (www.taz.de). These web pages are easily accessible. Don't expect to understand every single word of an article: concentrate on grasping the gist of it.

Now start the recording for Unit 9.

ACTIVITY 1 is on the recording.

ACTIVITY 2

Correct the statements which are false.

1 Frau Meier often enjoyed a leisurely breakfast.　T / F
2 Frau Meier spent a lot of time on the beach.　T / F
3 She often had dinner in a restaurant.　T / F
4 She went to see Siena and Florence.　T / F

DIALOGUE 1

○ Frau Meier, da sind Sie ja wieder! Wie war Ihr Urlaub?

■ Ach, Italien war toll!

○ Das ist ja schön. Was haben Sie denn so gemacht?

■ Also, morgens haben wir immer ganz gemütlich gefrühstückt. Danach haben wir immer am Strand gelegen. Nachmittags haben wir Kaffee getrunken. Ja, und abends haben wir oft in einem Restaurant gegessen.

○ Waren Sie denn nicht in Siena – oder in Florenz?

■ Ach, nein. Der Strand war viel zu schön!

VOCABULARY	
wie war Ihr Urlaub?	how was your holiday?
ja	yes [*here used to express surprise and for emphasis*]
wieder	again
war	was
toll	great [*colloquial*]
gemacht	done, made [*from* **machen**]
morgens	in the morning(s)
ganz	[*here =*] really, very
gemütlich	leisurely, relaxed
gefrühstückt	had breakfast [*from* **frühstücken**]
der Strand(-¨-e)	beach
gelegen	laid [*from* **liegen**]
liegen	to lie
nachmittags	in the afternoon(s)
getrunken	drunk [*from* **trinken**]
abends	in the evening(s)
gegessen	eaten [*from* **essen**]

✓ The perfect tense with *haben*

In English the simple past is used to talk about past events (e.g. 'he ate'): in German the perfect tense is mainly used in this context (e.g. **er hat gegessen** – 'he has eaten'). The perfect tense has two components: the present tense of either **haben** or **sein** and a past participle – the **ge-** form of the verb. (See pages 141 and 169 for the perfect tense with **sein**.)

> Wir **haben** in einem Restaurant **gegessen**.
> [*literally* We have in a restaurant eaten.]
> We ate in a restaurant.

Note that the past participle always goes to the end of the sentence. See page 125 for the endings of past participles.

The **haben** form is always the second element of the sentence (see page 127 for the position of the **haben** form in questions). This does not necessarily mean it is the second word of the sentence, as (for example) there could be a time phrase or two subjects in the initial position:

> **Gestern Abend haben wir** in einem Restaurant gegessen.
> Yesterday evening we ate in a restaurant.
> **Hans und Peter haben** im Restaurant gegessen.
> Hans and Peter ate in a restaurant.

If the sentence starts with a time phrase (e.g. **gestern Abend**), the subject (e.g. **wir**) follows the verb, as in the present tense:

> **Am Montagabend essen wir** in einem Restaurant.
> On Monday evening we'll eat in a restaurant.

✓ Time phrases

The same word is used for 'in the morning' and 'in the mornings', etc.

morgens in the (early) morning(s)   **nachmittags** in the afternoon(s)
vormittags in the morning(s)   **abends** in the evening(s)
[*time before lunch*]

ACTIVITY 3

Put the words in the correct order to complete the sentences.

1 sie/getrunken/haben/Kaffee
2 abends/Paul/Schweinefilet/gegessen/hat
3 morgens/ich/am Strand/gelegen/habe
4 hast/du/gegessen/Pizza
5 nachmittags/Tee/haben/getrunken/wir

🎧 Now do activities 4 and 5 on the recording.

Wie war Ihr Wochenende?

🔊 **ACTIVITY 6** is on the recording.

ACTIVITY 7

Correct the statements which are false.

1	Frau Sommer went on a bike trip.	T/F
2	Frau Sommer had a leisurely dinner with her husband.	T/F
3	On Saturday, Frau Meier had a lie in.	T/F
4	On Sunday, Frau Meier went on a hiking trip.	T/F

DIALOGUE 2

○ Na, Frau Sommer, wie war Ihr Wochenende?

■ Ja, es war toll. Am Samstag habe ich eine Radtour gemacht, und am Samstagabend haben mein Mann und ich gemütlich gegessen.

○ Und am Sonntag?

■ Am Sonntag haben wir eine Wanderung im Odenwald gemacht. Am Sonntagabend habe ich gelesen. Und Sie, Frau Meier?

○ Och, es war wie immer. Am Samstag haben wir lange geschlafen und nachmittags haben wir unsere Wohnung geputzt. Und am Sonntag waren wir auch im Odenwald.

■ Zum Wandern?

○ Nein – zum Kaffeetrinken!

VOCABULARY

das Wochenende(-n)	weekend
am Samstagabend	on Saturday evening
eine Radtour machen	to go for a bicycle ride, cycling tour
eine Wanderung machen	to go on a hiking trip
der Odenwald	*low mountain region in Germany*
geschlafen	slept [*from* **schlafen**]
schlafen (er schläft)	to sleep
lange schlafen	to have a lie in
die Wohnung(-en)	apartment
putzen	to clean

✓ The past participle of regular verbs

The past participle of regular verbs is formed as follows:

1 Take the stem of the verb (the infinitive minus the -en ending):

mach<u>en</u> (to do, to make) – **mach-**

2 Add **ge-** and **-t**:

<u>ge</u>mach<u>t</u> (made)

Note: for verbs whose stem ends in -**t**, add an extra **e**:

arbei<u>t</u>en – **<u>ge</u>arbei<u>tet</u>**

✓ The past participle of irregular verbs

The past participle of irregular verbs ends in -**en**. Quite a few change their vowel, or change or even add consonants:

lesen	**<u>ge</u>lesen** (read)
essen	**<u>ge</u>gessen** (eaten)
trinken	**<u>ge</u>trunken** (drunk)

From now on, vocabulary lists will show only those past participles with a different spelling from the stem, e.g.:

geschrieben   written [*from* **schreiben**]

For all other past participles, only the infinitive will be given in the vocabulary list. All irregular verbs will be marked with an asterisk (*). Bearing in mind the rules outlined above, you can then work out their past participles and check whether you got them right in the Grammar Summary (pages 235–6).

ACTIVITY 8

Form the past participle of these regular verbs.

1 wohnen   4 fragen
2 kaufen   5 arbeiten
3 spielen   6 holen

ACTIVITY 9

A lazy weekend! Translate what Frau Walter did into German.

1 She read.   4 On Saturday, she had a lie in.
2 She ate.   5 On Sunday evening, she cleaned her
3 She drank coffee.   apartment.

Now do activities 10 and 11 on the recording.

(♠) **ACTIVITY 12** is on the recording.

ACTIVITY 13

1 When did Hans and his wife watch the Jack Nicholson movie?
2 When might Achim go to the cinema?
3 Has Hans already bought a new computer?
4 What does Hans get congratulated on?

DIALOGUE 3

○ Achim, hast du schon den neuen Film mit Jack Nicholson gesehen?
■ Nein, warum?
○ Anna und ich haben ihn am Samstagabend gesehen. Es war toll!
■ Hmm, vielleicht gehe ich am Mittwochabend ins Kino. Habt ihr eigentlich schon einen neuen Computer gekauft?
○ Nein, noch nicht. Wir müssen im Moment ein bisschen sparen.
■ Warum denn?
○ Anna und ich wollen bald heiraten – und auf Hochzeitsreise gehen!
■ Was, wirklich? Mensch, Hans, herzlichen Glückwunsch!

VOCABULARY	
der Film(-e)	film, movie
eigentlich	actually
der Computer(-)	computer
im Moment	currently [*literally* at this moment]
ein bisschen	a little bit
sparen	to save
bald	soon
heiraten	to marry, to get married
die Hochzeitsreise(-n)	honeymoon
auf Hochzeitsreise gehen	to go on a honeymoon
herzlichen Glückwunsch!	congratulations!

⊘ Times of the day

The words for morning (**der Morgen**), afternoon (**der Nachmittag**), and evening (**der Abend**) can be combined with the weekdays to form a single word in German expressing the various times of a day:

der Samstag + der Morgen = **der Samstagmorgen** Saturday morning

⊘ Questions about the past

In questions in the perfect tense, the past participle always goes to the end of the question (as in statements). The **haben** form follows the question word; if there is no question word, it appears at the beginning of the question:

Wann **habt** ihr eine Wanderung **gemacht**?
When did you go on a hiking trip?
Hast du schon einen neuen Computer **gekauft**?
Have you already bought a new computer?

⊘ The simple past of *sein* ('to be')

When talking about the past, Germans mainly use the simple past of **sein** rather than its more complex perfect tense (see pages 141 and 159). The simple past of **sein** can be used to translate 'was/were', 'has/have been', or 'was/were being'. The simple past of **sein** has the following forms:

ich **war**	wir **waren**
du **warst**	ihr **wart**
er/sie/es **war**	sie **waren**
	Sie **waren**

ACTIVITY 14

Put the words in order to complete the questions.

1 lange / geschlafen / Sie / wie / haben / ?
2 du / gegessen / hast / schon / ?
3 du / Kaffee getrunken / schon / hast / ?
4 den Film / wann / ihr / gesehen / habt / ?

ACTIVITY 15

Where was everyone? Translate these sentences into German.

1 On Saturday, we were in Hamburg.
2 On Sunday, I was in the Odenwald.
3 Where were you, Frau Meier?
4 Where were you, Peter and Maria?

🎧 Now do activities 16 and 17 on the recording.

9.4 The Germans on holiday
Die Deutschen im Urlaub

Most German employees are entitled to 'holiday money' (**das Urlaubsgeld**), paid once a year by their employer. A two- to three-week holiday every year is still considered normal, even though increasing unemployment rates have reduced travelling overall.

Walter Hoffmann, 67 Jahre
Ich bin Hobby-Archäologe und habe dieses Jahr wieder Urlaub in Griechenland gemacht. Ich habe so viele interessante Dinge gesehen!

Gisela Koslowsky, 54 Jahre
Mein Mann und ich gehen gerne wandern – und wir sprechen leider nur Deutsch. Deshalb machen wir jedes Jahr Urlaub in Österreich. Da versteht uns jeder!

Karola Rösch, 35 Jahre
Unsere Kinder sind noch klein. Deshalb haben wir wieder an der Ostsee Urlaub gemacht. Die Kinder haben am Strand gespielt, ich habe gelesen und mein Mann hat oft Volleyball gespielt. Es war toll – ein perfekter Familienurlaub!

Ingo Altmann, 27 Jahre
Im Urlaub will ich Sonne haben! Deshalb fahre ich jedes Jahr ins Ausland. Dieses Jahr war ich mit meiner Frau in Italien. Jeden Tag hat die Sonne geschienen! Es hat uns sehr gut gefallen.

der Hobby-Archäologe(-n)	amateur archaeologist
Griechenland	Greece
sehen*	to see
sprechen*	to speak
Deutsch	German
Österreich	Austria
verstehen*	to understand
die Ostsee	Baltic Sea
perfekt	perfect
der Familienurlaub(-e)	family holiday, family vacation
die Sonne(-n)	sun
das Ausland	abroad
jeden Tag	every day
geschienen	shone [*from* scheinen]
scheinen*	to shine

ACTIVITY 18

Quickly scan the text and write down who spent his or her holiday at each of these places.

1 in Austria   _____
2 in Italy   _____
3 at the Baltic Sea _____
4 in Greece   _____

ACTIVITY 19

Read the text again and write down (in English) why each person chose that particular holiday destination.

ACTIVITY 20

Now find the German equivalents of these English phrases.

1 I saw so many interesting things.
2 The children played on the beach.
3 My husband often played volleyball.
4 We liked it a lot!

DIE WANDERUNG
THE HIKING TRIP

Es ist Samstagmorgen. Susanne serviert das Frühstück im Hotel. Peter möchte immer noch mit Susanne wandern gehen.

servieren	to serve
immer noch	still
wandern gehen	to go hiking
mal	just [*used to moderate the tone of a request*]
geben*	to give, to hand
sich freuen	to look forward to (something)
ich habe mich schon so gefreut!	I was so looking forward to it!
das tut mir Leid	I'm sorry about this
das macht nichts	that doesn't matter
mit/gehen*	to come too, to come along
doch	[*here =*] really
aus/sehen*	to look
toll aus/sehen* (er sieht toll aus)	to look great
besonders	particularly
tanzen gehen*	to go dancing
wie gesagt	as (I) said before
allein	alone
andere Leute	other people
viel Spaß!	have fun! [*literally* lots of fun!]

ACTIVITY 21

Listen to the story again and decide whether these statements are true or false.

1 Susanne will join Peter on the hiking trip. T/F
2 Peter is disappointed because Susanne can't come along. T/F
3 Susanne claims that she'll have to go to the bakery. T/F
4 Susanne pours some coffee over Peter. T/F
5 Susanne says that she's going out dancing that evening. T/F

ACTIVITY 22

Read this summary of the conversation between Susanne and Peter. Underline the events that did not happen.

Peter frühstückt im Hotel Gertrud. Er möchte mit Susanne wandern gehen, aber Susanne will nicht mitgehen. Susanne mochte eine neue Frisur und geht zum Friseur. Sie will abends mit Peter tanzen gehen.

STORY TRANSCRIPT

Peter	Hallo, Susanne!
Susanne	Morgen.
Peter	Und? Gehen wir heute wandern?
Susanne	Nein, leider nicht. Ich kann heute nicht. Kannst du mir mal deine Tasse geben?
Peter	Ja, klar. Hier ist sie. ... Schade! Ich habe mich schon so gefreut! ... Aua! Autsch, das ist heiß!
Susanne	Huch, oh, das tut mir aber Leid!
Peter	Das macht nichts. Mensch, war das heiß! Aber warum kannst du denn nicht mitgehen?
Susanne	Ich muss heute noch einkaufen. Und danach will ich zum Friseur gehen.
Peter	Schon wieder? Aber du brauchst doch keine neue Frisur! Du siehst doch toll aus!
Susanne	Ja, ... aber heute Abend gehe ich tanzen. Da will ich besonders gut aussehen. Also wie gesagt: ich kann nicht. Und du bist ja nicht allein. Es gehen ja genug andere Leute mit!
Peter	Schade.
Susanne	Ja, also dann, viel Spaß heute!
Peter	Danke. Bis später!

Test

Now it's time to test your progress in Unit 9.

1 Match these German phrases with the correct English version.

1	frühstücken	a	to clean the apartment
2	etwas Schönes machen	b	to buy a new coat
3	eine Radtour machen	c	to marry
4	eine Wanderung machen	d	to save
5	die Wohnung putzen	e	to have breakfast
6	einen neuen Mantel kaufen	f	to do something nice
7	sparen	g	to go for a cycling tour
8	heiraten	h	to go on a hiking trip

8

2 Pretend you did all the things mentioned in exercise 1. Say what you did using the past tense. (Hint: all verbs in exercise 1 are regular.)

8

3 Give the past participles of these irregular verbs.

1 lesen
2 trinken
3 essen
4 liegen
5 sehen

5

4 Put the words in the correct order to form questions.

1 Sie / getrunken / schon Tee / haben / Herr Meier / ?
2 du / gegessen / Pizza / hast / ?
3 wann / gesehen / den Film / ihr / habt / ?
4 schon / den neuen Film / Sie / haben / gesehen / ?
5 gekauft / warum / keinen / du / hast / neuen Computer / ?

5

5 Hans and Anna get asked a lot of questions about their wedding. Translate them into German, using the informal 'you'. (2 points for a correct answer, 1 point if you make one mistake.)

1 Where did you get married?
2 Did you buy a new suit and a new dress?
3 Did you eat in a restaurant?
4 Did you have coffee? (use **trinken**)
5 How was your honeymoon?

10

6 A friend is asking you what you did last weekend. Using your diary below, answer her questions. (2 points for a correct answer, 1 point if you make one mistake.)

Example: Hast du am Sonntagmorgen gearbeitet?
Nein, da habe ich lange geschlafen.

	Freitag	Samstag	Sonntag
Morgen		gemütlich gefrühstückt	lange geschlafen
Nachmittag	die Wohnung geputzt	eine Radtour gemacht	
Abend	neuen Film mit Jack Nicholson gesehen	Pizza gegessen	gelesen

1 Was hast du am Freitag gemacht? Am Freitgnachmittag habe ich …
2 Und am Freitagabend? Was hast du da gemacht? Am Freitagabend …
3 Hast du am Samstagmorgen gearbeitet? Nein, da …
4 Und was hast du am Samstagnachmittag gemacht? Ich …
5 Warst du am Sonntagabend im Kino? Nein, da …

10

TOTAL SCORE **46**

If you scored less than 36, go through the dialogues and the Language Building sections again before completing the Summary on page 134.

Summary 9

 Now try this final test summarizing the main points covered in the unit. You can check your answers on the recording. Use the formal **Sie** where necessary.

How would you:
1 ask someone how his weekend was?
2 say 'thank you, it was great'?
3 ask someone what she did on Saturday evening?
4 say that on Saturday evening, you watched a film.
5 ask someone how his holiday was?
6 ask someone why she can't come along?

REVISION

It's a good idea to make a list of past participles with their infinitives (e.g. **lesen – gelesen**) as you come across them. This might also help you keep practising talking about past events and situations. As you go through your daily routines, think of how you would say what you've just done in German: for example, **ich habe Tee getrunken**, etc.

For Unit 10, the present tense of **sein** (see Unit 2, page 19) will be very important. You may want to consult the relevant Language Building section again if you feel uncertain about it.

Making plans
Pläne schmieden

OBJECTIVES

In this unit you'll learn how to:

✓ make suggestions

✓ say what you usually do at certain times

✓ talk about events and situations in the past

✓ communicate on the phone

✓ cancel an appointment and give a reason

And cover the following grammar and language:

✓ **weil** ('because') to give reasons

✓ the present tense to talk about future events

✓ **und** ('and'), **aber** ('but'), **denn** ('then'), and **oder** ('or') to link sentences

✓ the perfect tense with **sein**

LEARNING GERMAN 10

If you have a satellite dish, you may want to tune in to one of the German channels that are transmitted via the ASTRA satellite. Even though you may not understand everything, it will give you a chance to listen to German spoken at natural speed. You could check out the two main public TV stations ZDF (frequency 10.964) and ARD (11.494). You could also try one of the private channels such as RTL (11.229, 11.214), SAT 1 (11.288). You will not always get high-quality TV, but soap operas and TV series may be fun to watch. Their language is usually not too elaborate and the pictures will help you to guess what has been said. International news may also be a good thing to watch, particularly if you have already heard the day's news in English.

Now start the recording for Unit 10.

Making plans

Sollen wir ins Theater gehen?

🎧 **ACTIVITY 1** is on the recording.

ACTIVITY 2

Complete the sentences.

1 Montags	a	wollen Daniel und Sabine ins Kino gehen.
2 Dienstags		
3 Am Freitagabend	b	geht Daniel immer tanzen.
	c	hat Daniel immer einen Kochkurs.

DIALOGUE 1

○ Sollen wir Montagabend ins Theater gehen?

■ Da kann ich leider nicht, weil ich montags immer tanzen gehe.

○ Und wie ist es am Dienstag? Am Dienstag um neunzehn Uhr dreißig läuft 'Romeo und Julia'.

■ Nein, da kann ich auch nicht, weil ich dienstags einen Kochkurs habe.

○ Also, dann musst du etwas vorschlagen.

■ Sollen wir am Freitagabend ins Kino gehen?

○ Hmm, hast du ein Kinoprogramm?

■ Ja, hier ist es. Also, um einundzwanzig Uhr läuft eine romantische Komödie.

○ Ja, das hört sich gut an. Das machen wir!

VOCABULARY

sollen wir … ?	[*here* =] shall we … ?
ins Theater gehen*	to go to the theatre
da kann ich leider nicht	unfortunately, I can't then [*colloquial*]
und wie ist es am Dienstag?	and what about Tuesday?
der Kochkurs(-e)	cookery class, cooking class
vorschlagen* (er schlägt vor)	to suggest
das Kinoprogramm(-e)	cinema programme, movie programme
romantisch	romantic
die Komödie(-n)	comedy

✅ The days of the week

Montag	Monday	**Freitag**	Friday
Dienstag	Tuesday	**Samstag**	Saturday
Mittwoch	Wednesday	(also: **Sonnabend**)	
Donnerstag	Thursday	**Sonntag**	Sunday

The days of the week are masculine.

As in English, adding an **-s** to the days of the week changes their meaning to 'on Mondays, etc.' In this form – **montags, dienstags**, etc. – the days no longer take a capital letter.

✅ Giving reasons using *weil*

You can use **weil** ('because') to give reasons. Note that **weil** affects the word order in the part of the sentence it introduces: it sends the verb that carries the personal ending (the form that stands next to the subject) to the end of the sentence:

Ich kann nicht kommen. Ich **gehe** tanzen.
Ich kann nicht kommen, weil ich tanzen **gehe**.
I can't come, because I'm going dancing.

Er kommt nicht mit. Er **will** nicht tanzen.
Er kommt nicht mit, weil er nicht tanzen **will**.
He won't come along, because he doesn't want to dance.

Sie ist zu spät gekommen. Sie **hat** zu lange geschlafen.
Sie ist zu spät gekommen, weil sie zu lange geschlafen **hat**.
She was late, because she slept for too long.

weil is a subordinating conjunction. See the Grammar Summary on page 235 for further information.

ACTIVITY 3

Link these sentences using **weil**.

1 Ich habe keine Wanderung gemacht. Ich war zu müde.
2 Er arbeitet nicht. Er will Tennis spielen.
3 Ich bin müde. Ich habe nicht lange geschlafen.
4 Ich habe Hunger. Ich habe nichts gegessen.
5 Ich will nicht ins Kino gehen. Ich will ins Theater gehen.

🎧 Now do activities 4 and 5 on the recording.

Talking about planned activities

Was machst du am Wochenende?

🔊 **ACTIVITY 6** is on the recording.

ACTIVITY 7

Correct the statements which are false.

1 Günther wants to surf and to row. T/F
2 Günther doesn't want Rolf and his wife to come along. T/F
3 Rolf's wife, Anna, usually plays tennis at the weekend. T/F
4 Rolf will give Günther a call. T/F

DIALOGUE 2

○ Was machst du denn am Wochenende, Günther?
■ Ich will an den Bodensee fahren.
○ Ach, zum Surfen?
■ Nein, ich will Rad fahren und ich nehme mein Ruderboot mit.
○ Das hört sich gut an!
■ Ja! Wollt ihr nicht auch mitkommen?
○ Hmm, da muss ich Anna fragen, samstags spielt sie nämlich immer Volleyball. Und sonntags geht sie oft zum Tennis. Ich rufe dich morgen Abend an!
■ Also gut. Bis morgen Abend, Rolf!

VOCABULARY	
surfen	to surf
Rad fahren* (er fährt Rad)	to ride a bike, to cycle
das Ruderboot(-e)	rowing boat, rowboat
mit/nehmen* (er nimmt mit)	to take along
das hört sich gut an!	that sounds good!
mit/kommen*	to come too, to come along
nämlich	namely [*here* = as]
Volleyball spielen	to play volleyball
an/rufen*	to call (by phone)
morgen	tomorrow

⊘ Talking about the future

Germans mostly use the present tense to talk about the future. The context or a time phrase usually makes it clear that the speaker is referring to a future event:

Am Montag fahre ich ab. I'll leave on Monday.
Ich räume **morgen** auf. I'll tidy up tomorrow.
Heute Abend gehe ich ins Kino. Tonight, I'll go to the cinema.

⊘ Linking sentences using co-ordinating conjunctions

und ('and') is a coordinating conjunction. You can use it to join two sentences:

(a) Ich gehe wandern. Ich will auch rudern.
(b) Ich gehe wandern **und** ich will auch rudern.
I'm going hiking and I want to row as well.

Note the word order: coordinating conjunctions don't count – **will** is still the second element.

Other common coordinating conjunctions are: **aber** ('but'), **oder** ('or'), and **denn** ('for', 'because').

Ich fahre heute nach Berlin, **aber** morgen fliege ich nach Prag.
Today, I'll go to Berlin, but tomorrow I'll fly to Prague.

Ich gehe schwimmen, **oder** ich gehe tanzen.
I'll go swimming or I'll go dancing.

Ich komme nicht mit, **denn** ich habe keine Zeit.
I won't come along, because I don't have time.

ACTIVITY 8

Join these sentences using the appropriate coordinating conjunction.

1 Ich kann nicht lange schlafen. Ich muss zur Arbeit fahren.
2 Wir wollen frühstücken. Dann müssen wir die Wohnung putzen.
3 Ich gehe ins Kino. Ich gehe Volleyball spielen.
4 Ich mag kein Fleisch. Ich mag Fisch.
5 Hans fährt nach Rom. Er will in die Museen gehen.

Now do activities 9 and 10 on the recording.

10.3 Cancelling an appointment
Wir kommen leider nicht mit!

ACTIVITY 11 is on the recording.

ACTIVITY 12

1 Why can't Anna come along to Lake Constance?
2 Did Rolf have a good day?
3 How did Rolf get to the office?
4 Did Rolf reach work on time?

DIALOGUE 3

○ Sommer.
■ Hallo Renate. Hier ist Rolf. Kann ich bitte mit Günther sprechen?
○ Günther ist gerade nicht hier.
■ Kannst du ihm etwas ausrichten?
○ Ja, natürlich.
■ Sag ihm bitte, wir kommen heute Abend leider nicht mit.
○ Warum denn nicht?
■ Ach, Anna hat am Wochenende ein Tennisturnier und ich habe einen furchtbaren Tag gehabt. Ich bin heute Morgen mit dem Zug zur Arbeit gefahren. Ich bin eine Stunde zu spät ins Büro gekommen!
○ Oh, Rolf, da kommt Günther gerade … Hier ist er …

VOCABULARY	
Sommer	*Renate's surname; instead of saying 'hello', Germans identify themselves when answering the phone*
hier ist Rolf	this is Rolf
mit … sprechen*	to talk to …
gerade	right now
etwas aus/richten (+ dative)	to pass a message on (to someone)
sag ihm bitte …	tell him, please [*informal imperative*]
das Tennisturnier(-e)	tennis tournament
furchtbar	awful, dreadful
mit dem Zug fahren*	to go by train
zur Arbeit fahren*	to go to work
zu spät kommen*	to be late [*literally* to come too late]

✅ The perfect tense with *sein*

Verbs indicating motion, in the sense of moving from A to B, form the perfect tense with the present tense of **sein** plus a past participle. The same rules about word order apply as for the perfect tense with **haben** (see Unit 9, pages 123, 127). The **sein** form appears as the second element of the sentence, and the past participle at the end:

Sie **sind** um neun Uhr **gekommen**. They came at nine o'clock.
Wir **sind** im Odenwald **gewandert**. We went hiking in the Odenwald.
Gestern ist er 1000 Meter **geschwommen**. Yesterday he swam 1000 metres.
Wann **ist** er nach Bremen **gefahren**? When did he go to Bremen?
Um wie viel Uhr **ist** sie **gekommen**? At what time did she come?

In questions without a question word, the **sein** form appears at the beginning:

Seid ihr nach Hause **gelaufen**? Did you walk home?
Ist er mit dem Rad **gefahren**? Did he go by bike?

Verbs indicating motion encountered so far: **gehen, fahren, kommen, mitkommen, laufen, schwimmen, wandern, Rad fahren**.

Note: Verbs that have or could have a direct object always form their past tense with **haben**. For example, **essen** can be used on its own, without a direct object – **ich esse** ('I'm eating'). However, it could also be used with a direct object: **ich esse Fisch** (I'm eating fish'). So it forms its perfect tense with **haben**:

Ich **habe** Fisch **gegessen**. I ate fish.

When you aren't sure whether to use **haben** or **sein** to form the perfect tense, ask yourself: is there or could there be a direct object in the sentence? If the answer is yes, use **haben**.

ACTIVITY 13

Using the following times, write down what Herr Specht did during the day, putting the verbs into the perfect tense.

Example: Um 7 Uhr: Tee trinken. Um sieben Uhr hat er Tee getrunken.

1 Um 8 Uhr: frühstücken
2 Um 9 Uhr: zur Arbeit fahren
3 Um 17 Uhr: nach Hause fahren
4 Um 18 Uhr: schwimmen gehen

🔊 Now do activities 14 and 15 on the recording.

10.4 Berlin, Culture Capital
Kultur-Hauptstadt Berlin

Berlin's bars, restaurants, and clubs are buzzing all night – there is no closing time in Berlin. It considers itself a **Weltstadt** ('cosmopolitan city'), and has something for everyone.

The following diary entries written by a traveller to Berlin tell you about just some of the things the city has to offer.

Freitag, 23.4.

Wir sind am Nachmittag am Flughafen Berlin Tegel angekommen und sind mit der Bahn in die Stadt gefahren. Unser Hotel ist gleich am Kudamm. Abends sind wir ins Theater des Westens gegangen und haben ein Musical gesehen. Es hat mir sehr gut gefallen, weil die Inszenierung sehr bunt und lebendig war. Anschließend haben wir in einer Bar 'Berliner Weiße' getrunken. Es hat toll geschmeckt! Um vier Uhr morgens sind wir wieder ins Hotel gegangen.

Sonnabend, 24.4.

Wir waren sehr müde, aber wir haben trotzdem eine Stadtrundfahrt gemacht! Wir haben den Reichstag und das Brandenburger Tor gesehen! Am Nachmittag haben wir in einem gemütlichen Cafe Kaffee getrunken und abends haben wir eine Revue im Friedrichstadtpalast gesehen. Danach sind wir ins Hotel gegangen und haben sofort geschlafen!

---

der Flughafen(-¨-)	*airport*
Berlin Tegel	*Berlin's airport*
die Bahn(-en)	*train*
der Kudamm	*short for* Kurfürstendamm, *a famous street in Berlin*
das Theater des Westens	*theatre in Berlin* [*literally* Theatre of the West]
das Musical(-s)	*musical*
die Inszenierung(-en)	*production*
bunt	*colourful*
lebendig	*lively*
anschließend	*afterwards*
die Bar(-s)	*bar*
die Berliner Weiße(-n)	*a local beer*

trotzdem	nevertheless, all the same
die Stadtrundfahrt(-en)	city sightseeing tour
eine Stadtrundfahrt machen	to go on a city sightseeing tour
der Reichstag	*seat of the German parliament, the* Bundestag
das Brandenburger Tor	Brandenburg Gate [*Berlin landmark*]
am Nachmittag	in the afternoon
die Revue(-s)	revue
der Friedrichstadtpalast	*large revue theatre in Berlin*

ACTIVITY 16

Which of these statements are true? Correct those which are false. Write your answers in English.

1 Herr Grün ist mit dem Bus nach Berlin gefahren.
2 Am Freitagabend hat er ein Musical gesehen.
3 Die Inszenierung hat ihm nicht gefallen, weil sie zu bunt war.
4 Er ist am Samstagmorgen um vier Uhr ins Hotel gegangen.
5 Am Samstag war er sehr müde und hat keine Stadtrundfahrt gemacht.
6 Am Samstagabend hat er in Friedrichshafen eine Revue gesehen.

ACTIVITY 17

Try translating the following sentences into German. You can use the vocabulary section below to help you. Then find the German equivalents in the text and check whether you got them right.

1 In the evening we went to the Theater des Westens.
2 I liked it a lot, because the production was very lively.
3 Afterwards, we had (use trinken) Berliner Weiße.
4 We saw the Reichstag and the Brandenburg Gate.

10.5 Hotel Gertrud

PETER HAT KOPFSCHMERZEN
PETER HAS A HEADACHE

Am Tag nach der Wanderung hat Peter Kopfschmerzen. Frau Semmler will ihm helfen, aber Susanne ist nicht sehr mitleidig.

der Kopfschmerz(-en)	headache
Kopfschmerzen haben	to have a headache [*literally* to have headaches]
am Tag nach der Wanderung	on the day after the hiking trip
mitleidig	compassionate, sympathetic
blass	pale
es geht mir (nicht) gut	I'm (not) well
die Kopfschmerztablette(-n)	painkiller
die Kneipe(-n)	pub, bar
in eine Kneipe gehen*	to go to a pub, bar
(viel) zu viel	(much) too much
deshalb	that's why, for that reason, because of that
dabei sein (es waren ... dabei)	to be there (there were ... there)
das ist nett	that's nice, that's kind
dass ...	that ...
gestern	yesterday
ich habe zu tun	I've got things to do
ach so	oh, I see [*colloquial*]

ACTIVITY 18

Listen to the story and underline the statements that are not true.

1 Peter hat Kopfschmerzen.
2 Susanne bringt ihm eine Kopfschmerztablette.
3 Peter ist 20 Kilometer gewandert.
4 Peter hat viel Bier getrunken und zu viel gegessen.
5 Susanne sagt, sie hat zu tun.
6 Peter sagt, er will ein bisschen Tennis spielen.

ACTIVITY 19

Now read through the story transcript and find the German equivalents of these English expressions.

1 We hiked 15 kilometres.
2 I had much too much wine.
3 There were many nice people there.
4 What a pity you weren't there yesterday!

STORY TRANSCRIPT

Frau Semmler	Hallo Herr Ritter, guten Morgen!
Peter	Hallo Frau Semmler.
Frau Semmler	Sie sehen aber blass aus!
Peter	Ja, es geht mir nicht gut. Ich habe furchtbare Kopfschmerzen!
Frau Semmler	Möchten Sie eine Kopfschmerztablette?
Peter	Ach ja, vielen Dank. Und einen Kaffee bitte!
Frau Semmler	Susanne! Kannst du Herrn Ritter bitte eine Kopfschmerztablette und einen Kaffee bringen? Und wie war denn Ihre Wanderung, Herr Ritter?
Peter	Es war toll! Wir sind 15 Kilometer gewandert und dann sind wir in eine Kneipe gegangen. Und ich habe viel zu viel Wein getrunken!
Frau Semmler	Ach, deshalb haben Sie jetzt Kopfschmerzen!
Peter	Ja, genau. Aber es war wirklich toll. Es waren viele nette Leute dabei und wir ...
Susanne	Hier bitte, die Kopfschmerztablette.
Peter	Danke Susanne, das ist nett. Schade, dass du gestern nicht dabei warst. Es war toll!
Susanne	Ach, es waren ja viele andere nette Leute dabei. Ich habe jetzt zu tun!
Peter	Ach so. Na dann bis später. Also, ich muss jetzt noch ein bisschen schlafen. Tschüss, Frau Semmler.
Frau Semmler	Bis später, Herr Ritter.

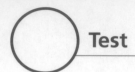

Test

Now it's time to test your progress in Unit 10.

1 Match the German phrases 1–10 with the correct English version a–j.

1	Rad fahren	a	to surf
2	mitnehmen	b	to ask
3	mitkommen	c	to take along
4	fragen	d	to go on a sightseeing
5	anrufen		tour
6	Kopfschmerzen haben	e	to have a headache
7	etwas ausrichten	f	to go to a pub
8	eine Stadtrundfahrt machen	g	to come along
9	in eine Kneipe gehen	h	to pass on a message
10	surfen	i	to ride one's bike
		j	to call

10

2 Which four verbs listed in 1 form their perfect tense with **sein**?

4

3 Write down the past participles of the following verbs. Be careful: verbs marked * are irregular.

1 Rad fahren*
2 fragen
3 haben*
4 gehen*
5 machen
6 surfen

6

4 Put the words in the correct order to form questions.

1 zu spät / gekommen / du / warum / bist / ?
2 ist / gekommen / er / zu spät / ?
3 ihr / gemacht / habt / eine Stadtrundfahrt / ?
4 wie lange / du / bist / geschwommen / ?
5 gefahren / bist / zur Arbeit / du / wie / ?

5

5 Complete the following letter using the appropriate forms of **haben** and **sein**.

Lieber Martin und liebe Ilse,

Wie geht es euch? Ich _ _ letzte Woche nach Italien gefahren. Ich _____ eine Woche Urlaub gemacht!

Ich _____ jeden Tag lange geschlafen und dann _____ ich an den Strand gegangen. Nachmittags _____ ich oft Rad gefahren und abends _____ ich oft in einem Restaurant gegessen.

Es war toll! Ich rufe euch nächste Woche an!

Euer Paul

| | 6 |

6 Link these sentences using **weil**.

1 Ich gehe heute nicht zur Arbeit. Ich habe Kopfschmerzen.
2 Ich bin nicht tanzen gegangen. Ich war müde.
3 Ich komme nicht mit. Ich will lieber lange schlafen.
4 Ich esse kein Fleisch. Ich bin Vegetarier.

| | 4 |

7 Link these sentences using **und, aber, oder,** or **denn**.

1 Ich fahre heute nach Bremen. Ich fahre morgen nach Bremen.
2 Ich mag kein Bier. Ich mag Wein.
3 Ich will tanzen gehen. Ich möchte essen gehen.
4 Ich fahre mit dem Zug zur Arbeit. Ich fahre nicht gern Auto.

| | 4 |

TOTAL SCORE | 39 |

If you scored less than 29, go through the dialogues and the Language Building sections again before completing the Summary on page 148.

Summary 10

Now try this final test summarizing the main points covered in the unit. You can check your answers on the recording.

How would you:
1 ask a friend what he's going to do at the weekend?
2 ask Frau Meier what she's going to do at the weekend?
3 suggest to your friend that you go to the cinema on Monday?
4 ask some friends if they want to come along?
5 say you don't want to come along, because you're tired?
6 say you have a headache?
7 ask your friend 'Can you pass a message on to her?'

REVISION

The next section will be a review section. If you still feel uncertain when talking about the past, you may want to work through the relevant Language Building sections and activities again. But don't worry too much, because there'll be lots of practice using the perfect tense in subsequent units. Look again at the verbs you already know, particularly those introduced in Units 9 and 10. Use them to say to yourself or your study partner what you did during the day, at the weekend, or on your last holiday.

Review 3

VOCABULARY

1 Match the German words 1–8 with the correct English version a–h.

1	mir	a	to/for him
2	dir	b	to/for me
3	ihm	c	to/for you (*formal*)
4	ihr	d	to/for you (*informal, pl.*)
5	uns	e	to/for you (*informal, sing.*)
6	euch	f	to/for them
7	ihnen	g	to/for her
8	Ihnen	h	to/for us

2 Circle the odd one out.

1 Rad fahren / surfen / in eine Kneipe gehen / Volleyball spielen

2 der Künstler / der Sportverein / die Kunstgalerie / das Bild

3 romantisch / heiraten / der Computer / die Hochzeitsreise

4 der Reichstag / der Fischmarkt / das Brandenburger Tor / der Kudamm

3 What do you like to do? Say whether you like or don't really like to do these activities.

Example: ins Café gehen – Ich gehe (nicht so) gerne ins Café.

1 tanzen
2 ins Kino gehen
3 Tennis spielen
4 ins Theater gehen
5 lesen

4 Frau Meier did lots of shopping! Supply the missing adjective endings.

1 Sie hat eine rot__ Bluse gekauft.
2 Sie hat einen blau___ Pullover gekauft.
3 Sie hat einen neu___ Mantel gekauft.
4 Sie hat einen schön___ Anzug gekauft.
5 Sie hat ein klein___ Auto gekauft.

5 Supply the missing endings or words.

1 Frau Meier gibt _____ (to us) eine Flasche Wein.
2 Ich gebe ____ (to them) eine Briefmarke.
3 Der Vater kauft d___ Tochter eine neue Bluse.
4 Die Kollegin hilft Herr___ Winn.
5 Peter und Anna, ich stelle _____ (to you) den Künstler vor.

6 In the following sentences, underline the indirect objects and circle the direct objects. Then translate the sentences. Pay attention to the word order!

1 I'll get you a cup of tea, Peter. (use **bringen**)
2 I'll introduce you to the artist, Peter.
3 She's buying him a new shirt.
4 The colleague helps her.
5 Herr Specht, can you get me a cup of coffee?

7 Listen to a group of people talking about their weekend.
  Who did what? Tick the appropriate answer.

	Frau Meier	Herr Winn	Frau Specht
lange schlafen	☐	☐	☐
eine Radtour machen	☐	☐	☐
nach Stuttgart fahren	☐	☐	☐
an den Bodensee fahren	☐	☐	☐
wandern	☐	☐	☐
schwimmen gehen	☐	☐	☐
in eine Kneipe gehen	☐	☐	☐
ein Tennisturnier haben	☐	☐	☐

8 Now write down what each of the people in 7 did at the
  weekend.

  Example: Frau … **hat** lange **geschlafen**, sie **hat** … und sie
  ist …

9 Now it's your turn! Tell a colleague what you did at the weekend. Read through this conversation and prepare your answers.

Your colleague: Hallo, guten Morgen!
You: 1 (Say good morning and ask him how he is.)

Your colleague: Danke gut. Wie war denn Ihr Wochenende?
You: 2 (Say 'thank you, very good').

Your colleague: Was haben Sie denn so gemacht?
You: 3 (Say on Saturday you went hiking [use **wandern gehen**].)

Your colleague: Schön! Und am Sonntag?
You: 4 (Say on Sunday you had a lie-in, and in the evening you went out to eat [use **essen gehen**]. Then ask him how his weekend was.)

Your colleague: Ach, wie immer, am Samstag habe ich die Wohnung geputzt und am Samstagabend habe ich gelesen.

Lost and found
Verloren und gefunden

OBJECTIVES

In this unit you'll learn how to:

- ✓ describe items
- ✓ ask for lost baggage
- ✓ say to whom certain items belong
- ✓ describe what people look like
- ✓ describe what you or others are wearing

And cover the following grammar and language:

- ✓ the genitive case of the definite and indefinite articles
- ✓ noun endings in the genitive singular
- ✓ adjective endings in the genitive and dative case
- ✓ **von** ('of') + dative instead of the genitive
- ✓ the simple past of **haben** ('to have')
- ✓ the perfect tense of **sein** ('to be'), **bleiben** ('to stay'), **werden** ('to become')

LEARNING GERMAN 11

When you listen to the dialogues on the recording, try to imitate the rhythm and intonation of the sentences, as well as the pronunciation of each individual word. The better you can reproduce pronunciation and intonation, the more 'native' your German will sound.

Now start the recording for Unit 11.

11.1 Lost baggage
Ich suche meinen Koffer!

ACTIVITY 1 is on the recording.

ACTIVITY 2

Correct the statements which are false.

1 Herr Lang accidentally picks up a suitcase that
   looks like his.   T / F
2 His suitcase has a blue stripe.   T / F
3 Herr Lang's papers are in his suitcase.   T / F
4 Herr Lang goes to the lost property office.   T / F
5 An elderly lady found Herr Lang's suitcase.   T / F

DIALOGUE 1

○ Entschuldigung, ich glaube, das hier ist nicht Ihr Koffer.

■ Aber mein Koffer ist blau, und er hat einen roten Streifen –
  und dies ist ein blauer Koffer mit einem roten Streifen.

○ Ja, aber das hier ist der Koffer der Dame dort drüben.

■ Ja, und wo ist mein Koffer? Meine Papiere sind in dem
  Koffer!

○ Fragen Sie doch mal im Fundbüro! Vielleicht ist er dort.

■ Guten Morgen. Ich suche einen blauen Koffer mit einem
  roten Streifen.

▼ Einen Moment bitte. … Ist das Ihr Koffer?

■ Ja! Ach, vielen Dank. Da bin ich aber froh!

▼ Da müssen Sie dem Herrn dort hinten danken. Er hat ihn
  gebracht.

VOCABULARY	
der Koffer(-)	suitcase
der Streifen(-)	stripe
dort drüben	over there
die Papiere (*pl.*)	(ID) papers
das Fundbüro(-s)	lost property office
froh	glad
da bin ich aber froh!	I'm so glad!
dort hinten	back there
gebracht	brought [*from* **bringen**]

✓ The genitive case

The genitive case of the definite and indefinite articles looks like this:

	m	f	n	m	f	n
Nominative	der	die	das	ein	eine	ein
Genitive	des	der	des	eines	einer	eines

In the plural, the definite article in the genitive is **der**:

> Das sind die Jacken **der** Kinder. These are the children's jackets.

The genitive case is equivalent to the English possessive (Mary's, the boys').

The genitive endings of possessive adjectives (**mein**, **dein**, etc.) will be covered in Unit 13. They are identical to the genitive endings of **ein**.

✓ Noun endings in the genitive singular

In the genitive singular, masculine and neuter nouns add -s: **des Autos, des Computers**.

Masculine and neuter monosyllabic nouns add -es: **des Mannes, des Kindes, des Fisches**.

Herr adds an **-n** in the genitive case:

> Das ist die Tasche **des** Herrn dort drüben. That is the gentleman's bag over there.

With proper nouns only, **-s** can be added to show possession:

> Das ist **Peters** Auto. That is Peter's car.
> Das ist **Frau Meiers** Handtasche. That is Frau Meier's handbag.

ACTIVITY 3

Lots of lost items! Use the genitive to indicate which items belongs to whom. Remember to add the appropriate noun endings as well.

> Example: das Auto (der Herr dort). Das ist das Auto **des** Herrn dort.

1 das Auto (der Mann dort drüben)
2 der Mantel (die Dame dort hinten)
3 der Anzug (ein Herr)
4 der Mantel (eine Frau)
5 die Jacke (ein Kind)

🎧 Now do activities 4 and 5 on the recording.

Wie sehen sie aus?

ACTIVITY 6 is on the recording.

ACTIVITY 7

Whom does each of the adjectives describe?

1 schlank ___ Frau Seese ___ Herr Seese
2 mittelgroß ___ Frau Seese ___ Herr Seese
3 grauhaarig ___ Frau Seese ___ Herr Seese
4 dick ___ Frau Seese ___ Herr Seese
5 ernst ___ Frau Seese ___ Herr Seese

DIALOGUE 2

○ Ach, Herr Müller, können Sie Herrn und Frau Seese vom Bahnhof abholen?

■ Ja natürlich. Wie sehen sie denn aus?

○ Sehen Sie das Foto der jungen Frau dort hinten? Das ist Frau Seese. Sie ist schlank, mittelgroß und trägt wahrscheinlich einen roten Mantel mit einem blauen Kragen.

■ Und Herr Seese?

○ Herr Seese ist fünfzig Jahre alt, grauhaarig und ein bisschen dick. Sie können ihn nicht verpassen. Er sieht immer sehr ernst aus!

VOCABULARY	
ab/holen	to collect, pick up, get
aus/sehen* (er sieht aus)	to look (like)
wie sehen sie denn aus?	what do they look like?
das Foto(-s)	photo
jung	young
schlank	slim
mittelgroß	medium-sized, of medium height
tragen* (er trägt)	to wear
wahrscheinlich	probably
der Kragen(-)	collar
grauhaarig	grey-haired
dick	fat, big
verpassen	to miss
ernst	serious

✓ Adjective endings in the genitive and dative case

The ending for adjectives in the genitive and dative case is **-en**, in the singular and plural. This rule applies for adjectives preceded by a definite article or an indefinite article:

Das ist die Brille **des** alten Mannes. These are the old man's glasses.
Das sind die Spielzeuge **der** kleinen Kinder. These are the small children's toys.
Die braune Reisetasche gehört **einem** alten Mann. The brown holdall belongs to an old man.
Sie trägt einen roten Mantel mit **einem** schwarzen Kragen. She's wearing a red coat with a black collar.

✓ Using *von* + dative instead of the genitive

The genitive case is used mostly in written German. In spoken German, possession is more usually indicated by **von** ('of'). Remember that articles following **von** have to be in the dative case, and that nouns in the dative plural have to end in **-n**:

Das ist die Jacke **von** Frau Meier. That's Frau Meier's jacket [*literally* the jacket of Frau Meier].
Das ist die Adresse **von einer Freundin**. That's the address of a (female) friend.
Das sind die Spielzeuge **von den Kindern**. These are the children's toys.

It's important not to let your worries about getting these endings right stop you from speaking German. Remember, you'll be understood even if you make mistakes. You could begin by concentrating on the endings in writing. Eventually, with a lot of exposure to the spoken language, you'll also get them right when speaking.

ACTIVITY 8

Supply the correct article and adjective endings:

1 Das sind die Jacken d_____ klein___ Kinder.
2 Die Reisetasche gehört d_____ jung___ Mann dort drüben.
3 Er trägt einen grauen Mantel mit ein__ gross__ Kragen.
4 Er ist mit ein__ jung__ Frau verheiratet.
5 Das ist das Auto von d___ Mann dort drüben.

🎧 Now do activities 9 and 10 on the recording.

Sie ist dunkelhaarig!

🎧 **ACTIVITY 11** is on the recording.

ACTIVITY 12

1 How long ago did Stefanie split up with her boyfriend?
2 When did Hugo get to know the new woman of his dreams?
3 How old is she?
4 What colour are her eyes?

DIALOGUE 3

○ Und Stefanie, hast du schon deinen Traummann kennen gelernt?

■ Nein, noch nicht. Ich hatte bis vor drei Monaten einen Freund – aber dann hatten wir Krach und es war aus! Und wie ist es mit deiner Traumfrau?

○ Ich glaube, ich habe sie am Dienstag kennen gelernt!

■ Wirklich? Und wie sieht sie aus?

○ Also, ihre Augen sind sehr blau. Außerdem ist sie dunkelhaarig und hat einen süßen Mund!

■ Und wie alt ist sie?

○ Fünf Tage!

■ Was? Mensch Hugo – du bist Vater geworden? Und du bist verheiratet? Herzlichen Glückwunsch!

VOCABULARY

der Traummann (-¨-er)	man of one's dreams
bis vor …	until … ago
der Freund(-e)	boyfriend, male friend
der Krach(-¨-e)	fight, row
Krach haben	to have a fight [*colloquial*]
es war aus	it was over [*colloquial*]
wie ist es mit … ?	what about … ?
die Traumfrau(-en)	woman of one's dreams
außerdem	moreover
dunkelhaarig	dark-haired
süß	sweet, cute
der Mund(-¨-er)	mouth
geworden	became [*from* **werden**]
werden* (er wird)	to become

✓ The simple past of *haben* ('to have')

When using **haben** to talk about things in the past, you can use the simple past tense instead of the more complicated perfect tense:

> Wir **hatten** Krach./Wir **haben** Krach **gehabt**. We had a fight.
> Ich **hatte** eine lustige Tante./Ich **habe** einen lustige Tante **gehabt**. I had a funny aunt.

To form the simple past of **haben**, add these endings to **hat-**:

ich **hatte**	wir **hatten**
du **hattest**	ihr **hattet**
er/sie/es **hatte**	sie **hatten**
	Sie **hatten**

✓ The perfect tense of *sein* ('to be'), *bleiben* ('to stay'), *werden* ('to become')

These verbs form their perfect tense with **sein**:

> **sein:** Ich **bin** in Hamburg **gewesen**. I was in Hamburg.
> **bleiben:** Wir **sind** zu Hause **geblieben**. We stayed at home.
> **werden:** Er **ist** Vater **geworden**. He became a father.

Note: **werden** is an irregular verb: **du wirst, er/sie/es wird**. For the remaining persons, add the present tense endings to the stem **werd-**.

ACTIVITY 13

A dreadful day for Herr Schulze! Translate what he did, using the simple past of **haben** where possible.

1 He drank too much wine.
2 He had a headache.
3 He stayed at home.
4 He had a fight with a friend.
5 He went to a pub and drank a lot of beer!

ACTIVITY 14

You're pointing out your colleagues to a friend. Translate these sentences. Watch out for the adjective endings!

1 The dark-haired lady with the red dress is Frau Wolf.
2 The young man with the blue jacket is Herr Müller.
3 Herr Schmidt is wearing a blue sweater.
4 Frau Sonne is wearing a green dress with a grey collar.

Now do activities 15 and 16 on the recording.

(11.4) German tennis players
Deutsche Tennisspieler

A friend needs help with a quiz about the careers of two of Germany's most prominent tennis players.

ACTIVITY 17

1 Which feature of many red-haired people does Boris Becker share?
2 At what age did he first win Wimbledon?
3 How often did he win Wimbledon altogether?

Boris Becker

Er hat eine große Nase und einen vollen Mund. Seine Haare sind rötlich, er hat Sommersprossen und manchmal trägt er einen Bart. 1985 hat er zum ersten Mal das Finale von Wimbledon gewonnen. Damals war er siebzehn Jahre und sieben Monate alt. Insgesamt hat er dreimal in Wimbledon gewonnen, zweimal bei den Australian Open und einmal bei den US Open.

der Tennisspieler(-)	tennis-player
die Nase(-n)	nose
voll	full
das Haar(-e)	hair
rötlich	reddish
die Sommersprosse(-n)	freckle
manchmal	sometimes
der Bart(-̈-e)	beard
zum ersten Mal	for the first time
das Finale(-s)	final
gewonnen	won [*from* **gewinnen**]
gewinnen*	to win
damals	at that time, then
insgesamt	altogether, in all
dreimal	three times
zweimal	two times, twice
einmal	once

ACTIVITY 18

1 What colour is Steffi Graf's hair?
2 How often has Steffi Graf won Wimbledon?
3 Steffi Graf was the second youngest player ever to receive a ranking in the world ranking list. How old was she at that time?
4 Roughly how many years (though not uninterrupted) has she been number one in the world ranking list?

Steffi Graf

Sie ist groß und ihre Haare sind blond und lang. Ihre Figur ist kräftig und sehr sportlich, denn sie ist eine sehr gute Tennisspielerin. Siebenmal hat sie das Finale von Wimbledon gewonnen, fünfmal die U.S. Open, fünfmal die French Open und viermal die Australian Open. Schon als Kind (mit 13 Jahren) war sie Nummer 124 in der Weltrangliste. Insgesamt war sie 365 Wochen lang die Nummer eins in der Weltrangliste.

groß	tall, big
blond	blond
lang	long
die Figur(-en)	figure
kräftig	strong
sportlich	sporty, athletic
siebenmal	seven times
fünfmal	five times
viermal	four times
als Kind	as a child
die Nummer (-n)	number
die Weltrangliste	world ranking list

ACTIVITY 19

How do you say eight times, nine times, and ten times in German? Can you work this out from the examples (three times, four times, etc.) above?

SUSANNE PACKT IHREN KOFFER
SUSANNE PACKS HER SUITCASE

Susanne packt ihren Koffer für ihre Reise nach Berlin. Sie sucht die passende Kleidung, denn sie trifft dort einen Mann und möchte schick aussehen.

packen	to pack
die Reise(-n)	journey, trip
passend	suitable, appropriate
was soll ich bloß anziehen?	what should I wear?
an/ziehen*	to put on [*clothes*]
auffällig	garish, loud [*colour*]
weiß	white
langweilig	boring
ganz nett	quite nice
das Telefon(-e)	telephone
angenehm	pleasant, agreeable
die Stimme(-n)	voice
braun	brown
das Kostüm(-e)	suit [*jacket and skirt*]
schwarz	black
der Hosenanzug(-¨-e)	trouser suit, pantsuit
meinen	to think
meinst du?	do you think so?
schon	[*here* =] hey presto!, in a flash
patent	capable

ACTIVITY 20

Susanne is going to meet a man in Berlin. What is his name, and what is he like? What does she finally decide to wear for the meeting? Listen to the dialogue and decide whether these statements are true or false.

1 Susanne will Herrn Meier treffen.   T/F
2 Herr Meier ist vierzig Jahre alt.   T/F
3 Er hat eine furchtbare Stimme.   T/F
4 Susanne findet das braune Kostüm schön.   T/F
5 Frau Semmler empfiehlt einen schwarzen
   Hosenanzug.   T/F

ACTIVITY 21

Listen to the dialogue again and complete the gaps using the words below. Watch out: you'll have to supply the correct endings!

braun/grün/weiß/angenehm/schwarz

1 ... den _____ Rock und die _____ Bluse?
2 Er hatte eine sehr _____ Stimme.
3 Warum ziehst du nicht das _____ Kostüm an?
4 Wie ist es mit dem _____ ___ Hosenanzug?
5 Dazu ziehst du die _____ Schuhe an.

ACTIVITY 22

Now read through the transcript of the dialogue and find the German equivalents of these English expressions.

1 No, that is too boring.
2 I don't know what I should wear.
3 Is Herr Meier nice?
4 Yes, I think he's quite nice.
5 ... and hey presto, you'll look smart and capable!

STORY TRANSCRIPT

Susanne	Was soll ich bloß anziehen? Das rote Kleid? Nein, das ist viel zu auffällig. Vielleicht den grünen Rock und die weiße Bluse? Nein, das ist zu langweilig.
Frau Semmler	Und? Hast du schon gepackt?
Susanne	Nein, noch nicht. Ich weiß nicht, was ich anziehen soll!
Frau Semmler	Ist Herr Meier denn nett?
Susanne	Ja, ich glaube er ist ganz nett, vielleicht fünfzig Jahre alt. Am Telefon hatte er eine sehr angenehme Stimme.
Frau Semmler	Warum ziehst du nicht das braune Kostüm an? Das sieht doch immer sehr nett aus!
Susanne	Braun? Nein, also Braun ist nun wirklich langweilig!
Frau Semmler	Und wie ist es mit dem schwarzen Hosenanzug? Der ist doch sehr schick!
Susanne	Meinst du?
Frau Semmler	Ja klar! Dazu ziehst du die schwarzen Schuhe und die weiße Bluse an – und schon siehst du schick und patent aus!
Susanne	Ja, das hört sich gut an, das mache ich! Puh, da bin ich aber froh! Dann kann ich ja jetzt meinen Koffer packen ....

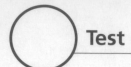

Test

Now it's time to test your progress in Unit 11.

1 Sort the words below into opposites.

Example: schwarz–weiß

> lustig alt blond klein jung schlank
> dunkelhaarig ernst
> groß interessant dick langweilig

6

2 Write down the German words for these colours. (Hint: some of them were first mentioned in Unit 4.)

1 red   5 brown
2 green   6 grey
3 blue   7 white
4 black   8 yellow

8

3 Complete the sentences using the most appropriate word.

patent/süß/attraktiv/kräftig/sportlich

1 Der Kuchen ist sehr _____.
2 Die neue Sekretärin ist wirklich sehr _____.
3 Boris Beckers Figur ist _____ und _____.
4 Der neue Freund von Frau Meier ist wirklich
   _____!

4

4 Complete the sentences by adding the missing endings to the articles and adjectives.

1 Die Bäckerei gehört ein____ jung____ Mann.
2 Der Name d____ Bäckerei ist 'Bäckerei Hahn'.
3 Der Name d____ Bäckers ist Hans Meier.
4 Das ist der Koffer d____ grauhaarig____ Dame.
5 Das ist die Reisetasche von d____ jung____ Mann.

8

5 Who's wearing what? Look at the pictures and write down what Frau Meier and Herr Weinert are wearing. (1 point for each correct item.)

Example: Frau Meier trägt eine grüne Jacke mit einem roten Kragen, … und …

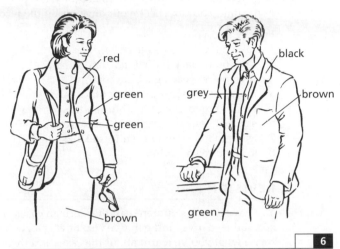

6

6 Translate the following description of a man called Eddie Schlecker, a notorious cake and sweets robber. Use the simple past of **haben** and **sein** and the perfect tense, where appropriate. (2 points for a correct sentence, 1 point if there is one mistake.)

Eddie Schlecker is 45 years old and very fat, because (use **denn**) he likes to eat a lot of cake. He is dark-haired. He is of medium height, has a big nose, and a full mouth. Eddie's father had a bakery. The father's name was Henry Schlecker, and the name of the bakery was 'Bäckerei Schlecker'. Eddie and his father often had fights (use **Krach haben**), because (use **weil**) he ate so much cake.

6

TOTAL SCORE 38

If you scored less than 28, go through the dialogues and the Language Building sections again before completing the Summary on page 166.

Summary 11

Now try this final test summarizing the main points covered in the unit. You can check your answers on the recording.

How would you:
1 say you're 45 years old?
2 say you're dark-haired, tall, and sporty?
3 say you're wearing a blue coat?
4 ask where the lost property office is?
5 say you're looking for a blue suitcase?
6 say that your papers are in the suitcase?
7 ask someone what his suitcase looks like?
8 say you're so glad?

REVISION

You have now encountered all the German cases –nominative, accusative, dative, and genitive – so now is a good time to revise what you've learnt about the cases and their usage! It is important to remember that there are different reasons for using a certain case; that is, certain words (verbs and prepositions) require specific cases, and certain functions in the sentence (subject, direct object, indirect object) require specific cases.

You may want to go to the Grammar Summary now and read through the sections on cases and prepositions, which summarize when to use which case. The Language Building section on page 111 lists verbs that take the dative case.

Don't be put off if you think you can't remember all of this now: frequent listening to the recordings and regular revision will help you get things right! And most importantly, don't let your concerns about getting the right endings stop you from speaking German. You'll be understood even if you do make mistakes.

Health and fitness
Gesundheit und Fitness

OBJECTIVES

In this unit you will learn how to:

✓ ask for remedies for common ailments

✓ talk about your diet and your (un)healthy lifestyle

✓ talk about obligations and past intentions

And cover the following grammar and language:

✓ past participles of regular verbs with a separable prefix

✓ past participles of irregular verbs with a separable prefix

✓ the modal verb **dürfen** ('to be allowed to')

✓ **dürfen** + negative to mean 'must not'

✓ the modal verb **sollen** ('to be supposed to')

✓ the simple past of modal verbs

LEARNING GERMAN 12

At this point in your study of German, the Grammar Summary at the back of this book will become more and more important to you. In it, the grammatical points discussed in the units are summarized in table format for ease of reference. Refer to the Grammar Summary to remind yourself of certain endings or other grammatical features. If you find that you need to refresh your memory on the underlying principles, go back to the Language Building sections in the relevant units. The grammar index at the very end of the book will tell you where to find what you're looking for.

Now start the recording for Unit 12.

12.1 At the pharmacy
In der Apotheke

ACTIVITY 1 is on the recording.

ACTIVITY 2

1 How did Frau Krause hurt her foot?
2 What kind of medicine is she given for her foot?
3 What else, besides her foot, is causing Frau Krause pain?
4 What other medicine does the pharmacist sell Frau Krause?

DIALOGUE 1

○ Guten Tag, Frau Krause. Was kann ich für Sie tun?
■ Ich bin heute Morgen hingefallen. Ich bin sofort aufgestanden, aber jetzt tut mir mein Fuß sehr weh!
○ Hmm, damit müssen Sie wahrscheinlich zum Arzt gehen, Frau Krause. Ich kann Ihnen nur eine schmerzstillende Salbe geben. Brauchen Sie sonst noch etwas?
■ Ja, mein Rücken tut auch ein bisschen weh. Haben Sie etwas gegen Rückenschmerzen?
○ Die Salbe hier ist gut für Ihren Fuß und für Ihren Rücken. Und hier sind auch noch ein paar Schmerztabletten. Aber gehen Sie bitte auch zum Arzt!

VOCABULARY	
die Apotheke(-n)	chemist's, pharmacy
hingefallen	fallen down [*from* hin/fallen]
hin/fallen* (er fällt hin)	to fall over, to fall down
sofort	immediately
aufgestanden	got up [*from* auf/stehen]
auf/stehen*	to get up
wehtun* (er tut weh)	to hurt
der Fuß(-̈-e)	foot
schmerzstillend	pain-killing
die Salbe(-n)	ointment
sonst	otherwise
der Rücken(-)	back
haben Sie etwas gegen … ?	do you have something for … ?
die Rückenschmerzen (*pl.*)	backache
ein paar	a few
die Schmerztablette(-n)	painkiller

✔ Past participles of regular verbs with a separable prefix

The past participles of regular verbs with a separable prefix end in **-t** and add **ge-** after the prefix. (Compare Unit 9, page 125.) The separable prefix is no longer 'separated':

auf/wachen (to wake up)   Ich bin **aufgewacht**. I woke up.

✔ How to find past participles of irregular verbs with a separable prefix

In the table of irregular verbs in the Grammar Summary, look under the verb without the prefix. For example, for **auf/stehen** look up the past participle of **stehen**, which is **gestanden**. Then add the prefix **auf: auf + gestanden = aufgestanden**.

Verbs indicating motion (**fahren, kommen, gehen, fallen,** etc.) plus a separable prefix form their perfect tense with **sein**:

Wir **sind** um neun Uhr **abgefahren**. We left at nine o'clock.
Wann **seid** ihr **angekommen**? When did you arrive?
Warum **bist** du **hingefallen**? Why did you fall down?

Verbs indicating a change of state form their perfect tense with **sein** as well, e.g. **auf/wachen** ('to wake up'), **ein/schlafen*** ('to fall asleep'), **sterben*** ('to die'):

Sind sie zu spät **aufgewacht**? Did they wake up too late?
Ist sie **eingeschlafen**? Did she fall asleep?
Ist sie **gestorben**? Did she die?

ACTIVITY 3

Using the following times and verbs, write down what Frau Krause did during the day.

Example: Um 6 Uhr: aufwachen. Um sechs Uhr ist sie aufgewacht.

1 Um 7 Uhr: aufstehen
2 Um 8 Uhr: frühstücken
3 Um 9 Uhr: hinfallen
4 Um 15 Uhr: zum Arzt fahren
5 Um 22 Uhr: einschlafen

Now do activities 4 and 5 on the recording.

12.2 A healthy diet
Eine gesunde Ernährung

ACTIVITY 6 is on the recording.

ACTIVITY 7

Tick the items Hanna is *not* allowed to have.

1 Kaffee __   5 Fisch __
2 Kuchen __   6 Eis __
3 Salat __   7 Sahne __
4 Fleisch __

DIALOGUE 2

■ Möchtest du auch einen Kaffee, Hanna?

○ Nein danke. Der Arzt sagt, ich soll keinen Kaffee trinken.

■ Möchtest du ein Stück Kuchen und einen Orangensaft?

○ Den Orangensaft nehme ich gerne, aber den Kuchen nicht.
Ich soll nämlich eine Diät machen – weil ich zu dick bin.

■ Was darfst du denn essen?

○ Salat, Obst, Gemüse, auch ein bisschen Fleisch und Fisch.
Aber kein Fett.

■ Darfst du denn noch Eis essen?

○ Nein, ich darf kein Eis essen, keine Schokolade – und keine
Sahne! Weißt du was? Ich glaube, ich nehme den Kuchen
doch!

VOCABULARY	
gesund	healthy
die Ernährung	diet
sollen	to be supposed to
dürfen (er darf)	to be allowed to
das Stück(-e)	piece
das Obst	fruit
das Gemüse(-)	vegetable
das Fett(-e)	fat
das Eis	ice cream
die Schokolade(-n)	chocolate
die Sahne	cream, whipped cream
doch	[*here* =] all the same, still

⊘ The modal verb *dürfen* ('may', 'to be allowed to')

Was **darfst** du **essen**? What are you allowed to eat?

ich **darf**	wir **dürfen**
du **darfst**	ihr **dürft**
er/sie/es **darf**	sie **dürfen**
	Sie **dürfen**

⊘ *dürfen* + negative = 'must not'

dürfen + a negative (either **kein** or **nicht**) means 'must not':

Du **darfst keinen** Alkohol **trinken**. You mustn't drink any alcohol.
Er **darf kein** Fett **essen**. He mustn't eat any fat.
Ich **darf nicht** so viel **essen**. I mustn't eat so much.
Sie **dürfen** hier **nicht rauchen**. You mustn't smoke here.

müssen + a negative means 'don't have to' (and not 'must not'):

Du **musst keinen** Kaffee **trinken**. You don't have to drink coffee.
Du **musst** nicht aufräumen. You don't have to tidy up.

⊘ The modal verb *sollen* ('to be supposed to')

ich **soll**	wir **sollen**
du **sollst**	ihr **sollt**
er/sie/es **soll**	sie **sollen**
	Sie **sollen**

Ich **soll** aufräumen. I'm supposed to tidy up.
Du **sollst** nicht lügen. You're not supposed to lie.
Das Wetter **soll** schön sein. The weather is supposed to be nice.

ACTIVITY 8

To recommend a healthy lifestyle, fill in the appropriate forms of **dürfen** (d) and **sollen** (s):

1 Sie _____ (d) nicht so viel rauchen!
2 Er _____ (d) nicht so viel essen!
3 Wir _____ (d) nicht so viel Alkohol trinken!
4 Ich _____ (s) viel wandern gehen.
5 Ihr _____ (s) viel schwimmen gehen.

ACTIVITY 9

Translate the sentences from activity 8 into English.

🎧 Now do activities 10 and 11 on the recording.

(12.3) Healthy living
Gesund leben

(🎧) **ACTIVITY 12** is on the recording.

ACTIVITY 13

Correct the statements which are false.

1   Barbara hat morgens Müsli gegessen.   T / F
2   Sie hat bei der Arbeit keinen Kaffee getrunken.   T / F
3   Rudi soll abnehmen.   T / F
4   Er hat in den letzten Wochen viel Sport gemacht.   T / F

DIALOGUE 3

○ Heute wollte ich mal ganz gesund leben. Ich wollte keinen Kaffee trinken und morgens ganz gesund frühstücken …

■ Und dann?

○ Zuerst konnte ich das Müsli nicht finden. Also habe ich gar nicht gefrühstückt. Und ohne Kaffee konnte ich bei der Arbeit kaum die Augen aufhalten. Also habe ich doch Kaffee getrunken.

■ Ich durfte die letzten Wochen auch keinen Kaffee trinken.

○ Warum denn nicht?

■ Der Arzt wollte es so! Außerdem sollte ich nicht so viel fernsehen, abnehmen und mehr Sport treiben.

○ Und, machst du jetzt mehr Sport?

■ Nein. Aber nächste Woche fange ich an! Dann lebe ich nur noch gesund!

VOCABULARY	
leben	to live
zuerst	first, at first
das Müsli(-s)	muesli
gar nicht	not at all
bei der Arbeit	at work
kaum	hardly, scarcely
das Auge(-n)	eye
offen halten* (er hält offen)	to keep open
außerdem	besides
fernsehen* (er sieht fern)	to watch TV
ab/nehmen* (er nimmt ab)	to lose weight
Sport treiben*	to do a sport, to play sports
Sport machen	to do a sport, to play sports
an/fangen* (er fängt an)	to begin

⊘ The simple past of modal verbs

When using modal verbs to talk about events in the past, you use the simple past rather than the perfect tense.

The word order rules for modal verbs in the present tense also apply in the simple past (see Units 2 and 3). Most importantly, the infinitive that accompanies the modal verb still appears at the end of the sentence:

Simple past: Ich **wollte** 2 Kilo **abnehmen**. I wanted to lose 2 kg.
Perfect tense: Ich **habe** 2 Kilo abnehmen **wollen**.

To form the simple past of modal verbs, add the endings below to these forms: **muss-, woll-, soll-, durf-, konn-**. Note that these endings are identical to the endings of **haben** in the simple past. For a full overview of the simple past of all modal verbs, see the Grammar Summary.

ich **mus**s**te**	ich **woll**te
du **mus**s**test**	du **woll**test
er/sie/es **mus**s**te**	er/sie/es **woll**te
wir **mus**s**ten**	wir **woll**ten
ihr **mus**s**tet**	ihr **woll**tet
sie **mus**s**ten**	sie **woll**ten
Sie **mus**s**ten**	Sie **woll**ten

Other modal verbs in the past tense:

Wir **sollten** nicht lachen. We weren't supposed to laugh.
Er **durfte** nicht sprechen. He wasn't allowed to talk.
Sie **konnte** nicht kommen. She couldn't (wasn't able to) come.
Konntet ihr nicht kommen? Weren't you able to come?

ACTIVITY 14

Write down the past tense of **sollen, dürfen**, and **können**, following the examples of **müssen** and **wollen** above.

ACTIVITY 15

Put these statements into the past.

Example: Ich will abnehmen! Ich **wollte** abnehmen!

1 Sie sollen keinen Kaffee trinken!
2 Ich darf nicht so viel essen.
3 Er muss mehr Sport machen.
4 Hilde will viel wandern gehen.
5 Herr und Frau Meier wollen rudern gehen.

🎧 Now do activities 16 and 17 on the recording.

(12.4) Natural remedies
Naturheilmittel

Natural remedies are very popular in Germany, and are sold over the counter in drugstores (**Drogerie**) and pharmacies. There is a herbal tea for almost every minor ailment, from coughs and colds to fever and stomach pains. The leaflet below gives you an idea of how Germans would treat common ailments.

A Eine Erkältung fängt oft mit Schnupfen an. Nehmen Sie schnell ein heißes Erkältungsbad mit ätherischen Ölen! Die Dämpfe machen Ihren Kopf und Ihre Nase wieder frei.

B Ihr Hals tut weh? Gegen Halsschmerzen hilft Salbei! Gurgeln Sie mehrmals täglich damit oder lutschen Sie Salbeipastillen! Auch heiße Erkältungstees und ein Schal können Ihnen helfen.

C Sie haben Husten? Dann trinken Sie heiße Hustentees und nehmen Sie Hustensaft. Wir empfehlen Hustensaft mit Thymianextrakt.

die Drogerie(-n)	drugstore, pharmacy [*sells medicines and remedies that are available without prescription, as well as cosmetics and household products*]
die Erkältung(-en)	cold
der Schnupfen(-)	runny nose

das Erkältungsbad(-¨-er)	*bath essence with essential oils for a cold*
ein Erkältungsbad nehmen	to take a bath for a cold
ätherisch	essential
das Öl(-e)	oil
der Dampf(-¨-e)	steam
der Kopf(-¨-e)	head
frei machen	to unblock
der Hals(-¨-e)	throat
die Halsschmerzen (pl.)	sore throat
der Salbei(-)	sage
gurgeln	to gargle
mehrmals täglich	several times a day
damit	with it
lutschen	to suck
die Pastille(-n)	pastille, lozenge
der Erkältungstee(-s)	*tea containing plant extracts for a cold*
der Schal(-s)	scarf
der Husten(-)	cough
der Hustentee(-s)	*tea containing plant extracts for a cough*
der Hustensaft(-¨-e)	cough syrup
empfehlen* [er empfiehlt]	to recommend
der Thymianextrakt(-e)	thyme extract

ACTIVITY 18

Read the leaflet and give the German for these instructions.

1 Have a hot bath with essential oils straightaway!
2 Gargle several times a day!
3 Suck sage pastilles!
4 Drink hot teas for a cough!
5 Take cough syrup!

ACTIVITY 19

Now match the following ailments to the remedies indicated in activity 18.

a Halsschmerzen
b Schnupfen
c Husten

GESUNDE ERNÄHRUNG?!
HEALTHY DIET?!

Hubert kommt ins Hotel Gertrud. Er will Susanne besuchen, aber Susanne ist in Berlin. Stattdessen kommt Hubert mit Frau Semmler ins Gespräch. Sie sprechen über gesunde Ernährung.

mit … ins Gespräch kommen*	to engage in conversation with
das Gespräch(-e)	conversation, discussion
sprechen* (er spricht)	to speak, to talk
sprechen über (+ accusative)	to speak/talk about
sprechen mit (+ dative)	to talk to
ein/laden* (er lädt ein)	to invite
das Essen(-)	food, meal
vegetarisch	vegetarian
… etwa nicht …?	not [*colloquial, for emphasis*]
fettarm	low-fat
das Bio-Gemüse (*sing.*)	organic vegetables
der Alkohol(-e)	alcohol
abschalten	to switch off, to relax [*colloquial*]
fit halten* (er hält fit)	to keep fit, to stay fit
zu/geben* (er gibt zu)	to admit
die Küche(-n)	kitchen, cuisine
bestimmt	certainly
übertreiben* mit	to overdo it with, to exaggerate about
der Gast(-̈-e)	guest
der Gruß(-̈-e)	greeting
viele Grüße an …	best wishes to … [*literally many greetings to …*]

ACTIVITY 20

Listen to the conversation between Hubert and Frau Semmler and tick the correct statements.

1 Hubert wants to invite Susanne
   a ___ to the cinema.   b ___ for a meal.
2 Hubert tells Frau Semmler about a new vegetarian
   a ___ café in Konstanz.   b ___ restaurant in Konstanz.

3 The new vegetarian place
  a ___ doesn't serve alcohol.   b ___ does serve alcohol.
4 Frau Semmler thinks people
  a ___ are right about a   b ___ overdo it with a low-
  low-fat diet.   fat diet.
5 Frau Semmler
  a ___ likes to eat meat.   b ___ doesn't like to eat
                                    meat.

ACTIVITY 21

Read this summary of the conversation between Hubert and
Frau Semmler. Underline the information that was NOT given
in the dialogue.

Hubert kommt ins Hotel Gertrud und will Susanne für 19 Uhr
in das Parasol, ein vegetarisches Restaurant in Konstanz
einladen. Leider ist Susanne schon seit drei Tagen in Berlin.

Das Essen im Parasol ist besonders gesund: es ist fettarm,
vegetarisch, und das Gemüse ist Bio-Gemüse. Außerdem gibt
es im Parasol keinen Alkohol und keinen Kaffee oder Tee.

Frau Semmler sagt, ohne Wein oder Tee kann sie abends gar
nicht abschalten.

STORY TRANSCRIPT

Frau Semmler	Hallo, Herr Wagner! Was kann ich für Sie tun?
Hubert	Ich wollte gerne mit Susanne sprechen. Ist sie da?
Frau Semmler	Leider nein, Susanne ist in Berlin. Soll ich ihr etwas ausrichten?
Hubert	Ja, ich wollte sie gerne zum Essen einladen. Es gibt jetzt ein vegetarisches Restaurant in Konstanz: das Parasol. Dort gibt es nur ganz gesundes Essen!
Frau Semmler	Ja, ist das Essen hier im Hotel nicht gesund?
Hubert	Doch, aber im Parasol ist es besonders gesund: fettarm, ohne Fleisch und das Gemüse ist Bio-Gemüse. Und Alkohol gibt es natürlich auch nicht.
Frau Semmler	Was, es gibt dort keinen Alkohol? Also, ohne mein Glas Wein kann ich abends gar nicht abschalten. Ein Glas Wein jeden Tag hält mich fit und gesund!
Hubert	Ach ja? Aber das müssen Sie zugeben: eine Küche ohne Fett und ohne Fleisch ist doch bestimmt sehr gesund.
Frau Semmler	Also, ich finde, die Leute übertreiben immer mit der fettarmen Ernährung. Und ich esse auch ganz gerne mal ein Stück Fleisch – und meine Gäste auch! Aber ich hab' jetzt leider zu tun …
Hubert	Ach so. Ja, dann tschüss, Frau Semmler. Und viele Grüße an Susanne.

Test

Now it's time to test your progress in Unit 12.

1   Cross out the odd one out in each group.

   1   der Hals / der Salbei / der Rücken / der Fuß
   2   das Eis / die Schokolade / der Fisch / die Sahne
   3   rauchen / Alkohol trinken / zu viel essen / Sport treiben
   4   das Auge / der Mund / die Salbe / die Nase
   5   der Husten / der Schnupfen / das Erkältungsbad / der Rücken

5

2   In this unit, you've encountered quite a few verbs with separable prefixes. Match the verbs 1–8 with the relevant prefix from a–h, then write down their meanings.

Example: ausgehen   to go out

1	fallen	a	auf
2	stehen	b	hin
3	geben	c	ab
4	nehmen	d	ein
5	fangen	e	fern
6	sehen	f	ein
7	laden	g	zu
8	schlafen	h	an

8

3   Write down the past participles of the verbs in 2. Hint: all of the verbs are irregular.

8

4   Which of these things are you not allowed to do, and which are you supposed to do if you want to live a healthy life? Fill in the appropriate form of **nicht dürfen** and **sollen**.

   1   Ich **darf nicht** rauchen.
   2   Ich _____so viel mit dem Auto fahren.
   3   Ich _____viel Salat essen.
   4   Ich _____ kein Eis essen.
   5   Ich _____viel wandern gehen.

4

5   In an e-mail, Renate talks about the busy day she had yesterday. Fill these words into the most appropriate gaps:

konnte / musste / konnte / wollten / sollte

Gestern war ein furchtbarer Tag! Ich **wollte** früh
aufstehen, aber dann habe ich zu lange geschlafen.
Ich 1 _____ schnell zur Arbeit fahren.
Ich 2 _____ bei der Arbeit kaum die
Augen offen halten, weil ich so müde war.
Und abends 3 _____ ich meine Eltern
besuchen! Sie 4 _____ mich zum Essen
einladen. Nach dem Essen 5 _____
ich nicht einschlafen, weil ich so satt war ... und
wie gehts dir heute?

Renate

5

6   Imagine you had an accident last weekend. Write a brief diary entry and note down how it happened. Use the perfect tense of the verbs and the past tense of the modal verbs below. The first sentence is done for you. (2 points for each correct sentence, 1 point if you make one mistake.)

Samstag, 15. März
Am Samstagmorgen bin ich früh aufgestanden. Ich ...

1   am Samstagmorgen: früh aufstehen
2   Sie wollten wandern gehen, aber ...
3   ... zuerst mussten Sie etwas einkaufen.
4   Also: in die Stadt gehen
5   Vor einer Bäckerei: hinfallen
6   wieder aufstehen, aber der linke Fuß tut sehr weh.
7   in einer Apotheke eine Salbe für den Fuß kaufen.

12

TOTAL SCORE **42**

If you scored less than 32, go through the dialogues and the Language Building sections again before completing the Summary on page 180.

Summary 12

 Now try this final test summarizing the main points covered in the unit. You can check your answers on the recording.

How would you:
1 ask the pharmacist whether she has anything for a runny nose?
2 ask her if she has any painkillers?
3 ask for a cough syrup?
4 say you're not allowed to drink any alcohol?
5 say you're not supposed to eat any fat?
6 say you wanted to go hiking?
7 say you had to go swimming?

REVISION

To practise the past tense of modal verbs, make a list of things you have to, or want to, or are supposed to do today. Then pick up your list at the end of the day and go over it again, this time saying what it was you wanted to, or had to, or were supposed to do.

Similarly, you can practise using the perfect tense of verbs with a separable prefix. Write down the verbs and their past participles that describe what you typically do during the day, e.g. get up, go shopping, fall asleep, watch TV, invite someone for a cup of tea, etc. Then tell yourself or your study partner about what you did yesterday.

At work
Bei der Arbeit

> **OBJECTIVES**
>
> In this unit you'll learn how to:
> - ✓ introduce yourself in a business environment
> - ✓ get through to someone on the phone
> - ✓ make an appointment
> - ✓ place an order
> - ✓ make comparisons
>
> And cover the following grammar and language:
> - ✓ possessive adjectives in the dative case
> - ✓ possessive adjectives in the genitive case
> - ✓ prepositions with the accusative
> - ✓ the comparative and superlative
> - ✓ irregular comparative and superlative forms

LEARNING GERMAN 13

Cultural knowledge can be quite important if you are involved in business and want to build up contacts with German business partners. You will probably find it helpful to talk to colleagues or friends who have been to Germany before. They can help you find out about the general conventions governing business conduct, or give insights into how German business people negotiate, for example. This unit will help you with writing business letters to German companies. More extensive guidelines on letter-writing can often be found in a good German–English dictionary.

🔊 Now start the recording for Unit 13.

13.1 Making a phone call

Hier ist Peter Hansen

ACTIVITY 1 is on the recording.

ACTIVITY 2

1 Where has Herr Kowalsky gone?
2 Is Herr Friedrichs in the office?
3 Whom does Herr Hansen talk to in the end?
4 What message does Herr Hansen leave?

DIALOGUE 1

○ Guten Tag, hier ist Peter Hansen von der Firma Hansen. Kann ich mit Herrn Kowalsky sprechen, bitte?

■ Herr Kowalsky ist heute leider nicht da. Möchten Sie mit seiner Sekretärin sprechen?

○ Nein danke. Können Sie mich mit seinem Kollegen, mit Herrn Friedrichs, verbinden?

■ Herr Friedrichs ist heute leider auch nicht im Hause. Er ist mit Herrn Kowalsky auf Geschäftsreise.

○ Ach so. Ja, dann verbinden Sie mich bitte mit der Sekretärin von Herrn Kowalsky.

▼ Guten Tag, Schönemann am Apparat.

○ Guten Tag, Frau Schönemann. Hier ist Herr Hansen von der Firma Hansen. Können Sie Herrn Kowalsky etwas ausrichten, bitte?

▼ Ja natürlich, Herr Hansen.

○ Sagen Sie ihm bitte, er soll mich morgen zurückrufen.

▼ Ja gut, Herr Hansen. Das sage ich ihm.

○ Vielen Dank, Frau Schönemann und auf Wiederhören!

VOCABULARY	
die Firma (die Firmen)	company
er ist nicht im Hause	he's not in [*literally* he's not in house]
die Geschäftsreise(-n)	business trip
verbinden*	to connect
am Apparat	on the line
zurück/rufen*	to call back

✅ Possessive adjectives in the dative case

Remember, possessive adjectives take the same endings as **ein**. In the dative case, these are as follows:

	m	f	n
singular	**seinem**	**seiner**	**seinem**

In the following examples, the prepositions **mit** and **von** take the dative case.

Ich spreche mit mein**em** Kollegen. I'm talking to my colleague.
Das ist die Jacke von mein**er** Sekretärin.
This is my secretary's jacket.
Das ist der Schlüssel von mein**em** Auto. This is the key to my car.

In the plural, the dative ending of the possessive adjective is always **-en**:

Sie spricht mit ihr**en** Kollegen. She's talking to her colleagues.
Sie kommen mit ihr**en** Kindern. They'll come with their children.

✅ Possessive adjectives in the genitive case

In the genitive, possessive adjectives again follow the **ein** pattern.

	m	f	n
singular	**ihres**	**ihrer**	**ihres**

Das ist das Auto mein**es** Kollegen. This is my colleague's car.
Das ist das Auto sein**er** Sekretärin. This is his secretary's car.
Das ist die Jacke unser**es** Kindes. This is our child's jacket.

In the plural, the genitive ending of the possessive adjective is always **-er**:

Das sind die Jacken unser**er** Kollegen. These are our colleagues' jackets.
Das sind die Spielzeuge mein**er** Kinder. These are my children's toys.

ACTIVITY 3

It's been a busy day for Herr and Frau Hansen! Fill in the missing endings.

1 Herr Hansen musste mit sein___ Kollegin Frau Schmidt sprechen.
2 Er hat die Telefonnummer sein__ Kollegin gesucht.
3 Frau Hansen hat die Jacken ihr__ Kinder gesucht.
4 Herr und Frau Hansen haben mit ihr___ Kindern gespielt.

Ⓐ Now do activities 4 and 5 on the recording.

13.2 Making an appointment
Einen Termin vereinbaren

 ACTIVITY 6 is on the recording.

ACTIVITY 7

Correct the statements which are false.

1 A delivery Herr Hansen received was more
   expensive than originally quoted.   T / F
2 Herr Kowalsky will come on 25th August.   T / F
3 Herr Kowalsky will come today.   T / F

DIALOGUE 2

■ Guten Morgen, Herr Hansen, hier ist Herr Kowalsky von
  der Firma Mitsch.
○ Ach, guten Morgen. Ja, Herr Kowalsky, ich möchte gerne
  einen Termin mit Ihnen vereinbaren.
■ Worum geht es denn, Herr Hansen?
○ Ihre letzte Lieferung war viel teurer als Ihr Angebot und
  wir hatten viele Probleme mit den Geräten.
■ Was? Das tut mir Leid, Herr Hansen. Sollen wir einen
  Termin für den 25. August vereinbaren?
○ Können Sie nicht früher kommen? Vielleicht morgen
  schon?
■ Das geht leider nicht. Aber ich kann heute noch kommen.
  Ich fahre heute Nachmittag durch die Stadt, dann kann ich
  bei Ihnen anhalten.

VOCABULARY	
der Termin(-e)	appointment
vereinbaren	to arrange
worum geht es denn?	what is it about then?
teurer	more expensive
als	than
das Angebot(-e)	[*here* =] quotation
das Problem(-e)	problem
das Gerät(-e)	piece of equipment
früher	earlier
das geht leider nicht	[*here* =] unfortunately, that's impossible
bei Ihnen	at your place [*i.e. Herr Hansen's company*]
an/halten* (er hält an)	to stop

✓ Prepositions with the accusative

These prepositions must always be followed by the accusative case:

durch through **für** for **gegen** against **ohne** without **um** around

Ich gehe **durch** die Stadt. I'll walk through the city.
Ich möchte ein Zimmer **für** den ersten August reservieren.
I'd like to book a room for the first of August.
Er ist **gegen** den neuen Chef. He's against the new boss.
Sie kommt **ohne** ihren Sohn. She'll come without her son.
Wir sind **um** den See gewandert. We hiked around the lake.

✓ The comparative

In German, the comparative is formed by adding the ending **-er** to the adjective or adverb:

früh – früher early, earlier   **spät – später** late, later
schnell – schneller fast, faster   **billig – billiger** cheap, cheaper

Heinz läuft **schneller** als Peter. Heinz runs faster than Peter.
Petra ist **kleiner** als Helga. Petra is smaller than Helga.
Diese Lieferung ist **teurer** als die letzte Lieferung. This delivery is more expensive than the last delivery.
Dieses Kleid ist noch **schöner** als das andere. This dress is even more beautiful than the other one.

ACTIVITY 8

Fill in the missing endings. Then translate the sentences into English.

1 Ich komme ohne mein___ Mann.
2 Es geht um Ihr__ Lieferung.
3 Wir sind durch ein__ schöne Stadt gefahren.
4 Ich suche eine Hose für mein___ Sohn.

ACTIVITY 9

Fill in the correct form of the adjective.

1 Peter läuft _____ (schnell) als Heinz.
2 Können Sie nicht _____ (früh) kommen?
3 Das rote Kleid ist viel _____ (schön)!
4 Frau Meier ist _____ (lustig) als Frau Gerber.

🔊 Now do activities 10 and 11 on the recording.

13.3 Placing an order
Ich möchte gerne etwas bestellen!

ACTIVITY 12 is on the recording.

ACTIVITY 13

1 Model No. 14 costs € ____ apiece.
2 Model No. 15 costs € ____ apiece.
3 Model No. 16 costs € ____ apiece.
4 Model No. 14 measures ___ metres by ___ metres.

DIALOGUE 3

- Seiler, guten Morgen.
- ○ Guten Morgen, Frau Seiler. Hier spricht Misch vom Hotel Weiß. Ich möchte gerne dreißig weiße Tischdecken bestellen.
- Gerne, Herr Misch. Wir haben drei verschiedene Modelle. Modell Nr. 14 ist aus Polyester und kostet 38 Euro pro Stück. Modell Nr. 15 ist ein bisschen größer, aber auch teurer: es kostet 48 Euro pro Stück und ist aus Baumwolle. Und Modell Nr. 16 ist am teuersten: 80 Euro pro Stück. Es ist aber auch am größten.
- ○ Wie groß ist denn das Modell 14?
- 1,60 Meter mal 1,30 Meter.
- ○ Das ist genau richtig. Also, dreißigmal das Modell Nr. 14 bitte. Wann können Sie denn liefern?
- Wir schicken die Tischdecken heute noch ab. Dann haben Sie sie morgen.

VOCABULARY	
die Tischdecke(-n)	tablecloth
verschieden	different
ist aus …	is made from …
der Polyester(-)	polyester
pro Stück	each, apiece
die Baumwolle (*pl.*)	cotton
am teuersten	most expensive
am größten	biggest
der Meter(-)	meter
-mal	times
genau richtig	just right
liefern	to deliver
ab/schicken	to dispatch, send off

✅ The superlative

To form the superlative, you use **am** and then add the ending **-sten** to the adjective or adverb:

billig – billiger – <u>am billigsten</u>	cheap, cheaper, the cheapest
schnell – schneller – <u>am schnellsten</u>	fast, faster, the fastest
schön – schöner – <u>am schönsten</u>	beautiful, more beautiful, the most beautiful

✅ Irregular comparative and superlative forms

Many monosyllabic adjectives take an umlaut (¨)in the comparative and superlative forms. Here are some common examples:

jung – jünger – am jüngsten	young, younger, the youngest
groß – größer – am größten	big, bigger, the biggest
warm – wärmer – am wärmsten	warm, warmer, the warmest
oft – öfter – am öftesten	often, more often, most often

Some comparatives and superlatives not only take an umlaut, but change consonants as well. The most common examples are:

nah – näher – am nächsten	near, nearer, the nearest
hoch – höher – am höchsten	high, higher, the highest

viel ('much') and **gut** ('good') are irregular:

viel – mehr – am meisten	much, more, the most
gut – besser – am besten	good, better, the best

The comparative and superlative of **gerne** are irregular as well:

Ich lese **gerne**. I like to read.
Ich gehe **lieber** schwimmen. I prefer to go swimming.
Ich spiele **am liebsten** Fußball. I like to play football most of all.

ACTIVITY 14

Make comparisons, using the correct form of the comparative and superlative.

Jacke A: €63. Jacke B: €65. Jacke C: €198. (**teuer**)
Jacke B ist **teurer als** Jacke A. Jacke C ist **am teuersten**.

1 Rock A: Größe 36. Rock B: Größe 40. Rock C: Größe 44. (**groß**)
2 Peter: 1,55 Meter. Uwe: 1,60 Meter. Bertie: 1,50. (**klein**)
3 Maria: 50 Jahre. Sabine: 55 Jahre. Stefan: 60 Jahre. (**alt**)
4 Uschi: 78 kg. Lotte: 85 kg. Hans: 98 kg. (**dick**)
5 Lutz: 65 kg. Karola: 63 kg. Anna: 60 kg. (**schlank**)

 Now do activities 15 and 16 on the recording.

187

(13.4) Business letters
Geschäftsbriefe

German conventions for writing formal or business letters are different from English ones, beginning with the way you address the envelope.

ACTIVITY 17

You want to write a letter to the company Habermann & Co. Read the guidelines below, then use them to help you address the envelope. The details you need are given below.

1 company name: Habermann & Co.
2 postal code: 50939 Köln in Germany (D)
3 house number: 67 c
4 street name: Schachtstraße
5 for the attention of Mr Herbert Habermann

So adressieren Sie einen Geschäftsbrief:

1 Schreiben Sie 'Herrn', 'Frau' oder 'Firma' in die erste Zeile, **über** den Namen des Adressaten oder der Firma.
2 'z.H. Frau Michele Glück' bedeutet 'zu Händen Frau Michele Glück'. Schreiben Sie 'z.H. Herrn/Frau …' **unter** den Firmennamen.
3 In der nächsten Zeile steht der Straßenname. Die Hausnummer steht **nach** dem Namen der Straße!
4 Darunter steht der Name der Stadt. Die Postleitzahl steht **vor** dem Namen der Stadt.
5 Schreiben Sie 'D', 'AU' oder 'CH' für Deutschland, Österreich oder die Schweiz **vor** die Postleitzahl.

der Geschäftsbrief(-e)	business letter
adressieren	to address
die Zeile(-n)	line
der Adressat(-en)	addressee
die Hand(-¨-e)	hand
zu Händen/z.H.	for the attention of [*literally* to the hands of]
der Firmenname(-n)	company name
der Straßenname(-n)	street name
die Hausnummer(-n)	house number
darunter	underneath
die Postleitzahl(-en)	postcode, ZIP code
Österreich	Austria
die Schweiz	Switzerland

ACTIVITY 18

Here are some ways of addressing people at the beginning of a letter, and of signing off at the end of the letter. Using the vocabulary you already know, cross out those phrases which do not belong in a formal business letter.

1 Sehr geehrte Damen und Herren
2 Liebe Frau Walzer
3 *Sehr geehrter Herr Meier*
4 Sehr geehrte Frau Walzer
5 ~~Lieber Herr Schmidt~~
6 *viele liebe Grüße*
7 ~~tschüss~~
8 **mit freundlichen Grüßen**
9 hochachtungsvoll

geehrt	honoured
liebe/lieber	dear [*when addressing a female/male friend*]
freundlich	friendly
hochachtungsvoll	[*here =*] yours faithfully [*literally* full of great respect]

WIE WARS IN BERLIN?
HOW WAS BERLIN?

Susanne kommt aus Berlin zurück und Frau Semmler fragt sie, wie ihre Reise war.

wie war's?	what was it like? [*short for* **wie war es?**]
anstrengend	strenuous, demanding
ganz gut	quite good, quite nice
naja	oh well [*colloquial*]
der Chef(-s)	boss
der Job(-s)	job
das Traumgehalt(-¨-er)	dream salary
anbieten*	to offer
nö	no [*colloquial for* **nein**]
jetzt nicht mehr	not any more
unbedingt	absolutely
das Spiel(-e)	game
im Spiel sein	to be involved [*literally* to be in the game] [*colloquial*]
Quatsch!	rubbish! [*colloquial*]
aus ... weg/gehen*	to go away from ...
der Unsinn	nonsense, rubbish
so ein Unsinn!	what nonsense!
aus/packen	to unpack

ACTIVITY 19

Listen to the dialogue and supply the missing words.

1 Berlin ist ja noch _____ als Konstanz.
2 Ich finde ihn (Herrn Meier) ein bisschen zu _____.
3 _____ Chefs sind einfach _____.
4 Ja, und Berlin? Das ist doch nun wirklich _____ als Konstanz.
5 Und Konstanz ist doch sehr _____!

ACTIVITY 20

Listen to the dialogue again and decide whether these statements are true or false.

1 Susanne thought Berlin was quite cheap.   T / F
2 She says Herr Meier was nice and younger than
   she'd expected.   T / F
3 Susanne had a romantic 'blind date' with Herr
   Meier.   T / F
4 Susanne had gone to Berlin for a job interview. T / F
5 Herr Meier had offered her a job with an excellent
   salary.   T / F
6 Susanne would like to live in Berlin.   T / F
7 Frau Semmler suspects a man is the reason why
   Susanne isn't too keen on Berlin.   T / F

STORY TRANSCRIPT

Frau Semmler	Susanne, da bist du ja wieder! Wie wars?
Susanne	Anstrengend! Und teuer! Berlin ist ja noch teurer als Konstanz!
Frau Semmler	Ja, klar. Aber wie wars denn nun mit Herrn Meier?
Susanne	Ganz gut. Er war sehr nett ...
Frau Semmler	Aber?
Susanne	Naja, ich finde ihn ein bisschen zu alt. Jüngere Chefs sind einfach netter.
Frau Semmler	Wie bitte? Und deshalb möchtest du den Job nicht haben? Hast du nicht gesagt: Herr Meier hat mir ein Traumgehalt angeboten?!
Susanne	Ja – aber die Firma war auch nicht so toll ...
Frau Semmler	Ja, und Berlin? Das ist doch nun wirklich interessanter als Konstanz. Möchtest du denn nicht mal in einer großen Stadt wohnen?
Susanne	Nö, jetzt nicht mehr. Ich finde Berlin zu groß. Und Konstanz ist doch sehr schön!
Frau Semmler	Also, das verstehe ich nicht. Du wolltest doch unbedingt nach Berlin gehen. Ist da etwa ein Mann im Spiel?
Susanne	Quatsch! Warum denn das?
Frau Semmler	Na, weil du nicht aus Konstanz weggehen möchtest ...
Susanne	Ach, so ein Unsinn. So, ich packe jetzt meinen Koffer aus. Bis später.

Test

Now it's time to test your progress in Unit 13.

1 Which is the odd one out?

   1 die Firma / die Geschäftsreise / die Hand / der Geschäftsbrief
   2 anrufen / verbinden / anhalten / zurückrufen
   3 das Angebot / liefern / die Lieferung / am Apparat
   4 schlank / dick / nett / teuer

4

2 Unscramble this conversation between a caller and a receptionist by numbering the sentences in the correct order.

   1 Meier und Co., guten Tag.
   2 Kann ich seine Sekretärin sprechen?
   3 Ach, guten Tag Herr Fischer, was kann ich für Sie tun?
   4 Ja, einen Moment bitte, ich verbinde Sie.
   5 Guten Tag, hier spricht Herr Fischer von der Firma Walter.
   6 Kann ich bitte Herrn Sommer sprechen?
   7 Es tut mir Leid, aber Herr Sommer ist auf Geschäftsreise.

7

3 Frau Specht is comparing herself to her colleagues at work. Fill in the appropriate forms of the adjectives in brackets.

Also, Frau Meier ist sehr _____ (nett), aber Frau Hahn ist noch _____ (nett). Ich finde mich aber am _____ (nett). Ich finde, ich sehe auch ganz gut aus. Frau Meier sieht noch _____ (gut) aus – na, und Frau Hahn sieht natürlich am _____ (gut) aus. Sie ist auch so _____ (schlank)! Am _____ (schlank) ist aber Frau Meier, das muss ich sagen. Ach, ich muss abnehmen!

7

4 Complete the endings in this phone conversation.

B: Guten Tag, ich möchte gerne Frau Petersen sprechen.
A: Es tut mir Leid, aber Frau Petersen ist nicht in ihr___ Büro. Möchten Sie ihr__ Sekretärin sprechen?

B: Nein danke. Kann ich ihr___ Kollegin, Frau Walter sprechen?

A: Frau Walter ist leider auf Geschäftsreise.

B: Haben Sie die Telefonnummer ihr___ Kollegen, Herrn Grün?

A: Ja, aber Herr Grün ist leider auch nicht im Hause.

B: Können Sie mich dann bitte mit ihr___ Sekretärin verbinden?

A: Ja, natürlich, ich verbinde Sie.

5

---

5 Herr Walter is telling his wife about his day. Write down what he says.

Example: Um acht Uhr aufstehen – Um acht Uhr bin ich aufgestanden.

1 Um 9 Uhr: frühstücken
2 Um 10 Uhr: mit einem Kollegen Kaffee trinken
3 Um 11 Uhr: einen Kollegen anrufen
4 Um 12 Uhr: essen
5 Um 15 Uhr: den Kollegen Tee bringen
6 Um 16 Uhr: Geschäftsbriefe schreiben

6

---

6 At the weekend, Herr and Frau Specht like to travel. Complete the sentences using the appropriate preposition from the list below.

durch/für/gegen/um

1 Herr Specht hat _____ den 30. August ein Zimmer am Bodensee reserviert.
2 Sie sind _____ den Bodensee gewandert.
3 Sie sind _____ die Stadt Konstanz nach Hause gefahren.
4 Leider sind sie dann _____ ihr Haus gefahren.

4

TOTAL SCORE **33**

If you scored less than 23, go through the dialogues and the Language Building sections again before completing the Summary on page 194.

Summary 13

Now try this final test summarizing the main points covered in the unit. You can check your answers on the recording.

How would you:
1 introduce yourself on the telephone as Herr Müller from Müller and Co.?
2 ask if you can speak to Herr Wolfram, please?
3 ask the receptionist if she can put you through to his colleague, Frau Walter, please?
4 ask the receptionist if she can pass on a message to her?
5 say 'Please could you tell her to call me back tomorrow?'
6 say 'I'd like to arrange an appointment with you'?
7 say you'd like to order 56 jackets in size 48?

REVISION

If you still feel uncertain about the use of possessive adjectives, you may want to go back to Unit 5, pages 63, 65, and 67. Make up simple sentences in which you have to use possessive adjectives. Imagine various items that belong to members of your family or to a friend. Then say to yourself: **Das ist Marias Tasche. Das ist ihre Tasche. Das ist Marias Buch. Das ist ihr Buch**, and so on. Then do the same for a male friend: **Das ist Peters Auto. Das ist sein Auto. Das ist Peters Lampe. Das ist seine Lampe**. You can then go on and think about sentences in which you have to use **unser** and **euer**.

You could also make comparisons between your colleagues at work. For further practice on comparatives and superlatives, why not get together with your study partner and talk about some common acquaintances? A is taller than B, but C is the tallest, etc.

▷ ▷ ▷ ▷ ▷ ▷ ▷ ▷ ▷ ▷ ▷ ▷ ▷ ▷ ▷

High days and holidays
Festtage und Feiertage

OBJECTIVES

In this unit you'll learn how to:

✓ talk about plans you have for special occasions

✓ wish someone a merry Christmas and a happy New Year

✓ express your plans and resolutions for the future

✓ read about things that happened in the past

And cover the following grammar and language:

✓ past participles without the **ge-** prefix

✓ the future tense

✓ past participles of mixed verbs

✓ the simple past of regular and irregular verbs

✓ the simple past of verbs with a separable prefix

LEARNING GERMAN 14

As this is the last unit of the course, you may be wondering how to work on your German after this. There are various possibilities you could consider. First, you could, of course, travel to a German-speaking country and finally enjoy the skills you've worked so hard to achieve! Second, you could try to find a German native speaker who wants to improve his or her English. He or she could speak about a certain topic in German to you, and you could reciprocate in English. Finally you could join a class and develop further the skills you've already acquired.

Now start the recording for Unit 14.

Was macht ihr über Weihnachten?

ACTIVITY 1 is on the recording.

ACTIVITY 2

1 Where does Inga want to go for Christmas?
2 Who recommended the hotel to her?
3 Does Inga like skiing?
4 Does Stefan join Inga for a coffee?

DIALOGUE 1

○ Na, Stefan, was macht Ihr über Weihnachten? Bleibt ihr wieder bei deinen Eltern unter dem Tannenbaum?

■ Nein, ich habe schon mit einem Hotel in Österreich telefoniert und ein Zimmer reserviert. Und ihr?

○ Wir wollen auch wegfahren – aber in die Sonne! Eine Kollegin hat mir ein Hotel auf Lanzarote empfohlen. Ich habe auch schon einen Prospekt von dort bekommen. Es sieht toll aus!

■ Aber dann könnt ihr dieses Jahr ja gar nicht Ski fahren!

○ Ach, ich fahre sowieso nicht gerne Ski. Ich habe meine alten Skier schon lange verkauft. So, jetzt gehe ich aber einen Kaffee trinken. Kommst du mit?

■ Nein, ich habe leider keine Zeit. Vielleicht nächstes Mal! Und frohe Weihnachten!

VOCABULARY

das Weihnachten(-)	Christmas
der Tannenbaum(-̈-e)	fir tree, [*here* =] Christmas tree
telefonieren	to make a phone call, to phone
weg/fahren* (er fährt weg)	to go away [*literally* to drive away]
der Ski(-er)	ski
sowieso	anyway
frohe Weihnachten!	merry Christmas!

✓ Past participles without the *ge-* prefix

Two kinds of verbs do not form their past participle with the prefix **ge-**.

1 Verbs with an infinitive ending in **-ieren**.
The past participle is formed by replacing the infinitive ending (**-ieren**) with **-iert**.

infinitive	*past participle*	*English verb*
reserv**ieren**	reserv**iert**	to reserve/reserved
telefon**ieren**	telefon**iert**	to phone/phoned
serv**ieren**	serv**iert**	to serve/served

2 Verbs starting with the non-separable prefixes **be-, emp-, ent-, er-, ge-, ver-, zer-**. Note that these verbs can be either (a) regular or (b) irregular.

(a) The past participle of regular verbs is formed by replacing the infinitive ending (**-en**) with **-t**.

infinitive	*past participle*	*English verb*
bestellen	bestell**t**	to order/ordered
verkaufen	verkauf**t**	to sell/sold
gehören	gehör**t**	to belong/belonged

(b) The past participle of irregular verbs ends in **-en** and a vowel change can take place in the stem. See the list of irregular verbs on pages 235–6.

infinitive	*past participle*	*English verb*
empfehlen	empf**ohlen**	to recommend/recommended
bekommen	bekommen	to receive/received
entscheiden	entsch**ieden**	to decide/decided

ACTIVITY 3

Using the diary below, say what you did over Christmas and New Year.

> Example: 24. Dezember: mein Radio verkaufen.
> Am vierundzwanzigsten Dezember habe ich mein Radio verkauft.

1 24. Dezember: einen neuen Mantel bekommen
2 25. Dezember: meine Schwester und ihre Familie besuchen
3 26. Dezember: meiner Mutter ein tolles Buch empfehlen
4 31. Dezember: meinen Freunden viel Sekt servieren
5 1. Januar: mit meinem Bruder in Amerika telefonieren

Now do activities 4 and 5 on the recording.

Happy New Year!
Ein frohes neues Jahr!

🎧 **ACTIVITY 6** is on the recording.

ACTIVITY 7

Correct the statements which are false.

1	Karin wants to lose 15 kg.	T/F
2	She wants to smoke less.	T/F
3	Herbert wants to spend more time with Karin.	T/F

DIALOGUE 2

■ Fünf, vier, drei, zwei, eins – PROST NEUJAHR!!!!!

○ Ein frohes neues Jahr wünsche ich dir, und alles Gute, mein Schatz!

■ Danke, gleichfalls! Und – was wirst du im nächsten Jahr besser machen?

○ Ich werde zehn Kilo abnehmen, ich werde mehr Sport treiben und ich werde nicht mehr rauchen!

■ Meinst du das ernst?

○ Ja, klar! Naja, ich habe es zumindest vor. Und du?

■ Ich? Ich werde mehr Zeit mit dir verbringen! Letztes Jahr habe ich viel zu wenig Zeit mit dir verbracht!

○ Das ist doch ein guter Vorsatz! Darauf trinken wir noch ein Glas Sekt!

VOCABULARY

Prost Neujahr!	Happy New Year! [*said as a toast*]
ein frohes neues Jahr!	a happy New Year!
alles Gute	all the best [*literally* everything good]
mein Schatz	my dear, my love [*literally* my treasure]
danke, gleichfalls	thank you, the same to you
meinen	to mean
meinst du das ernst?	are you serious?
zumindest	at least
vor/haben	to intend
letztes Jahr	last year
wenig	too little
verbringen (*mix.*)	to spend (time)
der Vorsatz(-¨-e)	intention, resolution
darauf trinken wir!	we'll drink to that!

✅ Talking about the future

German often uses the present tense to refer to things in the future. However, the future tense is also used if the context doesn't make it sufficiently clear that an action will take place in the future, or if the speaker wants to stress his or her determination to do something.

✅ The future tense

To form the future tense, you use the present tense of **werden** ('to become') plus an infinitive:

ich **werde**	wir **werden**
du **wirst**	ihr **werdet**
er/sie/es **wird**	sie **werden**
	Sie **werden**

The infinitive always goes to the end of the sentence. In a statement, the **werden** form is the second element:

Ich **werde** nächstes Jahr **abnehmen**. I'll lose weight next year.
Wir **werden** nicht nach Spanien **fahren**. We won't go to Spain.

In a question, the **werden** form goes either to the second or first position, depending on whether there is a question word or not:

Wann **wirst** du **heiraten**? When will you get married?
Wirst du ihn **heiraten**? Will you marry him?

✅ The past participles of mixed verbs

Some verbs, like **verbringen** ('to spend') and the modal verbs, are mixed, that is, they behave partly like regular, partly like irregular verbs. The past participles of mixed verbs have a vowel change, but still end in -t like those of regular verbs: **verbringen**, but **ich habe zu wenig Zeit mit dir verbracht**. Mixed verbs will be marked (*mix.*) in the vocabulary lists, and you can look up their past participles in the list of irregular verbs on pages 235–6.

ACTIVITY 8

Translate these New Year's resolutions into German, using the future tense.

1 Herbert will do more sport.
2 Marlene and Peter will go hiking a lot.
3 I'll spend more time with my family.
4 Erich won't smoke any more.
5 We will go swimming more often.

 Now do activities 9 and 10 on the recording.

No Merry Christmas

Kein frohes Weihnachten

ACTIVITY 11 is on the recording.

ACTIVITY 12

Correct the mistake in each of these statements:

1 Die Familie Horaz besuchte ein paar Freunde.
2 Sie fuhren gegen 19 Uhr ab.
3 Ein Mann stahl Geschenke im Wert von €3000.

DIALOGUE 3

○ Mensch, Rudi, das muss ich dir vorlesen!
„Die Familie Horaz besuchte am 24. Dezember ihre
Großmutter. Sie fuhren gegen 18 Uhr ab. Ein Mann
gelangte in das Haus der Familie und stahl Geschenke im
Wert von 300 Euro. Gegen 23 Uhr kam die Familie Horaz
nach Hause. Sie suchten nach ihren Geschenken und
konnten sie nicht finden."
Ist das nicht furchtbar?

VOCABULARY	
vor/lesen* (er liest vor)	to read aloud
die Großmutter(-̈-er)	grandmother
sie fuhren ab	they left [*from* ab/fahren]
ab/fahren* (er fährt ab)	to leave, depart
er gelangte	he got into [*from* gelangen]
gelangen	to reach, to arrive, [*here =*] to get into
er stahl	he stole [*from* stehlen]
stehlen* (er stiehlt)	to steal
das Geschenk(-e)	gift
der Wert(-e)	value
im Wert von ...	worth
er kam	he came [*from* kommen]
sie suchten nach ...	they looked for
suchen nach ...	to look for
sie konnten nicht	they couldn't [*from* konnen]

✅ The simple past of regular verbs

In written texts, Germans mostly use the simple past to refer to events in the past.

The simple past of regular verbs is formed by adding the endings below to the stem (e.g. **klettern**, stem **kletter-**). These endings are the same as for the simple past of **haben** and the modal verbs.

ich **kletterte**	wir **kletterten**
du **klettertest**	ihr **klettertet**
er/sie/es **kletterte**	sie **kletterten**
	Sie **kletterten**

✅ The simple past of irregular verbs

Irregular verbs usually change their vowel in the past tense. The past tense endings are identical to the present tense endings, but there are no endings in the **ich** and **er/sie/es** forms. In the list of irregular verbs on pages 235–6, you'll find the simple past of the **er/sie/es** forms of irregular verbs.

ich **stahl**	wir **stahlen**
du **stahlst**	ihr **stahlt**
er/sie/es **stahl**	sie **stahlen**
	Sie **stahlen**

Note: Mixed verbs change their vowel in the simple past, but carry the same endings as regular verbs: **verbringen** ('to spend time'), **ich verbrachte, du verbrachtest, er/sie/es verbrachte**, etc.

✅ The simple past of verbs with a separable prefix

Regular and irregular verbs with a separable prefix form their simple past in the same way as outlined above for regular and irregular verbs. The prefix goes to the end of the sentence:

regular **ein/kaufen**: Sie **kaufte** Nahrungsmittel **ein**.
She bought some food.

irregular **weg/laufen**: Er **lief** von zu Hause **weg**.
He ran away from home.

ACTIVITY 13

Here you'll have to do some guesswork. Try to work out the infinitives of these verbs in the simple past.

1 er sprach 3 er schlief
2 er rief an 4 er schwamm

🎧 Now do activities 14 and 15 on the recording.

14.4 Shrovetide
Die Fastnacht

There is an abundance of carnival and Shrovetide customs in Germany. Shrovetide clubs exist to organize festivities. Carnival jesters in fancy costumes celebrate **Karneval** all along the Rhine and the Isar, and **Fastnacht** in Southern Germany, Austria, and Switzerland.

ACTIVITY 16

This timetable lists last year's Shrovetide events in a village near Konstanz. Fill in the appropriate past tense endings.

Schmutziger Donnerstag
11 Uhr: das ganze Dorf tanz__ im Hemdglonkerumzug
16 Uhr: die Narren befrei___ die Schüler
19 Uhr: die Narren zog___ im Fasnetsumzug durch das Dorf

Sonntag
15 Uhr: die Narren stell__ den Narrenbaum auf
20 Uhr: die Narren verbrann__ (*mix.*) die Fasnet

Dienstag
19 Uhr: das Dorf tanz__ auf dem Bürgerball

Schmutziger Donnerstag	the Thursday before Ash Wednesday [*literally* dirty Thursday]
der Hemdglonkerumzug(-¨-e)	*procession of villagers dancingthrough the streets wearing white nightgowns*
der Narr(-en)	carnival jester, reveller
befreien	to free
der Schüler(-)	male pupil
sie zogen	they marched [*from* **ziehen**]
ziehen*	to pull, [*here* =] to march
der Fasnetsumzug(-¨-e)	*procession of the Shrovetide clubs in their costumes [dialect for* **der Fastnachtsumzug**]
das Dorf(-¨-er)	village
die Fasnet (*sing.*)	Shrovetide [*dialect for* **die Fastnacht**]
der Bürgerball(-¨-e)	villagers' ball [*literally* citizen ball]

ACTIVITY 17

The order of events in the timetable above is mixed up. With the help of the report below, put the events in the correct order.

Am Schmutzigen Donnerstag zogen die Narren mit der Musikkapelle zur Schule und 'befreiten' die Schüler. Nachmittags trugen die Narren und die Musikkapelle den 'Narrenbaum' durch das Dorf. Sie stellten den Baum am Marktplatz auf. Am Donnerstagabend fand dann der 'Hemdglonkerumzug' statt. Das ganze Dorf tanzte!
Am Sonntagnachmittag war wieder der Fasnetsumzug, und am Sonntagabend tanzten die Dorfbewohner auf dem Bürgerball. Am Dienstagabend war die Fasnet zu Ende: In einem Hemdglonkerumzug trugen die Dorfbewohner die Fasnet (symbolisiert durch eine Strohpuppe) durchs Dorf. Sie hängten sie am Narrenbaum auf und verbrannten sie.

der Narrenbaum(-¨-e)	tree stripped of its bark and put up in a central place [literally carnival jester tree]
der Baum(-¨-e)	tree
auf/stellen	to put up
sie verbrannten	they burnt [from verbrennen]
verbrennen (mix.)	to burn
die Musikkapelle(-n)	band of musicians
die Schule(-n)	school
sie trugen	they carried [from tragen]
tragen* (er trägt)	to carry, to wear
der Dorfbewohner(-)	villager
symbolisieren	to symbolize
symbolisiert durch	symbolized by
die Strohpuppe(-n)	straw doll
auf/hängen	to hang up, [here =] to hang

DAS ENDE DER GESCHICHTE...
THE END OF THE STORY ...

Es ist Sonntagmorgen im Hotel Gertrud. Susanne kommt
müde nach Hause. Sie war bis um sechs Uhr auf einem
Fastnachtsball. Frau Semmler möchte wissen, ob Susanne
nach Berlin geht oder nicht.

das Ende(-n)	end
die Geschichte(-n)	story
der Ball(-¨-e)	ball
ob	whether
endlich	at long last
auf keinen Fall	on no account
längst	a long time ago, long since
vergessen* (er vergisst)	to forget
übrigens	by the way
vorbei/kommen*	to drop in
der Gemüsefanatiker(-)	vegetable fanatic
du musst es ja wissen ...	you have to know what you're doing
duschen	to shower

ACTIVITY 18

There are mistakes in six of the following statements about the
dialogue. Underline them and correct them.

1 Es ist neun Uhr morgens.
2 Susanne war bis um sieben Uhr auf einem Ball.
3 Sie trägt noch ihr Abendkleid.
4 Herr Meier hat gestern Vormittag angerufen.
5 Susanne wird nach Berlin gehen.
6 Susanne möchte sich in Konstanz einen Job suchen.
7 Susanne hat Max (ihren Exmann) schon längst vergessen.
8 Hubert wird heute in das Hotel kommen.
9 Hubert und Susanne wollen an den Bodensee fahren.
10 Frau Semmler meint: Susanne möchte in Konstanz
   bleiben, weil Hubert in Konstanz wohnt.

ACTIVITY 19

So, what does the future hold for Susanne? Translate the sentences which follow and then tick those which you think will happen.

1 Susanne wird Vegetarierin werden, weil Hubert Vegetarier ist. ___

2 Sie wird Hubert heiraten. ___

3 Susanne und Hubert werden viele Kinder haben. ___

4 Susanne und Hubert werden viel Krach haben, weil Susanne nicht sehr gesund isst. ___

5 Susanne und Hubert werden Krach haben und Susanne wird nach Berlin gehen. ___

6 In Berlin wird Susanne Peter treffen und sie werden heiraten. ___

STORY TRANSCRIPT

Susanne	Mann, bin ich müde!
Frau Semmler	Susanne – da bist du ja endlich! Die Gäste wollen ihr Frühstück haben. Ja, wie siehst du denn aus? Es ist acht Uhr – und du bist noch im Kostüm?
Susanne	Ich war bis sechs Uhr auf dem Ball.
Frau Semmler	Was?! Ach übrigens, Herr Meier hat gestern Abend angerufen. Er wollte wissen, ob du nach Berlin kommst oder nicht. – Susanne?
Susanne	Hmmm? Wie bitte?
Frau Semmler	Herr Meier! Er will wissen, ob du nach Berlin kommst. – Susanne? Was wirst du denn nun machen?
Susanne	Ich werde auf keinen Fall nach Berlin gehen.
Frau Semmler	Und was ist mit dem Traumgehalt?
Susanne	Geld ist nicht alles! Ich werde mir hier in Konstanz einen Job suchen.
Frau Semmler	Wolltest du nicht auch nach Berlin gehen, weil du Max und die Scheidung vergessen wolltest?
Susanne	Max? Den habe ich schon längst vergessen! – Übrigens – heute nachmittag kommt Hubert hier vorbei. Wir gehen dann zusammen in die Stadt.
Frau Semmler	Aha! Also ist doch ein Mann im Spiel! War Hubert nicht auch gestern auf dem Ball?
Susanne	Hmmm.
Frau Semmler	Dieser Gemüsefanatiker?! Na, du musst es ja wissen, mein Schatz …
Susanne	Genau! Und jetzt gehe ich duschen – bis später!

Test

Now it's time to test your progress in Unit 14.

1 Match the German words 1–12 with the correct English version a–l.

1	das Weihnachten	a	to spend (time)
2	der Tannenbaum	b	grandmother
3	telefonieren	c	to mean
4	verkaufen	d	Christmas
5	bestellen	e	Christmas tree
6	meinen	f	to order
7	vorhaben	g	to phone
8	verbringen	h	to drop in
9	gelangen	i	to serve
10	die Großmutter	j	to sell
11	vorbeikommen	k	to reach, to arrive
12	servieren	l	to intend

12

2 Tick the correct verb form that goes with each person. Note: sometimes more than one answer is possible!

1	kletterte:	___wir	___ihr	___er
2	schliefen:	___sie	___Sie	___wir
3	riefen an:	___wir	___ihr	___sie
4	kauftest:	___du	___er	___Sie
5	fuhr Ski:	___ich	___du	___sie
6	telefonierte:	___ sie	___ihr	___wir

10

3 Unscramble these questions and statements about what the future holds.

1 wirst/wann/anrufen/du /?
2 fahren/ihr/wohin/werdet/?
3 ich/nach Spanien/fahren/werde
4 du/sie/wirst/heiraten/?
5 ihr/bei deinen Eltern/wohnen/werdet/?

5

4 Translate these sentences into German using the perfect tense to tell your German-speaking friend what you did today. (2 points for a correct sentence, 1 point if you make one mistake.)

1 I spent a lot of time with my family.
2 I called a friend. (use **telefonieren mit**)
3 I ordered a new car.
4 I gave a cup of tea to my wife. (use **servieren**)

| 8

5 In a letter to some friends, Frau Horaz tells them about the break-in at her family's house on Christmas Eve. Put the infinitives in brackets into the simple past.

Liebe Maria, lieber Ernst,

Wir 1 _____ (**haben**) wirklich ein furchtbares Weihnachten dieses Jahr! Am 24. Dezember 2 _____ (**fahren***) wir zu meiner Mutter nach Hamburg. Gegen 23 Uhr 3 _____ (**kommen***) wir wieder nach Hause. Wir 4 _____ (**gehen***) ins Haus und 5 _____ (**suchen**) unsere Geschenke, aber wir 6 _____ (**können**) nichts finden! Der Tannenbaum 7 _____ (**sein**) auch weg! 8_____ (**haben**) ihr denn ein schöneres Weihnachten?

Viele liebe Grüße,

deine Anni

| 8

TOTAL SCORE | 43

If you scored less than 33, go through the dialogues and the Language Building sections again before completing the Summary on page 208.

Summary 14

Now try this final test summarizing the main points covered in the unit. You can check your answers on the recording.

How would you:
1 ask a good friend what he's doing over Christmas?
2 ask two friends what they're doing over Christmas?
3 say that you want to go away? (use **wegfahren**)
4 wish a good friend a happy New Year?
5 wish a group of friends a happy New Year?
6 say 'I'll learn more German'?

REVISION

Congratulations on completing the course! After giving yourself a (well-deserved!) break to let things sink in, you may want to revise those areas you found particularly difficult before. Now you have an overview of the whole grammar and vocabulary content of this course, things you didn't understand before may well fall into place when you go back over them. You'll find that the connections and cross-references highlighted throughout mean much more to you. Most importantly, if you want to maintain or even expand your skills, don't get rusty, and try to think of ways to get back into the habit of doing some German at least once a week. For now: **Auf Wiedersehen und alles Gute!**

VOCABULARY

1 Answer these clues in German and complete the crossword.

1 Ich muss gurgeln und Salbeipastillen lutschen, denn mein _____ tut weh.
2 Es hat zwölf Monate.
3 Manfred (90 Kilo) ist dick, aber Heino (50 Kilo) ist _____ .
4 Ein Mann sucht seinen Koffer. Er findet ihn im _____ .
5 Hier können Sie Kopfschmerztabletten, Hustensaft usw. kaufen.
6 Sie können sie essen. Sie ist braun und süß, aber sie ist nicht gesund.
7 Es ist gesund und viele Leute essen es morgens zum Frühstück.
8 Sie kann groß und weiß sein und Sie finden sie oft auf einem Tisch. Was ist das?
9 Was ist am 25.und 26. Dezember?
10 Sie reisen. Sie brauchen einen _____ für Ihre Kleidung.

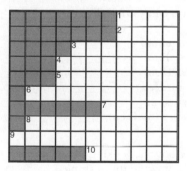

2 Match each phrase from 1–5 with a phrase from a–e to make correct sentences.

1 Acht Uhr ist zu spät, …
2 Herr Münch ist leider nicht hier, …
3 Um neun Uhr habe ich leider einen Termin, …
4 Ich möchte gerne Frau Kiesel sprechen, …
5 Frau Hansen ist auf Geschäftsreise, …

a können Sie vielleicht später kommen?
b soll ich Sie mit ihrer Sekretärin verbinden?
c können Sie mich mit ihr verbinden, bitte?
d kann ich ihm etwas ausrichten?
e können Sie nicht früher kommen?

GRAMMAR AND USAGE

3 Fill in the missing modal verbs in the appropriate tense (simple past or present).

1 Gestern (**wollen**)_____ ich mit meiner Schwester ins Kino, aber ich (**können**) _____ leider nicht gehen. Ich (**müssen**)_____ bis 21 Uhr arbeiten.
2 Wo warst du gestern? Du (**wollen**) _____ doch kommen?
3 Er (**sollen**) _____um 7 Uhr zu Hause sein. Er kam aber erst um 8 Uhr.
4 Inge (**wollen**) _____ gestern mit uns schwimmen gehen. Leider (**dürfen**) _____ sie nicht mitkommen.
5 Ich hatte leider keine Zeit. Ich (**wollen**) _____ am Abend zu meinen Eltern gehen.

4 Put the verbs in brackets into the simple past and write them in the gaps. Watch out: in three cases you won't need to fill in the second gap!

1 Um neun Uhr (**aufwachen**) _____ Frau Meier

_____.

2 Sie (**aufstehen**) _____ schnell _____.
3 Sie (**hinfallen**) _____ _____.
4 Sie (**verletzen**) _____ ihren Fuß _____.
5 Dann (**anrufen**) _____ sie im Büro _____.
6 Ihr Chef (**sein**) _____ auch krank _____.
7 Frau Meier (**bleiben**) _____ zu Hause

_____.

5 Three little boys are talking to each other. Complete the sentences following the example.

Example: 1 Unser Haus ist groß. 2 Unser Haus ist aber größer. 3 Unser Haus ist am größten.

1 Meine Freundin wohnt ganz nah.
2 Meine Freundin wohnt aber _____ .
3 Meine Freundin wohnt _____ .

4 Meine Mutter kocht gut.
5 Meine Mutter kocht aber _____ .
6 Meine Mutter kocht _____ .

7 Mein Fahrrad war teuer.
8 Mein Fahrrad war aber _____ .
9 Mein Fahrrad war _____ .

6 Link the sentences using **weil**.

1 Er kommt nicht mit. Er hat kein Auto.
2 Er kam nicht. Er hatte kein Auto.
3 Ich gehe jetzt nach Hause. Ich bin müde.
4 Ich kaufe die Blumen nicht. Sie sind zu teuer.
5 Sie konnte nicht mitkommen. Sie war krank.

7 Complete each sentence with the most appropriate preposition: **für, durch, ohne,** or **gegen**.

1 Ich bin _____ das Rauchen.
2 Sie tut alles _____ ihren Chef.
3 Wir kommen heute Abend _____ unsere Kinder.
4 Fahren Sie um diese Zeit besser nicht _____ die Stadt.
5 Er ist _____ einen Baum gefahren.

🎧 LISTENING

8 Listen to the story on the recording and answer the following questions.

1 Wer kommt aus der Bank?
2 Was hat sie in der rechten Hand?
3 Was für Kleidung trägt sie?
4 Wer kommt nach der jungen Frau aus der Bank?
6 Die junge Frau sieht die zwei Männer aus der Bank kommen. Was macht sie?
7 Wo hält das Auto?
8 Wer fährt das Auto?
9 Was macht der Mann mit der Frau?

9 The next day you read in the newspaper that the police are looking for witnesses who saw the incident. In 10 sentences, describe what happened, using the verbs below in the simple past. If you're not sure about some past forms, look them up on pages 235–6.

1	aus der Bank kommen	6	sehen
2	in der Hand haben	7	über die Straße gehen
3	tragen	8	anhalten
4	bis zur Ampel gehen	9	ins Auto ziehen
5	aus der Bank kommen	10	wegfahren

SPEAKING

10 The police are asking you to make a statement about the incident in 8 above. Without looking at the notes you made for 8, listen to the recording and answer the police officer's questions, using the simple past when talking about the incident.

11 You and a friend decide to have a healthy snack at a café. Translate the missing sentences and write them down. Then read through your answers a few times, go to the recording, and respond according to the cues. Try not to look at your notes.

Waitress: Möchten Sie etwas trinken?
You: 1 (A mineral water for me and a coke for my friend, please.)
Waitress : Tut mir Leid, Cola haben wir nicht. Wir haben nur Säfte, Wasser oder Tee.
You: 2 (Can you bring my friend a tea without milk? He mustn't drink any milk.)
Waitress : Natürlich. Möchten Sie auch etwas essen?
You: 3 (Can we have a muesli and a piece of cake with cream, please?)
Waitress : Gerne. Möchten Sie Apfelkuchen oder Erdbeerkuchen?
You: 4 (I prefer apple cake, but I would like a small piece, because I'm on a diet.)
Your friend: Warum machst du denn eine Diät?
You: 5 (I'm not allowed to smoke in the office any longer. Now I'm eating too much chocolate.)
Your friend: Ja, ich glaube, du bist auch schon dicker geworden.
You: 6 (My brother is getting married and I want to look good!)
Your friend: Dann fang doch jetzt mit der Diät an. Ich esse gerne deinen Apfelkuchen!

Answers

Unit 1

2   a afternoon; b evening; c morning
6   Ingrid Herbst – Berlin; Frau Jung – Frankfurt; Michael Weiss – Heidelberg; Karl Schmidt – Munich
7   1 Ich heiße Johann Herbst. I'm called Johann Herbst.
2 Mein Name ist Karin Müller. My name is Karin Müller.
3 Ich komme aus Berlin. I come from Berlin.
4 Wie heißen Sie? What are you called?
5 Woher kommen Sie? Where are you from?
11   *Susanne*: a cup of coffee with milk and sugar *Karin*: a cup of tea.
12   Eine Tasse Kaffee mit Milch und Zucker, ein Glas Orangensaft und ein Bier, bitte.
13   1 c; 2 a; 3 b
16   1 Pension; 2 Straße; 3 Einzelzimmer; 4 Doppelzimmer; 5 Hotel; 6 mit Dusche; 7 mit Bad
17   1 P; 2 S; 3 FS; 4 P; 5 FS; 6 S
18   Peter does not ask for a cup of tea.

Test

1   1 c; 2 f; 3 e; 4 b; 5 g; 6 h, 7 a
2   1 Ich heiße Ingrid Herbst. 2 Wie heißen Sie? 3 Woher kommen Sie? 4 Ich komme aus Frankfurt. 5 Ich trinke ein Glas Cola.
3   1 das Glas; 2 die Flasche; 3 die Tasse
4   1, 3, 5, 2, 4
5   1 Ich heiße …. 2 Eine Flasche Mineralwasser, bitte. 3 Ein Glas Orangensaft, bitte. 4 Eine Tasse Tee mit Milch, bitte. 5 Guten Abend.
6   Susanne: Hallo Karin! **Wie geht es dir?**
Karin: **Danke** gut, und dir?
Susanne: Auch **gut**, danke.
Karin: Was trinkst **du?**
Susanne: Ich **trinke** ein Bier.
Karin: **Ein Bier** und **ein** Glas Rotwein, bitte.

Summary 1

1 Guten Morgen, Guten Tag, Guten Abend 2 Wie heißen Sie? 3 Ich heiße Johann. 4 Wie geht es Ihnen? 5 Woher kommen Sie? 6 Ich komme aus England. 7 Was trinkst du? 8 Eine Tasse Kaffee mit Milch und Zucker, bitte. 9 Danke.

Unit 2

2   1 They plan to go to the cinema; 2 The film begins at nine o'clock; 3 Because

they're late; 4 At the cinema
3   1 Wann beginnt der Film? 2 Wie viel Uhr ist es? 3 Wir sind spät. 4 Du kannst eine Cola trinken. 5 Du kannst eine Tasse Kaffee trinken.
7   1 The post office closes at 17.00. 2 In the dialogue it is 4.45 p.m. 3 The bank closes at 14.00.
8   1 c; 2 d; 3 a; 4 b
9   die Post – **sie**; das Geld – **es**; das Kino – **es**; die Briefmarke – **sie**; der Film – **er**; der Tee – **er**
13   *Golden Eye*: 9.30, €8; *Das Piano*: 8.00, €8; *Dr Dolittle*: 6.00, Adults €8, Children €6
14   To negate the sentence you just add **nicht**. Make sure you put it in the right position. 1 Der Mann heißt **nicht** Müller. 2 Der Film beginnt **nicht** um 9.30.
3 Das ist **nicht** der James Bond Film. 4 Das ist **nicht** das Hotel Gertrud.
15   1 Trinken Sie eine Tasse Tee? 2 Haben Sie eine Briefmarke? 3 Können Sie Geld wechseln? 4 Kannst du eine Cola kaufen? 5 Beginnt der Film um acht Uhr?
18   1F 2T 3T 4F 5T
19   1 Pfund Spagetti – 99 Cent; 6 Baguettebrötchen – 80 Cent; 1 kg Bananen – 60 Cent; 5 Flaschen Bier €4; 5 Kilo-Packung Waschmittel – €7; 1 Flasche Wein – €2,10
20   1 FS; 2 S; 3 FS; 4 S; 5 FS; Order of sentences: 5, 2, 4, 1, 3.
21   1 T; 2 F; 3 T; 4 F; 5 T
22   Peter: 1 Heute Morgen: Going swimming; 2 Heute Abend: Going to the cinema Susanne: 1 Heute Nachmittag: Going to the hairdresser's

Test

1   Wo ist die Bank? Woher kommen Sie? Wann beginnt der Film? Wie viel kostet der Kaffee?
2   1 Der Wein **ist** aus Deutschland. 2 Die Kinder **sind** in England. 3 **Sind** Sie aus Hamburg? 4 Wir **sind** spät. 5 Wie viel Uhr **ist** es? 6 Hier **ist** nicht das Princess, Sie haben die falsche Nummer.
3   1 **der** Film 2 **das** Kino 3 **die** Minute 4 **das** Kind 5 **die** Telefonnummer
4   1 **Er** trinkt ein Bier. 2 **Es** kauft eine Cola. 3 **Sie** ist falsch. 4 **Sie** schließt um 14 Uhr. 5 **Er** beginnt um 21 Uhr.
5   1 Kann ich eine Tasse Kaffee kaufen? 2 Kann ich eine Cola und ein Mineralwasser bezahlen? 3 Wann beginnt der Film? 4 Wie viel kostet eine Eintrittskarte? 5 Haben Sie die richtige Telefonnummer?

6 Susanne: Hallo Claire. Wie geht es dir?
Claire: Danke gut, und dir?
Susanne: Auch gut. Beginnt der Film um
acht Uhr?
Claire: Nein, er beginnt nicht um acht Uhr.
Er beginnt um 8.30.
Susanne: Oh, wir können noch eine Tasse
Tee trinken.

Summary 2
1 eins, zwei, drei, vier, fünf, sechs, sieben,
acht, neun, zehn 2 Wie viel Uhr ist es? / Wie
spät ist es? 3 Es ist halb vier. 4 Wann hat die
Bank geöffnet? 5 Kann ich hier Briefmarken
kaufen? 6 Können Sie das bitte wiederholen?
7 Auf Wiederhören. 8 Wie viel kostet eine
Tasse Kaffee? 9 Wo kann ich Geld wechseln?

Unit 3

2 1S 2C 3S 4S 5C
3 1 **einen** Tee = DO. 2 **Der** Tee = S. 3 **Die**
Briefmarke = S. 4 **eine** Cola = DO. 5 **Der**
Pullover = S. 6 **Ich** = S
7 dreißig Brötchen, zwanzig Brezeln, ein
Vollkornbrot, einen Apfelkuchen.
8 a dreiundzwanzig; b fünfundreißig; c
sechsundsiebzig ; d neunundsechzig; e
einundneunzig
9 1 Einen Rotwein, bitte. 2 Einen Kaffee,
bitte. 3 Ein Vollkornbrot, bitte. 4 Eine
Tasse Tee, bitte.
13 1 p.m; 2 42; 3 44
14 1 Sie möchten Rotwein? 2 Eine Flasche
Rotwein kostet heute nur €2,10! 3 Sie
müssen Vollkornbrot kaufen! Es kostet nur
50 Cent. 4 Wir haben alles! 5 Das
Supermarkt-Team arbeitet für Sie!
17 *Schuhabteilung*: Kinderschuhe, Schuhe,
Stiefel; *Damenbekleidung*: Damenhosen,
Damenjacken, Blusen, Kleider, Pullover,
Röcke; *Herrenbekleidung*: Anzüge,
Herrensocken, Herrenmäntel, Hemden,
Pullover
18 1 You can try it first before buying it. 2 a
Würzburger Kämmerlein; b Forster
Ungeheuer; c Bernkasteler Witwe; d
Riesling Winzersekt.
19 30 Brötchen, 5 Brote, 20 Brezeln, 2
Pflaumenkuchen.
20 1 F (the baker delivered two plumcakes
instead of the three ordered); 2 T; 3 T; 4 F
(it cost 40 euros and 50 cents); 5 F

Test
1 1b dreiundzwanzig 23; 2a einundreißig 31;
3c zweiundneunzig 92; 4e sechsundsechzig
66; 5d fünfundsiebzig 75
2 1 das Würstchen: all the other goods can
be bought at the baker's
2 der Bäcker: all the other words are
related to the post office
3 der Supermarkt: all the other words have
to do with clothes shopping
4 suchen: it is the only verb

3 Here you had to make sure that you added
the appropriate endings for the masculine
direct objects in the sentence.
1 Ich muss ein**en** Brief nach England
schicken. 2 Ich suche ein**en** Rock in Größe
38. 3 Ich nehme **den** Apfelkuchen und **das**
Brot. 4 **Ein** Brief nach England kostet
siebzig Cent. 5 Ich nehme **den** Rock in
Größe 42.
4 1 Fünf Brötchen, ein Brot und einen
Apfelkuchen, bitte. 2 Ich brauche einen
Rock. 3 Entschuldigung, ich suche den
Wein. 4 Wie viel kostet ein Brief nach
England? 5 Der Rock ist zu klein / zu groß.
5 1 du musst 2 es / sie kostet 3 ich arbeite 4
du arbeitest 5 ich / er muss 6 Sie möchten
7 ich habe
6 b, e, a, f, h, c
7 The modal verb should take the second
position in the sentence; the infinitive
goes to the end.
1 Ich muss ein Brot kaufen. 2 Ich möchte
einen Brief nach England schicken. 3 Ich
muss einen Kaffee trinken. 4 Ich möchte
eine Flasche Wein kaufen. 5 Ich möchte
den Rock anprobieren.

Summary 3
1 dreißig , einundreißig, zweiundreißig,
dreiundreißig, vierundreißig, fünfundreißig. 2
15 Brötchen und ein Brot, bitte. 3 Ich suche
einen Mantel. 4 Kann ich den Mantel
anprobieren? 5 Wo sind die Umkleideräume?
6 Wie viel kostet der Mantel? 7 Wie viel kostet
ein Brief nach England?

Review 1
1 1 heiß (it's not a verb); 2 das Brötchen (it's
not a drink); 3 Auf Wiederhören (it's how
you say goodbye on the phone); 4 brauche
(it's not an adjective); 5 einen (it's not a
verb)
2 1 c; 2 e; 3 a; 4 d; 5 b
3 1 Er kostet € 25,50. 2 Er beginnt um 9 Uhr.
3 Ja, sie hat heute geöffnet. 4 Sie kosten
€ 1. 5 Es kostet 25 Cent. 6 Er kostet
€ 4,10. 7 Ja, er schmeckt sehr gut.
4 1 **einen** Tee; 2 **eine** Tasse Kaffee; 3 **einen**
Kaffee; 4 **einen** Rock; 5 **ein** Mineralwasser;
6 **eine** Briefmarke kaufen
5 1 Guten Tag, ich heiße Johann Müller. 2 Ist
das Herr Herbst? 3 Wie viel kosten die
Brötchen? 4 Kann ich den Rock
anprobieren? 5 Ich möchte einen Brief
nach England schicken. 6 Können Sie das
bitte wiederholen?
6 1 Woher kommen Sie? 2 Wie heißen Sie?
3 Wie viel kosten die Brötchen? 4 Wann
beginnt der Film? 5 Wie viel Uhr ist es?
6 Wo ist die Touristeninformation?
7 1 Möchten Sie eine Tasse Kaffee trinken?
2 Kaufst du eine Cola? 3 Wann kaufst du
die Brötchen? 4 Wie viel kosten die
Hemden? 5 Sind sie Herr Meier?
8 1 Anna called. 2 She has two tickets. 3
Titanic. 4 The film starts at seven thirty. 5

They will meet at six thirty. 6 They will meet at the Stadtcafé. 7 They will have a coffee before going to the cinema.

9 1 They have to buy bread and sausages. Wir müssen Brot kaufen! Und Würstchen. 2 She wants to go swimming in the morning. Ich möcht heute Morgen schwimmen gehen. 3 He has to work this morning. Ich muss heute Morgen arbeiten. 4 Her friend Katrin is coming at one thirty. Nein, heute Nachmittag um halb zwei kommt Katrin. 5 Ralf is finally going shopping. Dann muss ich gehen. 6 He´s also buying an apple cake. Und einen Apfelkuchen. 7 He takes ten euros. Hast du zehn Euro?

10 1 Wie viel kosten die Briefmarken? 2 Ist dort das Capitol? 3 Haben Sie den Rock in Größe 40? 4 Wie heißen Sie? 5 Wann beginnt der Film? 6 Woher kommen Sie? 7 Was darf es sein?

Unit 4

2 1 Rinderbraten – 3 times; 2 Forelle – 3 times; 3 Schweinefilet – 2 times; 4 Vorspeise once

3 You get two hints for which endings to use. Whenever people are being addressed as Herr or Frau, they are addressed formally, with Sie. The second clue is the verb ending. The verb ending for ihr is -t, the verb ending for Sie is -en.
1 Sabine und Elfie, was esst ihr? 2 Frau Meier, was nehmen Sie? 3 Meine Herrren, möchten Sie bestellen? 4 Hallo Lisa, hallo Rolf. Möchtet ihr etwas Fisch? 5 Heiko und Anna, fahrt ihr nach Hamburg?

4 lesen: ich lese, du liest, er/sie/es liest, wir lesen, ihr lest, sie lesen, Sie lesen
fahren ich fahre, du fährst, er/sie/es fährt, wir fahren, ihr fahrt, sie fahren, Sie fahren

8 1 F; 2 F; 3 T; 4 T

9 Direct objects: masculine einen / keinen; feminine eine / keine; neuter ein / kein
1 Er hat keinen Mantel. 2 Ich mag keinen Fisch. 3 Ich mag kein Fleisch. 4 Das ist keine Vorspeise, das ist ein Hauptgericht. 5 Er braucht keine Jacke.

10 1 He doesn't have a coat. 2 I don't like (any) fish. 3 I don't like (any) meat. 4 This isn't a starter, this is a main course. 5 He doesn't need a jacket.

14 1 They don't order dessert. 2 One of them has tea. 3 They had fillet of pork and roast beef. The third had trout. 4 The bill comes to 58 euros.

15 Adjective endings: after the der, die, and das: -e; after den and the plural die: -en.
1 Ich kaufe die gelbe Bluse. 2 Ich kaufe die roten Schuhe. Since die Schuhe is the plural, you have to add -en. 3 Ich kaufe den grauen Anzug. 4 Ich kaufe die blaue Hose. 5 Ich kaufe den grünen Rock.

18 1 In restaurants, you often have to wait and no waiter or waitress comes to your table. 2 You can wave and say: 'We would like to order, please'. 3 You can call a waiter with 'Herr Ober!' 4 Fräulein is outdated and antiquated – you shouldn't use it. 5 You can call 'Entschuldigung' and wave.

19 1 Pizza and Spaghetti Bolognese; 2 Kebab; 3 Bulette; 4 Pommes frites (sometimes just Pommes, pronounced as 'Pommas'); 5 Currywurst

20 Kebab: drei Euro fünfzig; Pizza, pro Stück – zwei Euro fünfundvierzig; Spaghetti Bolognese – vier Euro sechzig; Currywurst – zwei Euro dreißig; Pommes frites – drei Euro dreißig; Bulette – zwei Euro fünfundfünfzig

21 : cream of asparagus soup (Spargelcremesuppe) for a starter and a platter of assorted sausages and meats (Schlachtplatte) as a main course.
: a platter of mixed salad and raw vegetables (Salatplatte Gärtnerin) as a main course and no starter.

22 1 Einen Krabbencocktail und eine Spargelcremesuppe als Vorspeise, bitte. 2 Ein Wiener Schnitzel und ein Rinderfilet als Hauptgerichte, bitte. 3 Wir möchten ein Mousse au chocolat und einen Apfelkuchen mit Schlagsahne als Nachspeise, bitte.
The articles on the menu were given to you so that you could use the correct form of ein in your orders. Remember: whenever you ask for an item which is masculine you use einen, for feminine items you use eine, and for neuter items you use ein.

Test

1m; 2h; 3j; 4l; 5k; 6d; 7b; 8c; 9e; 10f; 11g; 12a
1 a, c, d; 2 b, f; 3 a, e; 4 b, f
Direct objects: masculine keinen, feminine keine, neuter kein
1 Ich mag keine Suppe! 2 Ich mag keine Vorspeise! 3 Ich esse keinen Rinderbraten! 4 Ich esse keinen Apfelkuchen! 5 Ich esse keine Nachspeise!
Sie – essen; er – nimmt; du – läufst; sie – empfiehlt (if you translate sie as she) or sie – empfehlen (if you translate sie as they); ich – sehe
Remember: the adjective ending after der, die, and das is –e; after den and the plural die it is -en.
1 Sie können die blaue Bluse und den roten Rock kombinieren.
2 Sie können die gelbe Hose und den braunen Mantel kombinieren.
3 Sie können den grauen Anzug und das blaue Hemd kombinieren.
4 Sie können auch die blauen Schuhe und das grüne Kleid kombinieren. (Der Schuh

in the plural becomes **die** Schuhe.)

6 Ober: **Ihr** möcht**et** bestellen?
Herr A: Ja, ich nehme den Rinderbraten.
Was **isst du**?
Herr B: Ich nehme das Schweinefilet in
Rahmsauce.
Herr A: Und was **nimmst du**?
Herr C: Ich nehme den Rehbraten.
Ober: Möcht**et ihr** auch eine Vorspeise?
Herr A: Nein, danke.

Summary 4

1 Ich möchte gerne bestellen, bitte. **2** Ich
nehme das Schweinefilet und eine Suppe,
bitte. **3** Ich nehme keine Vorspeise. **4** Ich mag
keinen Fisch, ich esse lieber Fleisch. **5** Ich bin
Vegetarier / Vegetarierin. **6** Danke, ich bin
satt. **7** Die Rechnung, bitte.

Unit 5

2 1 Walter März and Monika Spree are both
from the same town, Lüneburg. 2 Klaus
Spree is Monika's brother. 3 Klaus now
lives in England. 4 He asks for Klaus's
telephone number.

3 1 Er sucht sein**en** Bruder. (**-en** before
masculine direct object) / Sein Bruder ist
hier. 2 Ich suche mein**e** Eltern. / Ihre Eltern
sind hier. (**-e** before plurals) 3 Ich suche
sein**e** Schuhe. / Seine Schuhe sind hier. (**-e**
before plurals) 4 Ich suche Ihr**en** Anzug. (**-
en** before masculine direct object) / **Mein**
Anzug ist hier.

7 1 F; 2 T; 3 F; 4 T; 5 F

8 1 Sind das eure Hemden? Nein, das sind
nicht unsere Hemden. 2 Sind das eure
Schuhe? Nein, das sind nicht unsere
Schuhe. 3 Sind das eure Mäntel? Nein, das
sind nicht unsere Mäntel. 4 Wo sind eure
Socken? Unsere Socken sind hier. 5 Sind
das eure Hosen? Ja, das sind unsere Hosen.
In each sentence there are plural nouns.
Therefore the ending is always **-e** (eur**e**,
unser**e**).

12 1 Spain / Spanien; 2 America / Amerika; 3
Italy / Italien; 4 France / Frankreich.

13 1 Ihre; 2 meine; 3 deine; 4 deinen; 5 ihre.

16 a geöffnet; c Torten; b Speisekarte;
e Cocktailbar; d Live-Auftritte;
f Ausstellungen

17 *Stefanie Wagner* lives in Heidelberg, where
the Kaffeehaus is located. Her children like
cakes and gâteau, which are offered on
the menu. Stefanie likes to have a cocktail
once in a while, and both she and her
husband enjoy music, particularly jazz. The
Kaffeehaus offers all of this, which is why
you can recommend it to them.
Norbert Wichtig lives in Heidelberg as
well. His eldest son Hans is an artist. He
might therefore enjoy the exhibitions in
the Kaffeehaus. His daughter plays in a
band, so she might enjoy the concerts on

offer. Frau Wichtig enjoys cake and a cup
of coffee, while Norbert prefers soup or a
salad. All of these are obtainable at the
café.

18 1 P; 2 S; 3 P; 4 H; 5 S; 6 P

19 a 5; b 6; c 1; d 3; e 4; f 2

Test

1 my **mein**; your [*informal*] **dein**; his **sein**; her
ihr; its **sein**
our **unser**; your [*informal, pl.*] **euer**; their
ihr; your [*formal*] **Ihr**

2 *Mutter* Engländerin; *Vater* Franzose;
(Tochter und) *Mann* Amerikaner; (Sohn
und) *Frau* Deutsche; (Tochter und) *Mann*
Italiener

3 1 Das ist mein**e** Mutter. 2 Sind das Ihre
Kinder? 3 Da sind eure Eltern. **Eltern** is a
plural noun, so the ending of the
possessive adjective is **-e**. 4 Das sind unsere
Mäntel. **Mäntel** (coats) is in the plural, so
the ending of the possessive adjective is **-e**.
5 Ich sehe seinen Bruder. **Bruder** is a
masculine direct object, so the ending is
-en.

4 This is an informal situation in which
people address each other with **du**. 'Your'
therefore has to be translated with **dein**.
Note also that you had to add **-in** to the
nationality, since it is two women talking
to each other.
A: Hallo, woher kommst du?
B: Ich bin Amerikaner**in**. Und du?
A: Ich bin Französin. Wie lange bist du
schon hier?
B: Drei Trage. Und du?
A: Auch erst drei Tage. Was bist du von
Beruf?
B: Ich bin Sekretär**in**.
A: Interessant! Und wie lange willst du
bleiben?
B: Ich möchte für fünf Tage bleiben.
A: Ach, ist das deine Jacke?
B: Ja, vielen Dank!

5 Note the capital on **Ihr** in a formal context.
A: Woher komm**en** Sie?
B: Wir kommen aus den USA.
A: Und wie lange bleiben **Sie**?
B: Wir bleiben fünf Tage. Und **Sie**?
A: Ich bleibe noch eine Woche. Ach, sind
das **Ihre** Socken?
C: Nein, das sind nicht unsere Socken. Aber
ist das **Ihre** Jacke?
A: Ja, danke! Wissen **Sie** auch, wo mein
Mantel ist?
C: Ich glaube, er ist dort. Ja, hier ist **Ihr**
Mantel.

Summary 5

1 Was sind Sie von Beruf? **2** Ich bin Ingenieur /
Ingenieurin. **3** Wie lange sind Sie schon hier? **4**
Ich will fünf Tage bleiben. **5** Ich bin
Amerikaner / Amerikanerin. **6** Ich bin Britin /
Ich bin Brite. **7** Ich habe einen Sohn und eine
Tochter. **8** Ich bin verheiratet. **9** Ich bin
geschieden.

Unit 6

2 1 F (links); 2 F; 3 I; 4 T

3 1 an dem Marktplat;. 2 in der Elbestraße; 3 vor dem Kino; 4 neben dem Marktplatz; 5 auf der Straße

7 1 He tells him to go to the Hotel Adler. 2 No, he doesn't know the hotel. 3 The post office is next to the hotel. 4 Herderstraße. 5 He has to pay €7,20. 6 He pays €8.

8 1 **Wissen** Sie, wo der Bahnhof ist? 2 **Kennen** Sie den Mann? 3 Nein, aber ich **weiß**, wo er wohnt. 4 **Kennen** Sie Hamburg? 5 **Wissen** Sie, wo die Universität dort ist?
When talking about places you have visited or when asking someone if he knows the place (because he has been there before), you use **kennen**. However, if you ask someone if he knows where something is located you use **wissen**.

12 1 Rita ist Sekretärin. 2 Ihre Arbeit beginnt um halb acht. 3 Rita arbeitet bis halb fünf. 4 Nein, Rita hat kein Auto. 5 In der Mittagspause geht sie mit einer Kollegin in die Kantine.

13 1 mit einer Kollegin; 2 mit einem Bus; 3 in einem Büro; 4 in einem Hotel; 5 zu einem Konzert

16 1 Wir fahren mit dem Zug nach Davos 2 Ja, wir können die Stadt besichtigen. 3 Am zweiten Tag wandern wir 6 Stunden bis Arosa. 4 Wir essen in unserem Hotel zu Abend. 5 Am dritten Tag wandern wir 4 Stunden bis nach Lenzerheide. 6 Im Hotel in Lenzerheide essen wir Schweizer Spezialitäten. 7 Zwei Übernachtungen für zwei Personen im Doppelzimmer kosten € 410. 8 Zwei Übernachtungen im Einzelzimmer kosten € 230.

17 1 Peter möchte heute Abend in die Kunstgalerie 'Gallo' gehen. 2 Peters Freund heißt Michael. 3 Es gibt dort eine Fotoausstellung. 4 Frau Semmler kennt die neue Kunstgalerie nicht. 5 Ihr Friseur ist auch in der Kurfürstenstraße.

18 The gallery is in Kurfürstenstraße, on the right beside the Café Müller.

Test

1 1 Die Touristeninformation ist in der Bahnhofstraße. 2 Die Post ist neben der Bank. Die Pizzeria ist neben der Bank. 3 Die Bäckerei ist links neben der Metzgerei. 4 Die Pizzeria ist zwischen der Bank und dem Kiosk.

2 Ich komme zum Hotel Gertrud.

3 1 Er geht **zum** Bahnhof. 2 Wir essen **im** Restaurant. 3 Das Café ist neben **dem** Marktplatz. 4 Frau Kind kommt aus **dem** Haus. 5 Sie arbeitet **im** Büro.

4 1 Sie können in der Elbestraße eine Theaterkarte kaufen. Or you could say: In der Elbestraße können Sie eine

Theaterkarte kaufen. 2 Ich kenne das Hotel Adler nicht. Or: Das Hotel Adler kenne ich nicht. 3 Herr Maier ist in dem Hotel. Or: Herr Maier ist im Hotel. 4 Die Kinder warten neben dem Kino.

5 1 Die Kinder warten vor dem Haus. 2 Frau Meier kauft den Rock im Kaufhaus. 3 Inga kauft die Theaterkarten in der Elbestraße. 4 Petras Suppe ist auf dem Tisch. 5 Den James Bond Film gibt es im Kino.
1 Ich fahre mit … zur Arbeit. 2 Ich arbeite von … bis … Uhr. 3 In der Mittagspause esse ich … 4 Ich esse gerne … 5 Ja, ich gehe oft ins Restaurant / Nein, ich gehe nicht oft ins Restaurant.

7 1 Ich muss zum Supermarkt. 2 Kommst du zum Kino? 3 Ich fahre morgen zur Arbeit. 4 Ich komme zum Café Neubauer. 5 Gehen Sie bis zum Marktplatz.

Summary 6

1 Fahren Sie zum Theater, bitte. 2 Entschuldigung, wie komme ich zum Marktplatz? 3 Wo kann ich Karten für das Kino kaufen? 4 Das Hotel ist auf der rechten Seite. 5 Die Bäckerei ist neben der Touristeninformation. 6 Der Rest ist für Sie.

Unit 7

2 1 F (12.30); 2 T; 3 F; 4 T

3 1 Ich gehe heute Abend aus. 2 Peter bringt eine Flasche Wein mit. 3 Der Zug fährt um 3 Uhr ab. 4 Sabine kommt um 13 Uhr an. 5 Ich kann den Tee eingießen.

7 1 She wants to go to Freiburg. 2 Her train leaves at 9.37. 3 It arrives at 11.30. 4 No. 5 She pays by credit card.

8 1 Wann fährt **er** ab? 2 Er trinkt **ihn** nicht. 3 Wie viel kostet **sie**? 4 Woher kommt **er**? 5 Woher kommt **sie**?

12 3: Hans reserviert **ein Doppelzimmer** mit Bad.

13 1 Die Kinder spielen vor **dem** Museum. 2 Herr Müller geht ins Museum. 3 Er stellt das Glas auf **den** Tisch. 4 Das Glas ist auf **dem** Tisch.
Remember: whenever you can ask the question **wo?**, 'where?' (where are the children playing?), you have to use an article in the dative. When it is possible to ask **wohin?**, 'where to?' (where is Mr Müller going (to)?), you use an article in the accusative.

16 1 Um 10 Uhr kann ich im Bahnhof am Schalter eine Fahrkarte kaufen. 2 Um 24 Uhr kann ich am Fahrscheinautomaten eine Fahrkarte ziehen.

17 3 Wählen Sie zuerst Ihr Fahrtziel. 5 Dann drücken Sie: Erwachsener oder Kind? 1 Lesen Sie die Geldanzeige: wie viel müssen Sie bezahlen? 4 Werfen Sie das Geld ein. 2 Entnehmen Sie Ihr Ticket und das Wechselgeld.

18 1 Wie viel kostet eine Hin-und Rückfahrkarte nach Frankfurt? 2 Wann fährt der Zug ab? 3 Wann kommt der Zug in Frankfurt an? 4 Muss ich umsteigen? 5 Muss ich einen Sitzplatz reservieren? 6 Von wo fährt der Zug ab?

19 5, 4, 2, 3, 1

20 1 T; 2 F; 3 F; 4 T; 5 F; 6 T; 7 T

Test

1 1 Der Zug kommt um 7 Uhr an. 2 Er muss nicht umsteigen. 3 Ich mache die Flasche Wein auf. 4 Petra und Inge gehen heute Abend aus. 5 Der Zug fährt auf Gleis 5 ab?

2 1 Ich treffe **ihn** heute Abend. 2 Ich mag **sie**. 3 Susanne trinkt **ihn**. 4 Sie kauft **ihn** im Kaufhaus. 5 Er isst ihn später.

3 1 Er sieht mich. 2 Wir sehen sie im Kino. 3 Sie sieht ihn im Café. 4 Wir sehen euch im Theater. 5 Wir sehen dich in der Bäckerei.

4 1 Wie viel kostet eine Hin-und Rückfahrkarte? 2 Muss ich umsteigen? 3 Wann fährt der Zug (ab)? 4 Von wo fährt der Zug ab? 5 Muss ich reservieren?

5 1 Das Theater ist neben **der** Polizei. 2 Er geht **ins** Theater. 3 Wir warten vor **dem** Kino. 4 Der Kaffee ist in **der** Tasse. 5 Sie gehen heute in **den** James Bond Film.

6 1 Ja, ich nehme **ihn**. 2 Ja, ich bezahle **sie**. 3 Ja, ich kaufe **sie** jetzt. 4 Ja, ich sehe **sie**. 5 Ja, ich esse **ihn** mit Sahne.

Summary 7

1 Wann fährt der nächste Zug nach Mannheim ab? 2 Fährt der Zug nach Frankfurt? 3 Ich möchte eine Hin-und Rückfahrkarte kaufen. 4 Kann ich mit Kreditkarte bezahlen? 5 Ich möchte einen Sitzplatz in einem Nichtraucherabteil reservieren. 6 Wie viel kostet ein Doppelzimmer mit Bad? 7 Ich möchte für Dienstag, den 2. Januar ein Einzelzimmer reservieren. 8 Wie komme ich von der Touristeninformation zum Bahnhof?

Review 2

1 1 b; 2 d; 3 c; 4 e; 5 a; 6 f

2 1 Fisch (not a meat dish); 2 Engländerin (not a family member); 3 gesundheitsbewusst; 4 Kellnerin; 5 Deutschland (not a place in a town); 6 Arbeit (not a means of transport)

3 1 f; 2 d; 3 e; 4 c; 5 b; 6 a

4 1 ab; 2 mit; 3 um; 4 an; 5 aus

5 1 When will you arrive in New York? 2 When does she leave for Hamburg? 3 I think she'll go to Berlin tomorrow. 4 Are you coming to Hanover on 23 March? 5 I think they'll leave at 3 p.m.

6 1 er; 2 ihn; 3 ihn; 4 er; 5 es; 6 sie

7 1 9.00 Uhr; auf der; 2 9.15; auf dem; 3 9.30 zu dem (zum); 4 8.50; auf dem; 5 20.00; in das (ins); 6 in dem (im)

8 Ich mag **keinen** Fisch. 2 Ich gehe heute **nicht** ins Kino. 3 Es gibt hier **keinen** Wein. 4 Er ist **nicht** geschieden. 5 Wir haben heute leider **keinen** Apfelkuchen. 6 Ich mag ihn **nicht**.

9 1 Bäckerei; 2 Theater; 3 Hotel Gertrud; 4 Blumen

10 1 Sie sind im Bahnhof. 2 mit dem Zug; 3 Sie will ins Theater (gehen). 4 Er möchte ins Kino (gehen). 5 Er ist Lehrer.

11 1 meinen Mantel; 2 Ihr Mantel; 3 meine Schuhe; 4 Ihre Schuhe; 5 meinen Pullover

12 1 Was können Sie empfehlen? 2 Nein, ich mag kein Fleisch, ich esse lieber Fisch. 3 Gut, ich nehme die Forelle. 4 Ich kann keinen Alkohol trinken. Ich fahre. 5 Nein danke, ich bin satt. 6 Herr Ober, wir möchten zahlen, bitte.

Unit 8

2 1 Sandra's parents; 2 no; 3 the Parasol; 4 It has a large buffet and there's something to suit every taste. 5 Her parents often go to the theatre.

3 1 Er fährt ein neues Auto. 2 Ich suche einen roten Rock. 3 Er kennt ein gutes Restaurant. 4 Meine Kollegin hat eine schicke Frisur.

7 1 roast beef and a beer; 2 because Anna said that she doesn't eat meat; she prefers vegetables. 3 going to the theatre; 4 She knows the new gallery and she likes the pictures there.

8 1 Er kommt mit **mir** ins Kino. 2 Sie gibt **dir** die Eintrittskarten. 3 Ich gehe mit **ihnen** in die Galerie. 4 Sie spielt mit **ihm** Tennis. 5 Er gibt **ihr** seine Telefonnummer.

12 1 F (she likes Hamburg very much); 2 T; 3 F (she doesn't like swimming); 4 T; 5 T

13 1 Ich helfe der Frau. Ich helfe **ihr**. 2 Die Hose gefällt dem Mann. Die Hose gefällt **ihm**. 3 Wir danken den Musikern für das Konzert. Wir danken **ihnen** für das Konzert. 4 Er gibt den Kindern die Schokolade. Er gibt **ihnen** die Schokolade. 5 Er gibt dem Taxifahrer das Geld. Er gibt **ihm** das Geld.

16 1 1,7 Millionen Leute wohnen in Hamburg. 2 Auf dem Fischmarkt. 3 Nein, Sie können auch viele andere Dinge kaufen. 4 Am Jungfernstieg gibt es viele Cafes und Kaufhäuser. 5 Es heißt Hot Spice Museum.

17 Lisa geht gerne ins Theater. Sie geht gerne einkaufen. Sie geht nicht gerne essen. Sie geht gerne ins Café. Jannick geht nicht gerne ins Theater. Er geht nicht gerne einkaufen. Er geht gerne essen. Er geht gerne ins Museum. Er geht nicht gerne ins Café.

18 Lisa, du kannst ins Deutsche Schauspielhaus (Thalia Theater) gehen. Du kannst am Jungfernstieg einkaufen gehen.
Jannick, du kannst ins Hot Spice Museum gehen. Du kannst in am Jungfernstieg essen gehen.

19 1 DK; 2 T; 3 F (Saturday); 4 F (he's meeting the other walkers at 9.30); 5 T; 6 T; 7 F (Saturday morning, at breakfast)

20 6, 4, 1, 5, 2, 3

Test

1 1 Er gibt mir die Speisekarte. 2 Können Sie mir helfen? 3 Ich spiele nächste Woche mit ihm Tennis. 4 Die Schuhe gehören ihr. 5 Er gibt uns seine Eintrittskarten.

2 1 d; 2 c; 3 a; 4 b

3 1 Ich möchte einen **lustigen** Film sehen. 2 Das ist aber ein **schickes** Kleid. 3 Sie kauft ihrem Mann einen **neuen** Mantel. 4 Sie bestellt eine **gebackene** Forelle. 5 Kennen Sie schon meine **neue** Telefonnummer?

4 1 Die Bedienung gibt **ihm** den Kaffee. 2 Sie kauft **ihnen** ein Eis. 3 Er bestellt **ihr** eine Gemüsesuppe. 4 Ich gebe **ihm** die Briefmarken.

5 1 Die Bedienung gibt **ihn ihm**. 2 Sie kauft **es ihnen**. 3 Er bestellt **sie ihr**. 4 Ich gebe **sie ihm**.

6 1 Sie kauft einen blauen Rock. 2 Ich nehme die rote Hose. 3 Hans fährt ein neues Auto. 4 Das ist ein schöner Urlaub. 5 Ich treffe meine alte Freundin.

7 1 Er hilft **ihr**. 2 Sie hilft **ihnen**. 3 Wir helfen **ihm**. 4 Er hilft **ihr**. 5 Ich helfe **ihm**.

Summary 8

1 Ich muss am Samstag arbeiten. **2** Kennst du ein gutes Restaurant? **3** München gefällt mir sehr gut. **4** Seine neue Jacke gefällt mir nicht. **5** Ich kann dich meinen Freunden vorstellen. **6** Kannst du mir seine Telefonnummer geben? **7** Am Samstag spiele ich mit ihm Tennis.

Unit 9

2 1 T; 2 T; 3 T; 4 F (the beach was too nice!)

3 You had to make sure that the **haben** form appeared as the second element of the sentence, and the past participle at the end. If you started the sentence with a time phrase (as in 2, 3, 5), the subject had to follow the verb.
1 Sie haben Kaffee getrunken. 2 Abends hat Paul Schweinefilet gegessen. (Or: Paul hat abends Schweinefilet gegessen.) 3 Morgens habe ich am Strand gelegen. (Or: Ich habe morgens am Strand gelegen.) 4 Du hast Pizza gegessen. 5 Nachmittags haben wir Tee getrunken. (Or: Wir haben nachmittags Tee getrunken.)

7 1 T; 2 T; 3 T; 4 F (she went to drink coffee in the Odenwald)

8 1 gewohnt; 2 gekauft; 3 gespielt; 4 gefragt; 5 gearbeitet (don't forget that for verbs whose stem ends in **-t**, an -e precedes the final **-t**); 6 geholt

9 1 Sie hat gelesen. 2 Sie hat gegessen. 3 Sie hat Kaffee getrunken. 4 Am Samstag hat sie lange geschlafen. (Or: Sie hat am Samstag lange geschlafen.) 5 Am

Sonntagabend hat sie ihre Wohnung geputzt. (Or: Sie hat am Sonntagabend ihre Wohnung geputzt.)

13 1 on Saturday evening; 2 on Wednesday evening; 3 no, not yet; 4 Hans and Anna are planning to get married and go on honeymoon.

14 1 Wie lange haben Sie geschlafen? 2 Hast du schon gegessen? 3 Hast du schon Kaffee getrunken? 4 Wann habt ihr den Film gesehen?

15 1 Am Samstag waren wir in Hamburg. (Or: Wir waren am Samstag in Hamburg.) 2 Am Sonntag war ich im Odenwald. (Or: Ich war am Sonntag im Odenwald.) 3 Wo waren Sie, Frau Meier? (Since the person asked is formally addressed as Frau Meier, you have to use **Sie** for 'you'.) 4 Wo wart ihr, Peter und Maria? (The use of first names suggests the informal **ihr**. On the use of **ihr**, see Unit 4, p. 59, and Dialogue 5.2, p. 64.)

18 1 Gisela Koslowsky; 2 Ingo Altmann; 3 Karola Rösch; 4 Walter Hoffmann.

19 *Walter Hoffmann*: Greece, because he's an amateur archaeologist.
Gisela Koslowsky: Austria, because she and her husband can only speak German
Karola Rösch: the Baltic Sea because her children are still small and could play on the beach.
Ingo Altmann: Italy, because he wants lots of sunshine on holiday.

20 1 Ich habe so viele interessante Dinge gesehen! 2 Die Kinder haben am Strand gespielt. 3 Mein Mann hat oft Volleyball gespielt. 4 Es hat uns sehr gut gefallen.

21 1 F; 2 T; 3 F (she wants to go shopping and to the hairdresser); 4 T; 5 T

22 Susanne isn't going dancing with Peter this evening.

Test

1 1 e; 2 f; 3 g; 4 h; 5 a; 6 b; 7 d; 8 c

2 The hint that all the verbs are regular was to help you form the past participle. Remember: to form the past participle of regular verbs, add **ge-** and **-t** to the stem.
1 Ich habe **gefrühstückt**. 2 Ich habe etwas Schönes **gemacht**. 3 Ich habe eine Radtour **gemacht**. 4 Ich habe eine Wanderung **gemacht**. 5 Ich habe die Wohnung **geputzt**. 6 Ich habe einen neuen Mantel **gekauft**. 7 Ich habe **gespart**. 8 Ich habe **geheiratet**. (The stem of **heiraten** ends in **-t**, which is why you had to add the additional **-e**.)

3 1 gelesen; 2 getrunken; 3 gegessen; 4 gelegen; 5 gesehen

4 Here, you had to watch out for the word order. See page 127 if you still feel uncertain.
1 Haben Sie schon Tee getrunken, Herr Meier? 2 Hast du Pizza gegessen? 3 Wann

habt ihr den Film gesehen? 4 Haben Sie schon den neuen Film gesehen? 5 Warum hast du keinen neuen Computer gekauft?

5 When addressing more than one person informally (Anna and Hans), remember to use **ihr** for 'you'.
1 Wo habt ihr geheiratet? 2 Habt ihr einen neuen Anzug und ein neues Kleid gekauft? 3 Habt ihr in einem Restaurant gegessen? 4 Habt ihr Kaffee getrunken? 5 Wie war eure Hochzeitsreise?

6 1 Am Freitagnachmittag habe ich die (or: meine) Wohnung geputzt. 2 Am Freitagabend habe ich den (or: einen) neuen Film mit Jack Nicholson gesehen. 3 Nein, da habe ich gemütlich gefrühstückt. 4 Ich habe eine Radtour gemacht. 5 Nein, da habe ich gelesen.

Summary 9

1 Wie war Ihr Wochenende? 2 Danke, es war toll! 3 Was haben Sie am Samstagabend gemacht? 4 Am Samstagabend habe ich einen Film gesehen. 5 Wie war Ihr Urlaub? 6 Warum können Sie nicht mitgehen?

Unit 10

2 1 b; 2 c; 3 a

3 1 Ich habe keine Wanderung gemacht, weil ich zu müde war. 2 Er arbeitet nicht, weil er Tennis spielen will. 3 Ich bin müde, weil ich nicht lange geschlafen habe. 4 Ich habe Hunger, weil ich nichts gegessen habe. 5 Ich will nicht ins Kino gehen, weil ich ins Theater gehen will.

7 1 F (he wants to ride his bike and he's taking his rowing boat along); 2 F (he invites them to come along); 3 T; 4 T

8 1 Ich kann nicht lange schlafen, denn ich muss zur Arbeit fahren. 2 Wir wollen frühstücken und dann müssen wir die Wohnung putzen. 3 Ich gehe ins Kino oder ich gehe Volleyball spielen. 4 Ich mag kein Fleisch, aber ich mag Fisch. 5 Hans fährt nach Rom, denn er will in die Museen gehen.

12 1 Anna has a tennis tournament this weekend; 2 no; 3 by train; 4 no, he was an hour late

13 1 Um acht Uhr hat er gefrühstückt. (Or: Er hat um acht Uhr gefrühstückt.) 2 Um neun Uhr ist er zur Arbeit gefahren. (Or: Er ist um neun Uhr zur Arbeit gefahren.) 3 Um siebzehn Uhr ist er nach Hause gefahren. (Or: Er ist um siebzehn Uhr nach Hause gefahren.) 4 Um achtzehn Uhr ist er schwimmen gegangen. (Or: Er ist um achtzehn Uhr schwimmen gegangen.)

16 True statements are 2, 4, 6. False are: 1 (he didn't go by bus, he flew into Berlin); 3 (he liked the production, because it was so colourful and lively); 5 (despite being tired, he went on a sightseeing trip).

17 1 Abends sind wir ins Theater des Westens gegangen. (Note: **zum** instead of **ins** is possible as well.) 2 Es hat mir sehr gefallen, weil die Inszenierung sehr lebendig war. 3 Anschließend haben wir Berliner Weiße getrunken. 4 Wir haben den Reichstag und das Brandenburger Tor gesehen.

18 Untrue statements are 3 (he hiked 15 kilometres), 4 (he drank too much wine; also, he doesn't say that he had too much to eat), 6 (he says he'll go and get some sleep).

19 1 Wir sind 15 Kilometer gewandert. 2 Ich habe viel zu viel Wein getrunken. 3 Es waren viele nette Leute dabei. 4 Schade, dass du gestern nicht dabei warst!

Test

1 1 i; 2 c; 3 g; 4 b; 5 j; 6 e; 7 h; 8 d; 9 f; 10 a

2 Rad fahren, mitkommen, in eine Kneipe gehen, surfen – because all of these are verbs of motion.

3 1 Rad gefahren; 2 gefragt; 3 gehabt; 4 gegangen; 5 gemacht; 6 gesurft

4 1 Warum bist du zu spät gekommen? 2 Ist er zu spät gekommen? 3 Habt ihr eine Stadtrundfahrt gemacht? 4 Wie lange bist du geschwommen? 5 Wie bist du zur Arbeit gefahren?

5 Wie geht es euch? Ich **bin** letzte Woche nach Italien gefahren. Ich **habe** eine Woche Urlaub gemacht. Ich **habe** jeden Tag lange geschlafen und dann **bin** ich an den Strand gegangen. Nachmittags **bin** ich oft Rad gefahren und abends **habe** ich oft in einem Restaurant gegessen. Es war toll! Ich rufe euch nächste Woche an!

6 1 Ich gehe heute nicht zur Arbeit, weil ich Kopfschmerzen habe. 2 Ich bin nicht tanzen gegangen, weil ich müde war. 3 Ich komme nicht mit, weil ich lieber lange schlafen will. 4 Ich esse kein Fleisch, weil ich Vegetarier bin.

7 You probably noticed that in 1 and 3 you could use either **und** or **oder**. 1 Ich fahre heute nach Bremen, oder ich fahre morgen nach Bremen. 2 Ich mag kein Bier, aber ich mag Wein. 3 Ich will tanzen gehen und ich möchte essen gehen. 4 Ich fahre mit dem Zug zur Arbeit, denn ich fahre nicht gern Auto.

Summary 10

1 Was machst du am Wochenende? 2 Frau Meier, was machen Sie am Wochenende? 3 Sollen wir am Montag ins Kino gehen? 4 Wollt ihr mitkommen? 5 Ich möchte nicht mitkommen, weil ich müde bin. 6 Ich habe Kopfschmerzen. 7 Kannst du ihr etwas ausrichten?

Review 3

1 1 b; 2 e; 3 a; 4 g; 5 h; 6 d; 7 f; 8 c

2 1 in eine Kneipe gehen (the least active pastime of the four); 2 der Sportverein

(nothing to do with art); 3 der Computer (not related to a wedding); 4 der Fischmarkt (not in Berlin)

3 1 Ich gehe (nicht so) gerne tanzen. 2 Ich gehe (nicht so) gerne ins Kino. 3 Ich spiele (nicht so) gerne Tennis. 4 Ich gehe (nicht so) gerne ins Theater. 5 Ich lese (nicht so) gerne.

4 1 rote; 2 blauen; 3 neuen; 4 schönen; 5 kleines

5 1 uns; 2 ihnen; 3 der Tochter; 4 Herrn Winn (**helfen** requires the dative case; **Herr** adds an **-n** in the dative singular); 5 euch

6 You had to use the accusative case for the direct object, and the dative case for the indirect object. Whenever the indirect object is a pronoun, it precedes the noun/direct object.
1 Ich bringe <u>dir</u> **eine Tasse Tee**, Peter. 2 Ich stelle **dich** <u>dem Künstler</u> vor, Peter. 3 Sie kauft <u>ihm</u> **ein neues Hemd**. 4 Der Kollege (or: die Kollegin) hilft <u>ihr</u>. (**helfen** requires the dative case, therefore **ihr**.) 5 Herr Specht, können Sie <u>mir</u> **eine Tasse Kaffee** bringen?

7 *Frau Meier*: lange schlafen; eine Radtour machen; nach Stuttgart fahren
Herr Winn: an den Bodensee fahren; wandern; schwimmen gehen
Frau Specht: in eine Kneipe gehen; ein Tennisturnier haben

8 Frau Meier hat lange geschlafen, sie hat eine Radtour gemacht und sie ist nach Stuttgart gefahren.
Herr Winn ist an den Bodensee gefahren, er ist gewandert und er ist schwimmen gegangen.
Frau Specht ist in eine Kneipe gegangen und sie hat ein Tennisturnier gehabt.

9 1 Guten Morgen, wie geht es Ihnen? 2 Danke, sehr gut. 3 Am Samstag bin ich wandern gegangen. 4 Am Sonntag habe ich lange geschlafen, und abends bin ich essen gegangen. 5 Und wie war Ihr Wochenende?

Unit 11

2 1 T; 2 F (his suitcase has a red stripe); 3 T; 4 T; 5 F (a man found his suitcase)

3 You had to add the genitive endings -s or -es to the neuter or masculine singular nouns in brackets.
1 Das ist das Auto **des** Mannes dort drüben. 2 Das ist der Mantel **der** Dame dort hinten. 3 Das ist der Anzug **eines** Herrn. 4 Das ist der Mantel **einer** Frau. 5 Das ist die Jacke **eines** Kindes.

7 1 Frau Seese; 2 Frau Seese; 3 Herr Seese; 4 Herr Seese; 5 Herr Seese

8 1 Das sind die Jacken **der kleinen Kinder**. 2 Die Reisetasche gehört **dem jungen Mann** dort drüben. 3 Er trägt einen grauen Mantel mit **einem großen Kragen**. 4 Er ist

mit **einer jungen Frau** verheiratet. 5 Das ist das Auto von **dem** Mann dort drüben.

12 1 She split up with him three months ago. 2 He met her on Tuesday. 3 She is five days old. 4 She's got blue eyes.

13 You can use the simple past of **haben** whenever you use 'had' in English.
1 Er hat zu viel Wein getrunken. 2 Er hatte Kopfschmerzen. 3 Er ist zu Hause geblieben. 4 Er hatte Krach mit einem Freund. (Note that **mit** requires the dative case of **ein Freund: einem Freund**.) 5 Er ist in eine Kneipe gegangen und hat viel Bier getrunken!

14 Adjective endings: a reminder
– preceded by **der, die** (sing.), **das**, and **eine: -e**
– preceded by **den** or **einen** and in the dative case: **–en** For adjectives
– preceded by **ein** and followed by a masculine noun: **–er**
– preceded by **ein** and followed by a neuter noun: **–es**
1 Die dunkelhaarige Dame mit dem roten Kleid ist Frau Wolf. 2 Der junge Mann mit der blauen Jacke ist Herr Müller. 3 Herr Schmidt trägt einen blauen Pullover. 4 Frau Sonne trägt ein grünes Kleid mit einem grauen Kragen.

17 1 He has freckles. 2 He was 17 years and seven months old when he first won Wimbledon. 3 He won Wimbledon three times altogether.

18 1 Her hair is blond. 2 She won Wimbledon seven times. 3 She was 13 years old when she received a ranking. 4 She was number 1 for 365 weeks, which roughly equals seven years.

19 achtmal, neunmal, zehnmal (**mal** is the equivalent to English 'times', but note that it is added directly to the number).

20 1 T; 2 F (he is about fifty years old); 3 F (he has a very pleasant voice); 4 F (she thinks it boring, because it's brown); 5 T

21 1 ... **den** grünen Rock und **die** weiße Bluse? 2 Er hatte **eine** sehr **angenehme** Stimme. 3 Warum ziehst du nicht **das** braune Kostüm an? 4 Wie ist es mit **dem** schwarzen Hosenanzug? (**mit** requires the dative); 5 Dazu ziehst du die schwarzen Schuhe an.

22 1 Nein, das ist zu langweilig. 2 Ich weiß nicht, was ich anziehen soll. 3 Ist Herr Meier nett? 4 Ja, ich glaube er ist ganz nett. 5 ... und schon siehst du schick und patent aus!

Test

1 lustig–ernst; jung–alt; dick–schlank; langweilig–interessant; blond–dunkelhaarig; groß–klein

2 1 rot; 2 grün; 3 blau; 4 schwarz; 5 braun; 6 grau; 7 weiß; 8 gelb

3 1 Der Kuchen ist sehr **süß**. 2 Die neue Sekretärin ist wirklich sehr **patent**. 3 Boris

Beckers Figur ist **kräftig** und **sportlich**. 4
Der neue Freund von Frau Meier ist
wirklich **attraktiv**!

4   1 Die Bäckerei gehört **einem jungen** Mann.
(**gehören** requires the dative); 2 Der Name
der Bäckerei ist 'Bäckerei Hahn'. 3 Der
Name **des** Bäckers ist Hans Meier. 4 Das ist
der Koffer **der grauhaarigen** Dame. 5 Das
ist die Reisetasche von **dem jungen** Mann.
(**von** requires the dative)

5   *Frau Meier* trägt eine grüne Jacke mit
einem roten Kragen, einen brauen Rock
und eine grüne Bluse.
Herr Weinert trägt eine braune Jacke mit
einem schwarzen Kragen, ein graues
Hemd und eine grüne Hose.

6   Eddie Schlecker ist 45 Jahre alt und sehr
dick, denn er isst gern viel Kuchen. Er ist
dunkelhaarig. Er ist mittelgroß, hat eine
große Nase und einen vollen Mund. Eddies
Vater hatte eine Bäckerei. Der Name des
Vaters war Henry Schlecker und der Name
der Bäckerei war 'Bäckerei Schlecker'.
Eddie und sein Vater hatten oft Krach,
weil er so viel Kuchen gegessen hat.

Summary 11

1 Ich bin 45 Jahre alt. 2 Ich bin dunkelhaarig,
groß und sportlich. 3 Ich trage einen blauen
Mantel. 4 Entschuldigung, wo ist das
Fundbüro? 5 Ich suche einen blauen Koffer. 6
Meine Papiere sind in dem Koffer. 7 Wie sieht
Ihr Koffer aus? 8 Da bin ich aber froh!

Unit 12

2   1 She fell. 2 An ointment. 3 Her back. 4
Painkillers.

3   Remember, verbs indicating motion
(**hinfallen**) and change of state (**aufstehen**)
form their perfect tense with **sein**.
1 Um sieben Uhr ist Frau Krause
aufgestanden. 2 Um acht Uhr hat sie
gefrühstückt. 3 Um neun Uhr ist sie
hingefallen. 4 Um fünfzehn Uhr ist sie zum
Arzt gefahren. 5 Um zweiundzwanzig Uhr
ist sie eingeschlafen.

7   Hanna is not allowed to have: 1 Kaffee, 2
Kuchen, 6 Eis, 7 Sahne

8   1 Sie **dürfen** nicht so viel rauchen! 2 Er
darf nicht so viel essen! 3 Wir **dürfen** nicht
so viel Alkohol trinken! 4 Ich **soll** viel
wandern gehen. 5 Ihr **sollt** viel schwimmen
gehen.

9   1 You mustn't smoke so much! 2 He
mustn't eat so much! 3 We mustn't drink
so much alcohol! 4 I'm supposed to go
hiking a lot. 5 You're supposed to go
swimming a lot.

13   1 F (because she couldn't find the muesli);
2 F (she had coffee, because she couldn't
keep her eyes open without any coffee); 3
T; 4 F (he claims that he wants to start next
week)

14   **sollen**: ich sollte, du solltest, er/sie/es sollte,
wir sollten, ihr solltet, sie sollten, Sie
sollten
dürfen: ich durfte, du durftest, er/sie/es
durfte, wir durften, ihr durftet, sie
durften, Sie durften
können: ich konnte, du konntest, er/sie/es
konnte, wir konnten, ihr konntet, sie
konnten, Sie konnten

15   1 Sie **sollten** keinen Kaffee trinken. 2 Ich
durfte nicht so viel essen. 3 Er **musste**
mehr Sport machen. 4 Hilde **wollte** viel
wandern gehen. 5 Herr und Frau Meier
wollten rudern gehen.

18   1 Nehmen Sie schnell ein heißes
Erkältungsbad mit ätherischen Ölen! 2
Gurgeln Sie mehrmals täglich! 3 Lutschen
Sie Salbeipastillen! 4 Trinken Sie heiße
Hustentees! 5 Nehmen Sie Hustensaft!

19   a Halsschmerzen: 2, 3; b Schnupfen: 1;
c Husten: 4, 5

20   1 b; 2 b; 3 a; 4 b; 5 a

21   The information that was <u>not</u> given in the
dialogue is underlined:
Hubert kommt ins Hotel Gertrud und will
Susanne <u>für 19 Uhr</u> in das Parasol, ein
vegetarisches Restaurant in Konstanz
einladen. Leider ist Susanne schon <u>seit drei
Tagen</u> in Berlin. Das Essen im Parasol ist
besonders gesund: es ist fettarm,
vegetarisch, und das Gemüse ist Bio-
Gemüse. Außerdem gibt es im Parasol
keinen Alkohol und <u>keinen Kaffee oder
Tee</u>. Frau Semmler sagt, ohne Wein <u>oder
Tee</u> kann sie abends gar nicht abschalten.

Test

1   1 der Salbei (a remedy, not a body part); 2
der Fisch (not a sweet); 3 Sport treiben
(the only healthy activity here); 4 die Salbe
(a remedy, not a facial feature); 5 der
Rücken (nothing to do with a cold)

2   Only those verbs that appeared in Unit 12
are given here. Other combinations would
be possible too.
1 **hinfallen**, to fall down; 2 **aufstehen**, to
get up; 3 **zugeben**, to admit; 4 **abnehmen**,
to lose weight; 5 **anfangen**, to begin; 6
fernsehen, to watch TV; 7 **einladen**, to
invite; 8 **einschlafen**, to fall asleep.

3   1 **hingefallen**; 2 **aufgestanden**; 3
zugegeben; 4 **abgenommen**; 5
angefangen; 6 **ferngesehen**; 7 **eingeladen**;
8 **eingeschlafen**

4   1 Ich **darf nicht** rauchen. 2 Ich **darf nicht** so
viel mit dem Auto fahren. 3 Ich **soll** viel
Salat essen. 4 Ich **darf/soll** kein Eis essen. 5
Ich **soll** viel wandern gehen.

5   1 musste; 2 konnte; 3 sollte; 4 wollten; 5
konnte

6   1 Am Samstagmorgen bin ich früh
aufgestanden. 2 Ich wollte wandern
gehen, aber… 3 … zuerst musste ich etwas
einkaufen. 4 Also bin ich in die Stadt

gegangen. 5 Vor einer Bäckerei bin ich hingefallen. 6 Ich bin wieder aufgestanden, aber der linke Fuß hat sehr wehgetan. 7 In einer Apotheke habe ich eine Salbe für den Fuß gekauft.

Summary 12

1 Haben Sie etwas gegen Schnupfen? 2 Haben Sie Schmerztabletten? 3 Einen Hustensaft, bitte. 4 Ich darf keinen Alkohol trinken. 5 Ich darf kein Fett essen. 6 Ich wollte wandern gehen. 7 Ich musste schwimmen gehen.

Unit 13

2 1 Herr Kowalsky went on a business trip. 2 No, Herr Friedrichs went with Herr Kowalsky on the business trip. 3 He talks to Herr Kowalsky's secretary. 4 Herr Hansen wants Herr Kowalsky to return his call.

3 1 Herr Hansen musste mit seiner Kollegin sprechen. (**mit** requires the dative); 2 Er hat die Telefonnummer seiner Kollegin gesucht. (the genitive for possession); 3 Frau Hansen hat die Jacken ihrer Kinder gesucht. (the genitive for possession); 4 Herr und Frau Hansen haben mit ihren Kindern gespielt. (**mit** requires the dative)

7 1 T, 2 F (he'll come today, as he's passing by Herr Hansen's office anyway); 3 T

8 **ohne, um, durch, gegen, für** take the accusative.
1 Ich komme ohne meinen Mann (*m*). 2 Es geht um Ihre Lieferung (*f*). 3 Wir sind durch eine schöne Stadt (*f*) gefahren. 4 Ich suche eine Hose für meinen Sohn (*m*). 1 I'll come without my husband. 2 It's about your delivery. 3 We drove through a beautiful town. 4 I'm looking for some trousers for my son.

9 1 schneller; 2 früher; 3 schöner; 4 lustiger

13 1 €75; 2 €90; 3 €80; 4 1.60 by 1.30 metres

14 1 Rock B ist größer als Rock A. Rock C ist am größten. 2 Peter ist kleiner als Uwe. Bertie ist am kleinsten. 3 Sabine ist älter als Maria. Stefan ist am ältesten. 4 Lotte ist dicker als Uschi. Hans ist am dicksten. 5 Karola ist schlanker als Lutz. Anna ist am schlanksten.

17 Firma Habermann & Co.
z.H. Herrn Herbert Habermann
Schachtstraße 67 c
D-50939 Köln

18 2, 5, 6, and 7 do NOT belong in a formal business letter:

19 1 teurer; 2 alt; 3 Jüngere, netter; 4 interessanter; 5 schön

20 1 F (she thought it was more expensive than Konstanz); 2 F (she thinks he's quite nice, but a bit too old); 3 F (she had a job interview); 4 T; 5 T; 6 F (not any more; she thinks it's too big); 7 T

Test

I 1 die Hand; 2 anhalten; 3 am Apparat; 4 teuer (it doesn't describe a person)

2 1, 5, 3, 6, 7, 2, 4

3 Also, Frau Meier ist sehr **nett**, aber Frau Hahn ist noch **netter** ('even nicer'). Ich finde mich aber **am nettesten**. Ich finde, ich sehe auch ganz gut aus. Frau Meier sieht noch **besser** aus – na, und Frau Hahn sieht natürlich **am besten** aus. Sie ist auch so **schlank**! **Am schlanksten** ist aber Frau Meier, das muss ich sagen. Ach, ich muss abnehmen!

4 A: Es tut mir Leid, aber Frau Petersen ist nicht in **ihrem** Büro.
A: Möchten Sie **ihre** Sekretärin sprechen?
B: Nein danke. Kann ich **ihre** Kollegin, Frau Walter sprechen?
B: Haben Sie die Telefonnummer **ihres** Kollegen, Herrn Grün? (the genitive for possession – 'of')
B: Können Sie mich dann bitte mit **ihrer** Sekretärin verbinden? (**mit** takes the dative)

5 Remember: if you don't know the past participle of a verb, check the list of irregular verbs in the Grammer Summary. If it isn't there, the verb is likely to be regular, forming its past participle by adding **ge-** and **-t** to the stem.
1 Um 9 Uhr habe ich gefrühstückt. 2 Um 10 Uhr habe ich mit einem Kollegen Kaffee getrunken. 3 Um 11 Uhr habe ich einen Kollegen angerufen. 4 Um 12 Uhr habe ich gegessen. 5 Um 15 Uhr habe ich den Kollegen Tee gebracht. 6 Um 16 Uhr habe ich Geschäftsbriefe geschrieben.

6 1 für; 2 um; 3 durch; 4 gegen

Summary 13

1 Guten Tag, hier spricht Herr Müller von der Firma Müller & Co. 2 Kann ich mit Herrn Wolfram sprechen, bitte? 3 Können Sie mich mit seiner Kollegin, Frau Walter, verbinden, bitte? 4 Können Sie ihr etwas ausrichten, bitte? 5 Sagen Sie ihr bitte, sie soll mich morgen zurückrufen. 6 Ich möchte gerne einen Termin mit Ihnen vereinbaren. 7 Ich möchte gerne 56 Jacken in Größe 48 bestellen.

Unit 14

2 1 To Lanzarote. 2 A colleague. 3 No, she sold her old skis a long time ago. 4 No, he doesn't have time right now.

3 1 Am <u>vierundzwanzigsten</u> Dezember habe ich einen neuen Mantel **bekommen**. 2 <u>Am fünfundzwanzigsten</u> Dezember habe ich meine Schwester und ihre Familie **besucht** 3 Am <u>sechsundzwanzigsten</u> Dezember habe ich meiner Mutter ein tolles Buch **empfohlen**. 4 Am <u>einunddreißigsten</u> Dezember habe ich meinen Freunden viel Sekt **serviert**. 5 Am <u>ersten</u> Januar habe ich mit meinem Bruder in Amerika **telefoniert**.

7 1 F (she wants to lose 10 kg); 2 F (she wants to give up smoking completely); 3 T

8 1 Herbert wird mehr Sport treiben (or: machen). 2 Marlene und Peter werden viel wandern gehen. 3 Ich werde mehr Zeit mit meiner Familie verbringen. 4 Erich wird nicht mehr rauchen. 5 Wir werden öfter schwimmen gehen.

12 1 Die Familie Horaz besuchte **ihre Großmutter**. 2 Sie fuhren gegen **18 Uhr** ab. 3 Ein Mann stahl Geschenke im Wert von **€300**.

13 1 sprechen; 2 anrufen; 3 schlafen; 4 schwimmen

16 tanzte; befreiten; zogen; stellten; verbrannten; tanzte

17 **Schmutziger Donnerstag**: 11 Uhr: die Narren befreiten die Schüler. 16 Uhr: die Narren stellten den Narrenbaum auf. 19 Uhr: das ganze Dorf tanzte im Hemdglonkerumzug. **Sonntag**: 15 Uhr: die Narren zogen im Fastnetsumzug durch das Dorf. 20 Uhr: das Dorf tanzte auf dem Bürgerball. **Dienstag**: 19 Uhr: die Narren verbrannten die Fasnet.

18 1 Es ist **acht Uhr** morgens. 2 Susanne war bis **um sechs Uhr** auf einem Ball. 3 Sie trägt noch ihr **Kostüm**. 4 Herr Meier hat **gestern Abend** angerufen. 5 Susanne wird **nicht** nach Berlin gehen. 9 Hubert und Susanne wollen **zusammen in die Stadt gehen**.

19 Susanne will become a vegetarian, because Hubert is a vegetarian. 2 She will marry Hubert. 3 Susanne and Hubert will have many children. 4 Susanne and Hubert will have lots of fights, because she doesn't eat very healthily. 5 Susanne and Hubert will have a fight and Susanne will go to Berlin. 6 In Berlin, Susanne will meet Peter and they'll get married.

Test

1 1 d; 2 e; 3 g; 4 j; 5 f; 6 c; 7 l; 8 a; 9 k; 10 b; 11 h; 12 i

2 1 er kletterte; 2 **sie** ('they') schliefen, **Sie** schliefen, **wir** schliefen; 3 **wir** riefen an, **sie** ('they') riefen an; 4 **du** kauftest; 5 **ich** fuhr Ski, **sie** ('she') fuhr Ski; 7 **sie** ('she') telefonierte.

3 1 Wann wirst du anrufen? 2 Wohin werdet ihr fahren? 3 Ich werde nach Spanien fahren. 4 Wirst du sie heiraten? 5 Werdet ihr bei deinen Eltern wohnen?

4 1 Ich habe viel Zeit mit meiner Familie verbracht. 2 Ich habe mit einem Freund/einer Freundin telefoniert. 3 Ich habe ein neues Auto bestellt. 4 Ich habe meiner Frau eine Tasse Tee serviert.

5 1 hatten; 2 fuhren; 3 kamen; 4 gingen; 5 suchten; 6 konnten; 7 war; 8 hattet

Summary 14

1 Was machst du über Weihnachten? **2** Was macht ihr über Weihnachten? **3** Ich will wegfahren. **4** Ich wünsche dir ein frohes neues Jahr. **5** Ich wünsche euch ein frohes neues Jahr! **6** Ich werde mehr Deutsch lernen!

Review 4

1 1 HALS 2 JAHR 3 SCHLANK 4 FUNDBÜRO 5 APOTHEKE 6 SCHOKOLADE 7 MÜSLI 8 TISCHDECKE 9 WEIHNACHTEN 10 KOFFER

2 1 e; 2 d; 3 a; 4 c; 5 b

3 1 wollte; konnte; musste; 2 wolltest; 3 sollte; 4 wollte; durfte; wollte

4 Um neun Uhr wachte Frau Meier auf. 2 Sie stand schnell auf. 3 Sie fiel hin. 4 Sie verletzte ihren Fuß. 5 Dann rief sie im Büro an. 6 Ihr Chef war auch krank. 7 Frau Meier blieb zu Hause.

5 2 näher, 3 am nächsten, 5 besser, 6 am besten, 8 teurer, 9 am teuersten

6 1 Er kommt nicht mit, weil er kein Auto hat. 2 Er kam nicht, weil er kein Auto hatte. 3 Ich gehe jetzt nach Hause, weil ich müde bin. 4 Ich kaufe die Blumen nicht, weil sie zu teuer sind. 5 Sie konnte nicht mitkommen, weil sie krank war.

7 1 gegen; 2 für; 3 ohne; 4 durch; 5 gegen

8 1 Eine junge Frau. 2 Einen kleinen Koffer. 3 Sie trägt eine blaue Jacke und einen gelben Rock. 4 Zwei Männer. 5 Sie geht schnell über die Straße. 6 Das Auto hält vor der Frau. 7 Ein dicker Mann fährt das Auto. 8 Er zieht die Frau in das Auto.

9 1 Eine Frau kam aus der Bank. 2 In der Hand hatte sie einen Koffer. 3 Sie trug eine blaue Jacke und einen gelben Rock. 4 Sie ging bis zur Ampel. 5 Zwei Männer kamen aus der Bank. 6 Die junge Frau sah die zwei Männer. 7 Die junge Frau ging über die Straße. 8 Vor ihr hielt ein auto an. 9 Ein Mann zog sie ins Auto. 10 Das Auto fuhr weg.

10 1 Ein Mineralwasser für mich und für meinen Freund eine Cola, bitte. 2 Können Sie meinem Freund einen Tee ohne Milch bringen? Er darf keine Milch trinken. 3 Können wir ein Müsli und ein Stück Kuchen mit Sahne haben, bitte? 4 Ich esse lieber Apfelkuchen. Aber ich möchte ein kleines Stück, weil ich eine Diät mache. 5 Ich darf im Büro nicht mehr rauchen und jetzt esse ich zu viel Schokolade. 6 Mein Bruder heiratet und ich möchte gut aussehen.

Grammar summary

The definite and indefinite articles

The definite article **(der, die, das)** and the indefinite article **(ein, eine, ein)** have to agree in gender, number, and case with the noun they accompany. The indefinite article can only be singular.

	sing			*pl*
	m	*f*	*n*	
Nominative	**der/ein**	**die/eine**	**das/ein**	**die**
Accusative	**den/einen**	**die/eine**	**das/ein**	**die**
Dative	**dem/einem**	**der/einer**	**dem/einem**	**den**
Genitive	**des/eines**	**der/einer**	**des/eines**	**der**

Nouns

In German, all nouns have a gender, either masculine, feminine, or neuter. Gender affects the form of the accompanying words such as adjectives, possessive forms, etc.

Some rules for the gender of nouns

1 Names of months, days of the week, and times of day are masculine, with the exception of **die Nacht**.

2 Nouns ending in **-in**, **-keit**, **-heit**, **-ung**, **-ie**, **-ion** are feminine. Many nouns ending with **-e** are feminine as well.

3 Nouns ending in **-chen** are always neuter.

Compound nouns

When two nouns are combined to form a single noun, the second part of the noun determines the gender.

der Fußball + das Spiel **das Fußballspiel** football match

Plurals

There are a number of ways of forming the plural of nouns in German. Here are a few rules to help you. In the six plural types listed below, (¨) means that the vowel takes an umlaut in the plural form.

1	ending (**-e**) with umlaut (**-¨-e**)	**der Abend** **der Saft**	**die Abende** **die Säfte**
2	ending (**-er**) with umlaut (**-¨-er**)	**das Kind** **das Weinglas**	**die Kinder** **die Weingläser**
3	no ending (**-**) with umlaut (**-¨-**)	**der Kellner** **der Vater**	**die Kellner** **die Väter**
4	ending (**-n**)	**die Kartoffel**	**die Kartoffeln**
5	ending (**-en**)	**die Frau**	**die Frauen**
6	ending (**-s**)	**das Auto**	**die Autos**

Many masculine nouns add the plural ending **-e**. Almost all feminine nouns end in **-en**, or **-n** if **-e** is already part of the noun: **die Salbe(-n)**, 'ointment'.

Cases

The case of a word is the form it takes according to its function in a sentence. The case is usually indicated by the ending. There are four cases: *nominative*, *accusative*, *dative*, and *genitive*.

The *nominative* case is used for the subject.
> **Der Junge** geht nach Hause. The boy is going home.

The *accusative* case is used for the direct object.
> Ich sehe **den Jungen**. I see the boy.

The *dative* case is used for the indirect object.
> Ich gebe **dem Jungen** einen Apfel. I give an apple to the boy.

The *genitive* case is used to express possession.
> Die Freunde **des Jungen**. The boy's friends.

		sing.		*pl.*
	m	*f*	*n*	
Nominative	der Kuchen	die Zeitung	das Brot	die Brote
Accusative	den Kuchen	die Zeitung	das Brot	die Brote
Dative	dem Kuchen	der Zeitung	dem Brot	den Broten
Genitive	des Kuchens	der Zeitung	des Brotes	der Brote

1 In the genitive singular, masculine and neuter nouns add an **-s**. Many monosyllabic nouns/nouns ending in **-s**, **-ß**, or **-z** add **-es**.

   der Brot   des Brot**es**   das Haus   des Haus**es**

2 Some masculine nouns add an **-n** or **-en** in the accusative, dative, and genitive.

   der Herr, den Herr**n**, dem Herr**n**, des Herr**n**

3 All nouns in the dative plural add an **-n**.

   den Männer**n**, den Kinder**n**, den Frau**en**

Pronouns

	Nominative	Accusative	Dative
(*sing.*)	**ich** I	**mich** me	**mir** (to/for) me
	du you	**dich** you	**dir** (to/for) you
	er he/it	**ihn** him/it	**ihm** (to/for) him/it
	sie she/it	**sie** her/it	**ihr** (to/for) her/it
	es it	**es** it	**ihm** (to/for) it
(*pl.*)	**wir** we	**uns** us	**uns** (to/for) us
	ihr you	**euch** you	**euch** (to/for) you
	sie they	**sie** them	**ihnen** (to/for) them
formal	**Sie** you	**Sie** you	**Ihnen** (to/for) you

Possessive adjectives

Possessive adjectives must agree in gender, number, and case with the noun they accompany. Possessive adjectives are also called **ein** words because they have the same endings as the indefinite article **ein** (see page 225). The plural form is identical in all three genders. Thus in the nominative the possessive adjectives are:

	sing.			*pl.*
	m	*f*	*n*	
my	mein	meine	mein	meine
your	dein	deine	dein	deine
his	sein	seine	sein	seine
her	ihr	ihre	ihr	ihre
its	sein	seine	sein	seine
our	unser	unsre	unser	unsre
your	euer	eure	euer	eure
their	ihr	ihre	ihr	ihre
your	Ihr	Ihre	Ihr	Ihre

Note that some forms of **unser** and **euer** drop the **e**.

Here is a table showing the possessive adjective **mein** in all four cases. The other possessive adjectives follow this example.

	sing.			*pl.*
	m	*f*	*n*	
Nominative	mein	meine	mein	meine
Accusative	meinen	meine	mein	meine
Dative	meinem	meiner	meinem	meinen
Genitive	meines	meiner	meines	meiner

Prepositions

Certain prepositions need to be followed by a specific case.

Prepositions + accusative

durch through	**ohne** without	**gegen** against, towards
für for	**um** around, at	**bis** until, by

Er geht **durch den** Park. He walks through the park.
Wir gehen **ohne ihn** ins Kino. We're going to the cinema without him.

Prepositions + dative

aus from, out of	**seit** since, for	**mit** with	**zu** to, at
bei with, at, near	**von** from, of	**nach** after, to	
gegenüber opposite			

Wir fahren immer **mit dem** Zug. We always go by train.
Nach dem Film sind wir nach Hause gegangen. After the film we went home.

Two-way prepositions
Some prepositions are followed either by the accusative or the dative.

an on, at	unter under	über over, above
hinter behind	zwischen between	neben next to, beside
in in	auf on	vor on front of, before

1 The dative is used to say where something is located – answering **wo?** ('where?'):

Ich bin **auf** dem Marktplatz. I'm in the market place.
Hans spielt **im** Haus. Hans is playing in the house.

2 The accusative is used with a verb indicating movement from one place to another – answering **wohin?** ('where to?'):

Ich gehe **auf** den Marktplatz. I'm going to the market place.
Hans geht **in** das Haus. Hans is going into the house.

Some prepositions are contracted with the following article.

an + dem → **am**	in + dem → **im**	zu + dem → **zum**
zu + der → **zur**	bei + dem → **beim**	

Adjectives

An adjective can either precede or follow the noun. When it precedes the noun, it has to agree in gender, number, and case with the noun. When it comes after the noun, it takes no ending.

Das ist **ein schönes Haus.**   Das Haus ist **schön.**
This is a nice house.   The house is nice.

The adjective ending changes depending on the type of article that precedes it.

Adjective with definite article

	sing.			pl.
	m	*f*	*n*	
Nominative	neue	neue	neue	neuen
Accusative	neuen	neue	neue	neuen
Dative	neuen	neuen	neuen	neuen
Genitive	neuen	neuen	neuen	neuen

*Adjective with indefinite article, possessive adjectives, and **kein***

	sing.			pl.
	m	*f*	*n*	
Nominative	neuer	neue	neues	neuen
Accusative	neuen	neue	neues	neuen
Dative	neuen	neuen	neuen	neuen
Genitive	neuen	neuen	neuen	neuen

Comparatives and superlatives

Comparatives

The comparative ('bigger than', 'less than', etc.) is formed by adding the ending **-er** to the adjective or adverb:

klein **kleiner**   früh **früher**

Dieses Kleid ist noch **schöner** als das andere.

This dress is even more beautiful than the other one.
Heinz läuft **schneller** als Peter. Heinz runs faster than Peter.

Superlative
To form the superlative ('the biggest', 'best', 'most beautiful') you
use **am** and add the ending **-sten** to the adjective or adverb:

billig **am billigsten**   klein **am kleinsten**
Sabine läuft **am schnellsten**. Sabine runs the fastest.

Irregular comparative and superlative forms
Many adjectives and adverbs of one syllable take an umlaut in the
comparative and superlative forms. Adjectives and adverbs ending
in a **t** add an **e** in the superlative form.

groß	größer	am größten	big, bigger, the biggest
alt	älter	am ältesten	old, older, the oldest

Some comparatives and superlatives also change consonants as
well.

nah	näher	am nächsten	near, nearer, the nearest
hoch	höher	am höchsten	high, higher, the highest

Other irregular forms:

viel	mehr	am meisten	much, more, the most
gut	besser	am besten	good, better, the best
gerne	lieber	am liebsten	like, prefer, like the best

Verbs

The present tense of regular verbs
Regular verbs, e.g. **machen** ('to make', 'to do'), add the following
endings to their stem to form the present tense:

ich **mache**	wir **machen**
du **machst**	ihr **macht**
er/sie/es **macht**	sie **machen**
	Sie **machen**

Note: verbs whose stem ends in **-t** (e.g. **arbeiten**, 'to work'), add
an extra **-e** in the **du, er/sie/es**, and **ihr** forms of the verb: **du
arbeitest, er/sie/es arbeitet, ihr arbeitet**.

The present tense of irregular verbs
Irregular verbs, e.g. **nehmen** ('to take'), add the same present
tense endings as regular verbs, but many change their stem in the
du and **er/sie/es** forms. The **er/sie/es** forms of common irregular
verbs are listed in the table on pages 235–6.

ich **nehme**	wir **nehmen**
du **nimmst**	ihr **nehmt**
er/sie/es **nimmt**	sie **nehmen**
	Sie **nehmen**

haben ('to have'), *sein* ('to be'), and **werden** ('to become') are completely irregular in the present tense.

ich **habe**	wir **haben**	ich **bin**	wir **sind**
du **hast**	ihr **habt**	du **bist**	ihr **seid**
er/sie/es **hat**	sie **haben**	er/sie/es **ist**	sie **sind**
	Sie **haben**		Sie **sind**
ich **werde**	wir **werden**		
du **wirst**	ihr **werdet**		
er/sie/es **wird**	sie **werden**		
	Sie **werden**		

Verbs with a separable prefix

In the present and simple past tenses, as well as in the imperative, the separable prefix goes to the end of the sentence.

Present tense: Ich **stehe** nicht gerne früh **auf**. I don't like getting up early.

Past tense: Ich **stand** noch nie gerne früh **auf**. I never liked getting up early.

Imperative: **Stehen** Sie **auf**! Get up!

The perfect tense

The perfect tense is formed using the present tense of either **sein** or **haben** and a past participle.

Ich **bin** zu spät **gekommen**. I came too late.
Ich **habe** ein neues Auto **gekauft**. I bought a new car.

The following verbs form their perfect tense with **sein**.

1 Verbs describing motion or a change of place, e.g. **kommen** ('to come'), **fahren** ('to go'), **gehen** ('to walk'), plus all their combinations with separable prefixes or other verbs.

Wir **sind** tanzen **gegangen**. We went dancing.
Wann **seid** ihr **angekommen**? When did you arrive?

2 Verbs describing a change of state, e.g. **einschlafen** ('to fall asleep'), **aufstehen** ('to get up').

Sind sie zu spät **aufgewacht**? Did they wake up too late?

3 **sein** ('to be'), **bleiben** ('to stay'), and **werden** ('to become')
sein: Ich **bin** in Hamburg **gewesen**. I was in Hamburg.
bleiben: Wir **sind** zu Hause **geblieben**. We stayed at home.
werden: Er **ist** Vater **geworden**. He became a father.

All other verbs form their perfect tense with **haben**.

The past participles of regular verbs
ge- and **-t** are added to the stem of the verb:

kaufen → gekauft bought   **lachen → gelacht** laughed

The past participles of verbs whose stem ends in **-t** add an extra **-e**: **arbeiten → gearbeitet** ('worked').

The past participles of Irregular verbs
ge- and -en are added to the stem. The past participles of
irregular verbs often change their vowels, or sometimes even
consonants. The past participles of irregular verbs used in this
course are listed on pages 235–6.

fahren → **gefahren** driven   **nehmen** → **genommen** taken

The past participles of mixed verbs
ge- and -t are added to the stem, as for regular verbs, but there is
also a spelling change in the stem.

bringen → **gebracht** brought

In the vocabulary glossary all mixed verbs are marked (*mix.*). Their
past participles are listed on pages 235–6.

The past participles of verbs with a separable prefix
1 For regular verbs, **ge-** is added after the prefix and -t is added
to the stem:

aufmachen → **aufgemacht** opened

2 For irregular verbs, **ge-** is added after the prefix and -en is
added to the stem; the stem often changes its spelling:

abfahren → **abgefahren** departed
annehmen → **angenommen** accepted

To form the past participle of an irregular verb with a separable
prefix, look up the past participle of the verb on pages 235–6. and
add the prefix. For instance, the past participle of **weggehen** is
weggegangen ('went away').

The past participles of verbs with a non-separable prefix
1 For regular verbs with non-separable prefixes (**be-, emp-, ent-,
er-, ge-, ver-, zer-**) -t is added to the stem (-et for stems ending
in -t)

verkaufen → **verkauft** sold   **behaupten** → **behauptet** to assert

2 For irregular verbs with a non-separable prefix, -en is added to
the stem; the stem often changes.

zerbrechen → **zerbrochen** broken
empfehlen → **empfohlen** recommended

The past participles of verbs with stems ending in -ieren
The prefix **ge-** is not added; -iert is added to the end of the stem.

telefonieren → **telefoniert** phoned
servieren → **serviert** served

The simple past tense
The following rules also apply to regular and irregular verbs with
a non-separable prefix.

1 *Regular verbs*
To form the simple past of regular verbs, e.g. **kaufen**, 'to buy', add
these endings to their stems:

ich **kaufte** I bought		wir **kauften** we bought	
du **kauftest** you bought		ihr **kauftet** you bought	
er/sie/es kauf**te** he/she/it bought		sie **kauften** they bought	
		Sie **kauften** you bought	

Verbs with a stem ending in -t add an extra e: ich **arbeitete**

2 *Irregular verbs*

In the simple past, irregular verbs, e.g. **nehmen**, add no ending in the **ich** and **er/sie/es** forms, and often change their vowel or even consonants. The **er** and **ich** forms of irregular verbs in the simple past are given in the table on pages 235–6. To form the simple past of the remaining persons, add the present tense endings:

ich **nahm** I took	wir **nahmen** we took
du nahm**st** you took	ihr **nahmt** you took
er/sie/es **nahm** he/she/it took	sie **nahmen** they took
	Sie **nahmen** you took

3 *haben and sein*

ich **hatte**	wir **hatten**	ich **war**	wir **waren**
du **hattest**	ihr **hattet**	du **warst**	ihr **wart**
er/sie/es **hatte**	sie **hatten**	er/sie/es **war**	sie **waren**
	Sie **hatten**		Sie **waren**

4 *Verbs with a separable prefix*

Regular verbs take the same endings as for **kaufen**. Again, an extra -**e** is added if the stem of the verb ends in -**t**. The separable prefix goes to the end of the sentence.

vor/bereiten: Ich bereit**ete** das Essen **vor**. I prepared the meal.

To form the simple past of irregular verbs with a separable prefix, look up the past tense form of the verb on pages 235–6 and add the same endings as for **nehmen**. The separable prefix goes to the end of the sentence.

ab/fahren: Wir fuhr**en** um acht Uhr **ab**. We left at eight o'clock.

4 *Mixed verbs*

Mixed verbs, e.g. **verbringen** ('to spend time'), take the same endings as for **kaufen**. However, they change their vowel and sometimes even consonants:

ich **verbrachte** I spent	wir **verbrachten** we spent
du **verbrachtest** you spent	ihr **verbrachtet** you spent
er/sie/es **verbrachte** he/she/it spent	sie **verbrachten** they spent
	Sie **verbrachten** you spent

The future tense

German often uses the present tense to talk about the future, especially if it is obvious that the future is meant.

Ich **fahre** nächstes Jahr nach Italien. I'm going to Italy next year.

If the reference to the future is not clear, or in order to express a strong future intention, German uses the future tense. This is formed using the present tense of **werden** plus the infinitive.

Ich **werde** nächstes Jahr **abnehmen.** I'll lose weight next year.
Wann **wirst** du **heiraten**? When will you get married?

Modal verbs

Present tense
The **ich, du,** and **er/sie/es** forms of the modal verbs **mögen** ('to like'), **müssen** ('to have to'), **dürfen** ('to be allowed to'), **können** ('to be able to'), **wollen** ('to want to'), and **sollen** ('to be supposed to') – change their vowel, with the exception of **sollen**. The **ich** and **er/sie/es** forms take no ending; the remaining persons take the regular present tense endings.

	mögen	müssen	dürfen	können	wollen	sollen
ich	mag	muss	darf	kann	will	soll
du	magst	musst	darfst	kannst	willst	sollst
er/sie/es	mag	muss	darf	kann	will	soll
wir	mögen	müssen	dürfen	können	wollen	sollen
ihr	mögt	müsst	dürft	könnt	wollt	sollt
sie	mogen	müssen	dürfen	können	wollen	sollen
Sie	mögen	müssen	dürfen	können	wollen	sollen

ich möchte ('I would like to') is actually a subjunctive form of **mögen.** In the present tense, it follows the pattern of a regular verb with a stem ending in **-t,** but the **er/sie/es** form is identical to the **ich** form: **ich möchte, du möchtest, er/sie/es möchte,** etc.

Usage
Modal verbs are generally used with an infinitive, which appears at the end of the sentence.

Ich **möchte** nichts **trinken.** I don't want anything to drink.

Only **mögen** appears regularly without an infinitive.

Ich **mag** kein Fleisch. I don't like meat.   Ich **mag** ihn. I like him.

Simple past tense of modal verbs
The simple past endings of the regular verbs are added to these forms: **moch-, muss-, durf-, konn-, woll-, soll-.**

	mögen	müssen	dürfen	können	wollen	sollen
ich	mochte	musste	durfte	konnte	wollte	sollte
du	mochtest	musstest	durftest	konntest	wolltest	solltest
er/sie/es	mochte	musste	durfte	konnte	wollte	sollte
wir	mochten	mussten	durften	konnten	wollten	sollten
ihr	mochtet	musstet	durftet	konntet	wolltet	solltet
sie	mochten	mussten	durften	konnten	wollten	sollten
Sie	mochten	mussten	durften	konnten	wollten	sollten

The simple past of the modal verbs is often used rather than the more complicated perfect tense:

Perfect tense: Ich **habe** noch einkaufen **müssen**. I had to go shopping.

Simple past: Ich **musste** noch einkaufen. I had to go shopping.

The imperative

The imperative is used to give an instruction or order.

> **Kommen Sie** herein! Come in! [*literally* Come you in!]
> **Gehen Sie** um die Ecke. Go round the corner.

The imperative of **sein** ('to be') is **seien**.

Negatives

kein is used with nouns to mean 'no', 'not any', 'not a'. In the singular, the endings of **kein** are identical with those of **ein** (see page 225), and in the plural with those of the possessive adjectives (see page 227).

> Ich möchte **keinen** Wein. I don't want any wine.

nicht is used with verbs to mean 'not':

> Ich trinke **nicht**. I don't drink.

Word order

Position of the verb

1 *In statements and in questions with a question word*
The verb takes the second position in the sentence.

> Er **hatte** kein Auto. He didn't have a car.
> Wann **fahren** Sie ab? When are you leaving?

Note that it is not necessarily the second **word** in the sentence, but the second piece of information or idea. You could, for instance, have a time phrase in front of the verb:

> Morgen Nachmittag **gehe** ich schwimmen. Tomorrow afternoon, I'll go swimming.

If there is a second verb (a past participle or an infinitive), it goes to the end of the sentence (the verb <u>underlined</u> in the examples below). The verb carrying the personal ending takes the second position in the sentence (the verbs in **bold**).

> Ich **habe** gestern <u>eingekauft</u>. Yesterday, I went shopping.
> Wo **werden** sie <u>heiraten</u>? Where will they get married?

2 *In questions without a question word*
The verb carrying the personal ending occupies the first position in the sentence.

> **Kommst** du morgen? Are you coming tomorrow?

If there is a second verb (a past participle or an infinitive), it goes to the end of the sentence.

3 Position of the verb after subordinating conjunctions

After the subordinating conjunctions **weil** ('because'), **dass** ('that'), and **ob** ('whether') the verb carrying the personal ending goes to the end of the sentence.

Er kommt nicht. Er **ist** krank. He won't come. He's ill.
Er kommt nicht, weil er krank **ist**. He won't come, because he's ill.

Position of objects in the sentence
In German, the indirect object (IO) precedes the direct object (DO).

subject	IO	DO
Peter erzählt	den Kindern	eine Geschichte.
Peter tells the children a story.		
Er erklärt	ihnen	die Geschichte.
He explains the story to them.		

Only when the direct object is a pronoun does it precede the indirect object.

subject	DO	IO	
Er erklärt	sie	den Kindern.	
He explains it to the children.			
Er liest	sie	ihnen	vor.
He reads it to them.			

Table of irregular verbs

The **er/sie/es** form is listed in the table.

Infinitive	Present tense	Simple past	Past participle	
beginnen	beginnt	begann	hat begonnen	to begin
bekommen	bekommt	bekam	hat bekommen	to receive
beschreiben	beschreibt	beschrieb	hat beschrieben	to describe
bieten	bietet	bot	hat geboten	to offer
bitten	bittet	bat	hat gebeten	to ask
bleiben	bleibt	blieb	ist geblieben	to stay
braten	brät	briet	hat gebraten	to roast
bringen	bringt	brachte	hat gebracht	to bring
denken	denkt	dachte	hat gedacht	to think
dürfen	darf	durfte	hat gedurft	to be allowed
empfangen	empfängt	empfing	hat empfangen	to receive
empfehlen	empfiehlt	empfahl	hat empfohlen	to recommend
erfahren	erfährt	erfuhr	hat erfahren	to find out
erkennen	erkennt	erkannte	hat erkannt	to recognize
essen	isst	aß	hat gegessen	to eat
fahren	fährt	fuhr	ist gefahren	to drive
fallen	fällt	fiel	ist gefallen	to fall
fangen	fängt	fing	hat gefangen	to catch
finden	findet	fand	hat gefunden	to find
fliegen	fliegt	flog	ist geflogen	to fly
geben	gibt	gab	hat gegeben	to give

Infinitive	Present tense	Simple past	Past participle	
gehen	geht	ging	ist gegangen	to go
gewinnen	gewinnt	gewann	hat gewonnen	to win
gießen	gießt	goss	hat gegossen	to pour
haben	hat	hatte	hat gehabt	to have
halten	hält	hielt	hat gehalten	to hold
heißen	heißt	hieß	hat geheißen	to be called
helfen	hilft	half	hat geholfen	to help
kennen	kennt	kannte	hat gekannt	to know
kommen	kommt	kam	ist gekommen	to come
können	kann	konnte	hat gekonnt	to be able to
laden	lädt	lud	hat geladen	to load
lassen	lässt	ließ	hat gelassen	to let
laufen	läuft	lief	ist gelaufen	to run
lesen	liest	las	hat gelesen	to read
liegen	liegt	lag	hat gelegen	to lie
mögen	mag	mochte	hat gemocht	to like
müssen	muss	musste	hat gemusst	to have to
nehmen	nimmt	nahm	hat genommen	to take
rufen	ruft	rief	hat gerufen	to call
scheinen	scheint	schien	hat geschienen	to shine
schlafen	schläft	schlief	hat geschlafen	to sleep
schließen	schließt	schloss	hat geschlossen	to close
schreiben	schreibt	schrieb	hat geschrieben	to write
schwimmen	schwimmt	schwamm	ist geschwommen	to swim
sehen	sieht	sah	hat gesehen	to see
sein	ist	war	ist gewesen	to be
sitzen	sitzt	saß	hat gesessen	to sit
sollen	soll	sollte	hat gesollt	to be supposed to
sprechen	spricht	sprach	hat gesprochen	to talk
stehen	steht	stand	hat gestanden	to stand
stehlen	stiehlt	stahl	hat gestohlen	to steal
sterben	stirbt	starb	ist gestorben	to die
tragen	trägt	trug	hat getragen	to carry
treffen	trifft	traf	hat getroffen	to meet
trinken	trinkt	trank	hat getrunken	to drink
tun	tut	tat	hat getan	to do
vergessen	vergisst	vergaß	hat vergessen	to forget
verlieren	verliert	verlor	hat verloren	to lose
verstehen	versteht	verstand	hat verstanden	to understand
vorschlagen	schlägt vor	schlug vor	hat vorgeschlagen	to suggest
wachsen	wächst	wuchs	ist gewachsen	to grow
waschen	wäscht	wusch	hat gewaschen	to wash
werden	wird	wurde	ist geworden	to become
werfen	wirft	warf	hat geworfen	to throw
wissen	weiß	wusste	hat gewusst	to know
ziehen	zieht	zog	hat gezogen	to pull

Vocabulary

- irregular verbs are asterisked, e.g. **nehmen*** to take
- mixed verbs are marked(*mix.*), e.g. **bringen** (*mix.*) to bring, to get
- separable prefixes are indicated by a slash (/), e.g. **auf/wachen***, to wake up
- all plural endings and/or spelling changes in the plural are given in brackets, e.g. **der Mann(-¨-er)**, man (See the Grammar Summary, page 225, for general rules on forming the plural of nouns.)
- (*sing.*) indicates that a noun exists only in the singular
- (*pl.*) indicates that a noun exists only in the plural

A

ab/fahren*	to leave, depart
ab/holen	to collect, pick up
ab/nehmen*	to lose weight
ab/schicken	to dispatch, to send off
der Abend(-e)	evening
aber	but
die Abfahrtszeit(-en)	departure time
ab/schalten	to switch off, to relax
die Abteilung(-en)	department
die Adresse(-n)	address
der Alkohol(-e)	alcohol
allein	alone
alles	all
als	than, as
alt	old
der Amerikaner(-)	(male) American
die Amerikanerin(-nen)	(female) American
die Ampel(-n)	traffic lights
an	at, next to, on
an/bieten*	to offer
an/fangen*	to begin
an/halten*	to stop
an/rufen*	to ring
an/ziehen*	to put on [clothes]
ander	other
das Angebot(-e)	offer, quotation
angenehm	agreeable
an/kommen*	to arrive
die Ankunftszeit(-en)	arrival time
an/probieren	to try on
anschließend	afterwards
anstrengend	strenuous
der Anzug(-¨-e)	suit
der Apfelkuchen(-)	apple cake
die Apotheke(-n)	pharmacy, drugstore
die Arbeit(-en)	work
arbeiten	to work

der Arzt(-¨-e)	(male) medical doctor
die Ärztin(-nen)	(female) medical doctor
ätherisch	essential
attraktiv	attractive
auch	also
auf	on (top of)
auf keinen Fall	on no account
auf Wiederhören	goodbye [*on the phone*]
auf Wiedersehen	goodbye
auf/hängen (mix.)	to hang (up)
auf/machen	to open
auf/räumen	to tidy up
auf/stehen*	to get up
auf/stellen	to put up
auf/wachen	to wake up
auffällig	garish
das Auge(-n)	eye
aus	from, out of
aus/gehen*	to go out
aus/packen	to unpack
aus/sehen*	to look (like)
das Ausland	abroad
außerdem	moreover
die Ausstellung(-en)	exhibition
das Auto(-s)	car

B

die Bäckerei(-en)	bakery
das Bad(-¨-er)	bath
das Baguettebrötchen(-)	bread roll
der Bahnhof(-¨-e)	station
bald	soon
die Banane(-n)	banana
die Bank(-en)	bank
bar	cash
die Bar(-s)	bar
der Bart(-¨-e)	beard
der Baum(-¨-e)	tree
die Baumwolle (pl.)	cotton
beantworten	to answer

237

die **Bedienung(-en)**	service	**danke, gleichfalls**	thank you, the
befreien	to free		same to you
beginnen*	to begin	**danken**	to thank
bei	at	**dann**	then
bei Ihnen	at your place, at	**daraufhin**	thereupon
	your company	**darunter**	underneath
beliebt	popular	**das**	that
der **Beruf(-e)**	occupation	**dass**	that
berühmt	famous	**dazu**	with it, with them
besichtigen	to go sightseeing	**dein**	your [informal]
besonders	particularly	**denn**	for, because, then
besser	better	**deshalb**	for that reason
bestellen	to order	**Deutsch**	German
bestimmt	certainly	der **Deutsche(-n)**	(male) German
der **Besuch(-e)**	visit	die **Deutsche(-n)**	(female) German
besuchen	to visit	**Deutschland**	Germany
bezahlen	to pay	der **Dezember**	December
das **Bier**	beer	die **Diät(-en)**	diet
billig	cheap	**dick**	fat, big
bis	until	der **Dienstag(-e)**	Tuesday
bis morgen!	see you	**dieser**	this
	tomorrow!	das **Ding(-e)**	thing
bis später!	see you later!	**direkt**	direct
bitte	please	**doch**	all the same, but
blass	pale	der **Donnerstag(-e)**	Thursday
blau	blue	das **Doppelzimmer(-)**	double room
bleiben*	to stay	das **Dorf(-¨-er)**	village
blond	blond	**dort**	there
die **Bluse(-n)**	blouse	**dort drüben**	over there
brauchen	to need	**dort hinten**	back there
braun	brown	**dorthin**	there
die **Brezel(-n)**	pretzel	**dritte**	third
der **Brief(-e)**	letter	**drücken**	to push [*a button*]
die **Briefmarke(-n)**	stamp	**durch**	through
die **Brille(-n)**	glasses	**dürfen** (*mix.*)	to be allowed to
bringen*	to bring	die **Dusche(-n)** shower	
der **Brite(-n)**	British (male)	**duschen**	to shower
die **Britin(-nen)**	British (female)		
das **Brot(-e)**	(loaf of) bread	**E**	
das **Brötchen(-)** roll			
der **Bruder(-¨-)**	brother	**eigentlich**	actually
das **Büfett(-s)**	buffet	**ein bisschen**	a little bit
die **Bulette(-n)**	rissole	**eine Radtour machen**	to go for a bicycle
bunt	colourful		ride, cycling tour
das **Büro(-s)**	office	**eine Wanderung machen**	to go on a hiking
der **Bus(-se)**	bus		trip
		die **einfache(-n) Fahrkarte(-n)**	single ticket, one-
C			way ticket
		ein frohes neues Jahr!	Happy New Year!
das **Café(-s)**	café	**ein/gießen***	to pour
der **Chef(-s)**	boss	**ein/kaufen**	to shop
der **Computer(-)**	computer	die **Einkaufspassage(-n)**	shopping mall
		ein/laden*	to invite
D		**ein paar**	a few
		ein/schlafen*	to fall asleep
da	there	die **Eintrittskarte(-n)**	ticket
dabei	with	**ein/werfen***	to insert
	him/her/it/them	das **Einzelzimmer(-)**	single room
dabei sein*	to be there	das **Eis (sing.)**	ice cream
damals	at that time, then	die **Eltern (pl.)**	parents
die **Dame(-n)**	woman, lady	**empfehlen***	to recommend
danach	after that	**empfindlich**	sensitive
danke	thank you	**endlich**	at long last

England	England	der Friseur(-e)	hairdresser
der Engländer(-)	English (male)	die Frisur(-en)	hairdo
die Engländerin(-nen)	English (female)	froh	glad
entnehmen*	to take out	frohe Weihnachten!	merry Christmas!
entscheiden*	to decide	früh	early
Entschuldigung!	excuse me!	früher	earlier, in the past
er	he	das Frühstück(-e)	breakfast
die Erdbeere(-n)	strawberry	das Fundbüro(-s)	lost property
das Ereignis(-se)	event		office
die Erkältung(-en)	cold	für	for
die Ernährung (sing.)	diet	furchtbar	awful, dreadful
ernst	serious	der Fuß(-̈-e)	foot
erst	only, not until		
der Erwachsene(-n)	adult	**G**	
es	it		
es gefällt mir	I like it	ganz	really, very, whole
es geht mir (nicht) gut	I'm (not) well	ganz besonders	particularly
es gibt (dort)	there is, there are	ganz schön	quite [colloquial]
essen*	to eat	gar nicht	not at all
das Essen(-)	food, meal	der Gast(-̈-e)	guest
etwas	something	gebacken	baked
etwas gerne tun*	to like doing	geben*	to give
	something	gefallen*	to please
etwas unternehmen*	to do something	gegen	against
euer	your (informal, pl.)	gehen*	to go
		gehören	to belong to
F		gelangen	to reach, to
			arrive, to get into
fahren*	to drive, to go [in	gelb	yellow
	a vehicle], to run	das Geld(-er)	money
	[of a train]	der Geldschein(-e)	bank note
der Fahrkartenschalter(-)	ticket office	das Gemüse(-)	vegetable(s)
der Fahrschein(-e)	ticket	die Gemüsesuppe(-n)	vegetable soup
das Fahrtziel(-e)	destination	gemütlich	leisurely, relaxed
falsch	wrong	genau	exactly
die Familie(-n)	family	genug	enough
fern/sehen*	to watch TV	gerade	right now
fett	fat	geradeaus	straight
das Fett(-e)	fat	das Gerät(-e)	piece of
fettarm	low-fat		equipment
die Figur(-en)	figure	gerne	certainly, with
der Film(-e)	film, movie		pleasure
finden*	to find	das Geschäft(-e)	shop, store
die Firma (die Firmen)	company	der Geschäftsbrief(-e)	business letter
der Fisch(-e)	fish	die Geschäftsreise(-n)	business trip
die Flasche(-n)	bottle	das Geschenk(-e)	gift
das Fleisch (sing.)	meat	die Geschichte(-n)	story
die Forelle(-n)	trout	geschieden	divorced
das Foto(-s)	photo	geschlossen	closed
fragen	to ask	der Geschmack(-̈-er)	taste
Frankreich	France	das Gespräch(-e)	conversation,
der Franzose(-n)	French (male)		discussion
die Französin(-nen)	French (female)	gestern	yesterday
Frau	Mrs	gesund	healthy
die Frau(-en)	woman, wife	gesundheitsbewusst	health conscious
das Fräulein(-)	Miss	die Getränkekarte(-n)	drinks list
frei	vacant	getrennt	separate(ly)
frei haben*	to be off	gewinnen*	to win
der Freitag(-e)	Friday	das Gewürz(-e)	spice
der Freund(-e)	(boy)friend	das Glas(-̈-er)	glass, jar
die Freundin(-nen)	(girl)friend	glauben	to think
freundlich	friendly	gleich	right away
frisch	fresh		

gleich neben	right next to
das Gleis(-e)	(railway) track
grau	grey
Griechenland	Greece
groß	big
Großbritannien	Great Britain
die Größe(-n)	size
die Großmutter(-¨-er)	grandmother
grün	green
der Gruß(-¨-e)	greetings
grüßen	to greet
gut	good

H

haben*	to have
das Hähnchen(-)	chicken
halb	half
halbtrocken	medium dry
der Hals(-¨-e)	throat
die Halsschmerzen (pl.)	sore throat
die Hand(-¨-e)	hand
die Handtasche(-n)	handbag
das Hauptgericht (-e)	main course
das Haustier(-e)	pet
heiraten	to get married
heiß	hot
heißen*	to be called
helfen*	to help
das Hemd(-en)	shirt
heraus/finden	to find out
her/kommen	to come here
Herr	Mr
der Herr(-en)	man, gentleman
herzlich	warm, kind
herzlich willkommen!	welcome!
herzlichen Glückwunsch!	congratulations!
heute	today
heutzutage	nowadays
hier	here
die Hin- und Rückfahrkarte(-n)	return ticket, round-trip ticket
hin/fallen*	to fall down, to fall over
hinter	behind
hoch	high
die Hochzeitsreise(-n)	honeymoon
höher	higher
die Hose(-n)	trousers, pants
der Hosenanzug(-¨-e)	trouser suit, pantsuit
das Hotel(-s)	hotel
der Hunger (sing.)	hunger
Hunger haben*	to be hungry
der Husten(-)	cough
der Hustensaft(-¨-e)	cough syrup

I

der IC-Zuschlag(-¨-e)	Intercity surcharge
die Idee(-n)	idea
Ihr	your [formal]

ihr	her, their
im Moment	currently
im Angebot	on offer
immer	always
immer geradeaus	straight ahead
in	in
in Ordnung sein	to be all right
der Ingenieur(-e)	(male) engineer
die Ingenieurin(-nen)	(female) engineer
insgesamt	altogether, in all
die Inszenierung(-en)	production
interessant	interesting
Italien	Italy
der Italiener(-)	(male) Italian, Italian (restaurant)
die Italienerin(-nen)	(female) Italian

J

die Jacke(-n)	jacket
das Jahr(-e)	year
der Januar	January
jeder	every
jetzt	now
der Job(-s)	job
jung	young

K

der Kaffee(-s)	coffee
die Kantine(-n)	canteen
die Kasse(-n)	ticket counter
kaufen	to buy
das Kaufhaus(-¨-er)	department store
kaum	hardly, scarcely
kein	not a, not any, no
der Kellner(-)	waiter
die Kellnerin(-nen)	waitress
kennen (mix.)	to know [person]
kennen lernen	to get to know, to meet (for the first time)
das Kilo(-)	kilo
das Kind(-er)	child
das Kino(-s)	cinema, movie theatre
das Kleid(-er)	dress
klein	small
klettern	to climb
die Kneipe(-n)	pub, bar
der Koffer(-)	suitcase
der Kollege(-n)	(male) colleague
die Kollegin(-nen)	(female) colleague
kommen*	to come
die Komödie(-n)	comedy
die Konditorei(-en)	cake shop
können (mix.)	to be able
das Konzert(-e)	concert
die Konzertkarte(-n)	concert ticket
der Kopf(-¨-e)	head
der Kopfschmerz(-en)	headache

Kopfschmerzen haben*	to have a headache
die Kopfschmerztablette(-n)	painkiller
kosten	to cost
das Kostüm(-e)	suit [*jacket and skirt*]
Krach haben*	to have a fight [*colloquial*]
der Krach(-̈-e)	fight, row
kräftig	strong
der Kragen(-)	collar
die Kreditkarte(-n)	credit card
die Kreuzung(-en)	crossroads
die Küche(-n)	kitchen, cuisine
die Kunstgalerie(-n)	art gallery
der Künstler(-)	artist

L

lang	long
lange schlafen*	to lie in
längst	a long time ago
langweilig	boring
laufen*	to run, to be on
leben	to live
lebendig	lively
die Lebensmittel (pl.)	groceries
der Lehrer(-)	(male) teacher
die Lehrerin(-nen)	(female) teacher
leicht	easily
leider	unfortunately
lesen*	to read
letzter	last
die Leute (pl.)	people
lieber	preferably, rather
liefern	to deliver
die Lieferung(-en)	delivery
liegen*	to lie
links	left
los/gehen*	to set off
lustig	amusing, funny

M

machen	to make, to do
-mal	times
mal	once in a while
manche	some
manchmal	sometimes
der Mann(-̈-er)	man, husband
der Mantel(-̈-)	coat
der Marktplatz(-̈-e)	market place
mehr	more
mein	my
meinen	to mean, to think
der Meter(-)	meter
die Metzgerei(-en)	butcher's
die Milch (sing.)	milk
die Million(-en)	million
das Mineralwasser(-̈-)	mineral water
die Minute(-n)	minute
mit	with
mit/kommen*	to come too

mit/nehmen*	to take along
mit/bringen*	to bring along
mitleidig	sympathetic
der Mittag(-e)	noon
das Mittagessen(-)	lunch
die Mittagspause(-n)	lunch break
mittelgroß	of medium height
der Mittwoch(-e)	Wednesday
das Modell(-e)	style, model
möchte	would like
mögen (mix.)	to like
der Moment(-e)	moment
der Monat(-e)	month
der Montag(-e)	Monday
morgen	tomorrow
müde	tired
der Mund(-̈-er)	mouth
das Museum (Museen)	museum
das Müsli(s)	muesli
müssen (mix.)	must, have to
die Mutter(-̈-)	mother

N

na?	well? why?
nach	to, after
der Nachmittag(-e)	afternoon
die Nachspeise(-n)	dessert
nächste	next
die Nacht(-̈-e)	night
nah	near
näher	nearer
der Name(-n)	name
die Nase(-n)	nose
natürlich	of course
neben	beside, next to
nehmen*	to take, to have
nein	no
nett	nice, kind
nicht	not
das Nichtraucherabteil(-e)	non-smoking compartment
nichts	nothing
noch etwas?	anything else?
noch nicht	not yet
die Nummer(-n)	number
nur	only

O

ob	whether
das Obst (sing.)	fruit
oder	or
öffnen	to open
die Öffnungszeit(-en)	opening time
oft	often
ohne	without
das Öl(-e)	oil
der Orangensaft(-̈-e)	orange juice
Österreich	Austria
die Ostsee	Baltic Sea

P

ein paar	a few
packen	to pack
die Packung(-en)	pack
die Papiere (*pl.*)	(ID) papers
der Parkplatz(-¨-e)	car park, parking lot
passen	to fit
passend	suitable
passieren	to happen
patent	capable
die Pension(-en)	guest house
perfekt	perfect
die Person(-en)	person
das Pfund(-e)	pound
der Plan(-¨-e)	plan
die Platzreservierung(-en)	seat reservation
die Polizei (sing.)	police
die Post	post office
die Postkarte(-n)	postcard
die Postleitzahl(-en)	post code, ZIP code
der Preis(-e)	price
pro	per
pro Stück	each, apiece
probieren	to try
das Problem(-e)	problem
der Programmierer(-)	(male) programmer
die Programmiererin(-nen)	(female) programmer
der Prospekt(-e)	brochure
Prost Neujahr!	Happy New Year!
prost!	cheers!
der Pullover(-)	pullover
putzen	to clean

R

Rad fahren*	to cycle
rauchen	to smoke
das Raucherabteil(-e)	smoking compartment
die Rechnung(-en)	bill, check
rechts	right
der Reis (sing.)	rice
die Reise(-n)	journey, trip
reisen	to travel
die Reisetasche(-n)	holdall
reservieren	to reserve, to book
der Rest	change [*money*]
das Restaurant(-s)	restaurant
richtig	right
das Rindfleisch (sing.)	beef
der Rock(-¨-e)	skirt
romantisch	romantic
rot	red
der Rotwein(-e)	red wine
der Rücken(-)	back
die Rückenschmerzen (*pl.*)	backache
rudern	to row

rufen*	to call
ruhig	quiet
ruhig halten*	to keep still

S

sagen	to say
die Sahne	(whipped) cream
die Sahnetorte(-n)	gâteau
der Salat(-e)	salad
die Salbe(-n)	ointment
der Salbei(-)	sage
der Samstag(-e)	Saturday
satt	full
schade	that's a pity
der Schal(-s)	scarf
der Schalter(-)	ticket office
der Scheck(-s)	cheque
scheinen*	to shine
schick	chic, stylish
schicken	to send
schlafen*	to sleep
schlagen*	to hit
schlank	slim
schließen*	to close
die Schmerztablette(-n)	painkiller
schnell	fast, quickly
der Schnupfen(-)	runny nose
die Schokolade(-n)	chocolate
schon	already
schön	nice, beautiful
der Schotte(-n)	Scottish (male)
die Schottin(-nen)	Scottish (female)
schreiben*	to write
der Schuh(-e)	shoe
die Schule(-n)	school
der Schüler(-)	male pupil
schwarz	black
das Schweinefilet(-s)	fillet of pork
die Schweiz	Switzerland
die Schwester(-n)	sister
das Schwimmbad(-¨-er)	swimming pool
schwimmen*	to swim
sehen*	to see
sehr	very
sein	his, its
sein*	to be
seit	since
seitdem	since then
die Seite(-n)	side
der Sekretär(-e)	(male) secretary
die Sekretärin(-nen)	(female) secretary
servieren	to serve
sie	they
sitzen*	to sit
der Sitzplatz(-¨-e)	seat
Ski fahren*	to ski
so	like this, so
die Socke(-n)	sock
sofort	immediately
der Sohn(-¨-e)	son

sollen*	to be supposed to
der Sommer(-)	summer
der Sonnabend(-e)	Saturday
die Sonne(-n)	sun
der Sonnenschein (*sing.*)	sunshine
die Sonnenterrasse(-n)	patio
der Sonntag(-e)	Sunday
sonst	otherwise
sowieso	anyway
Spanien	Spain
der Spanier(-)	(male) Spaniard
die Spanierin(-nen)	(female) Spaniard
sparen	to save
spät	late
die Speisekarte(-n)	menu
das Spiel(-e)	game
spielen	to play
das Spielzeug(-e)	toy
Sport treiben*/machen	to play sports
sportlich	sporty, athletic
der Sportverein(-e)	sports club
sprechen* mit (+ *dative*)	to talk to
sprechen* über (+ *accusative*)	to speak, to talk about
die Stadt(-"-e)	town
die Stadtrundfahrt(-en)	city sightseeing tour
stattdessen	instead
stehlen*	to steal
stellen	to put
sterben*	to die
der Stiefel(-)	boot
die Stimme(-n)	voice
der Strand(-"-e)	beach
die Straße(-n)	street
der Straßenname(-n)	street name
der Streifen(-)	stripe
das Stück(-e)	piece
die Stunde(-n)	hour
suchen (nach)	to look for
der Supermarkt(-"-e)	supermarket
surfen	to surf
süß	sweet, cute
symbolisieren	to symbolize

T

der Tag(-e)	day
täglich	daily
die Tankstelle(-n)	service station, gas station
der Tannenbaum(-"-e)	Christmas tree
die Tante(-n)	aunt
tanzen	to dance
die Tasche(-n)	bag
die Tasse(-n)	cup
der Tee(-s)	tea
das Telefon(-e)	telephone
telefonieren	to call (phone)
die Telefonnummer(-n)	telephone number
der Termin(-e)	appointment
teuer	expensive

das Theater(-)	theatre
die Theaterkasse(-n)	box office
der Tisch(-e)	table, desk
die Tischdecke(-n)	tablecloth
die Tochter(-"-e)	daughter
toll aus/sehen*	to look great
toll	great [*colloquial*]
der Tomatensalat(-e)	tomato salad
die Torte(-n)	gâteau, cake
die Touristeninformation(-en)	tourist information office
tragen*	to carry, to wear
das Traumgehalt(-"-er)	dream salary
treffen*	to meet
trinken*	to drink
trocken	dry
trotzdem	nevertheless
tschüs!	bye!
tun	to do
tut mir Leid	I'm sorry
der Typ(-en)	type, kind

U

über	over, above
überhaupt	at all
die Übernachtung(-en)	overnight stay
übertreiben* mit	to exaggerate
übrigens	by the way
um	around, at
der Umkleideraum(-"-e)	changing room, dressing room
um/steigen*	to change trains
unbedingt	absolute(ly)
und	and
unser	our
der Unsinn (*sing.*)	nonsense
unter	under
unterwegs	on the way
Urlaub machen	go on vacation
der Urlaub(-e)	holiday, vacation
die USA (*pl.*)	the USA

V

das Vanilleeis (*sing.*)	vanilla ice cream
der Vater(-"-)	father
der Vegetarier(-)	vegetarian
vegetarisch	vegetarian
der Veranstaltungskalender (-)	calendar of events
verbinden*	to connect
verbrennen (mix.)	to burn
verbringen (mix.)	to spend (time)
vereinbaren	to arrange
vergessen*	to forget
verheiratet	married
verkaufen	to sell
vermissen	to miss
verpassen	to miss
verreisen	to go away
verschieden	different
verstehen*	to understand

243

viel	much	der Winter(-)	winter
viel Spaß!	have fun!	wirklich	really
vielleicht	perhaps	wissen*	to know [a fact]
vierte	fourth	wo	where
voll	full	die Woche(-n)	week
das Vollkornbrot(-e)	wholewheat bread	das Wochenende(-n)	weekend
		woher	where from
von	from	wohnen	to live
vor	before, in front of	die Wohnung(-en)	apartment
vor/haben	to intend	wollen*	to want to
vor/lesen*	to read aloud	worum	what about
vor/stellen	to introduce	das Würstchen(-)	sausage, hotdog
vorbei	past		
vorbei/kommen*	to drop in	**Z**	
der Vorsatz(-¨-e)	resolution		
vor/schlagen*	to suggest	die Zahl(-en)	number
vorsichtig	careful	zahlen	to pay (for)
die Vorspeise(-n)	starter, appetizer	zeigen	to show
		die Zeile(-n)	line
W		die Zeit(-en)	time
		die Zeitschrift(-en)	magazine
wählen	to choose	zerbrechen*	to break
wahrscheinlich	probably	ziehen*	to pull, to march
der Wald(-¨er)	forest	ziemlich	quite
wandern	to hike	das Zimmer(-)	room
wann	when	zu	to, too
warm	warm	zu Abend essen*	to have dinner
warten	to wait	zu/geben*	to add, to admit
warum	why	der Zucker (sing.)	sugar
was	what	zuerst	first, at first
was darf es sein?	what would you like to order?	der Zufall(-¨-e)	coincidence
		der Zug(-¨-e)	train
was macht das?	what does that come to?	die Zugverbindung(-en)	rail connection
		zum Beispiel	for instance
das Wechselgeld	change [money]	zum Glück	luckily [colloquial]
wechseln	to exchange	zumindest	at least
weg/fahren*	to go away [in a vehicle]	zurück/rufen*	to call back
		zusammen	together
weg/gehen*	to go away	zweite	second
weh/tun*	to hurt	zwischen	between
das Weihnachten(-)	Christmas		
weil	because		
der Wein(-e)	wine		
weiß	white		
der Weißwein(-e)	white wine		
wenig	little		
wer	who		
werden*	to become		
wie	how		
wie alt?	how old?		
wie bitte?	I beg your pardon?		
wie geht es dir?	how are you? [informal]		
wie geht es Ihnen?	how are you? [formal]		
wie spät ist es?	what time is it?		
wie viel	how much, how many		
wie viel Uhr ist es?	what time is it?		
wieder	again		
wiederholen	to repeat		
winken*	to wave		

Glossary of grammatical terms

Accusative case: The case used for the direct object.

Ich sehe **den Mann.** I see the man.

Adjective: A word used to give information about a noun.

der **kleine** Hund the small dog
der **blaue** Rock the blue skirt

Adverb: A word used to give information about a verb, an adjective, or another adverb.

Er arbeitet **schnell.** He works quickly.
Er ist **sehr** groß. He's very tall.
Er fährt **zu** schnell. He's driving too fast.

Agree: To match another word in number (singular or plural), gender (masculine or feminine), or grammatical person ('I', 'you', etc.)

Article: In English 'the' is the definite article and 'a' and 'an' are the indefinite articles.

Case: The case of a noun, adjective, or pronoun is the form used to show its function in a sentence. The case is usually indicated by the ending of the word. See also *Accusative case; Dative case; Genitive case; Nominative case*

Comparative: The form of an adjective or adverb used to express higher or lower degree. See also *Superlative*.

Das Flugzeug ist **schneller als** der Zug. The plane is faster than the train.

Compound noun: A noun formed from two or more words.

der Käse + das Brot
das Käsebrot cheese sandwich
der Abend + das Essen
das Abendessen dinner

Conjunction: A word used to combine sentences.

Ich gehe schwimmen, **oder** ich gehe tanzen.

I'll go swimming or I'll go dancing.
Ich kann heute nicht kommen, **weil** ich arbeiten muss.
I can't come today because I have to work.

Dative case: The case used for the indirect object.

Ich gebe **dem Mann** einen Apfel. I give an apple to the man.

Definite article: In English, the definite article is 'the'. The German equivalents are **der, die,** and **das.**

Direct object: The noun, pronoun, or phrase directly affected by the action of the verb. See *Accusative case*.

Wir essen **den Kuchen.** We eat the cake.

Ein words: Words taking the same endings as **ein,** e.g. **kein,** possessive adjectives (**mein, dein,** etc.)

Ending: A letter or letters added to the stem of the verb to show the tense, subject, and number; also to nouns and adjectives, to show the number, gender, and case.

er arbeit**et,** wir arbeit**en** he works, we work
die blau**en** Schuhe the blue shoes

Feminine: One of the three genders in German.

Future tense: The form of a verb used to express what will happen in the future.

Ich **werde** nächstes Jahr **abnehmen.** I'll lose weight next year.

Gender: In German, all nouns have a gender, either masculine, feminine, or neuter. Gender also affects the form of accompanying words such as adjectives, possessive forms, etc.

Genitive case: The genitive case is used to express possession.

Das sind die Kinder **meiner Freundin.** These are my friend's children.

245

Imperative: The form of a verb that is used to express orders or instructions, or to suggest that someone does something.

Gehen Sie um die Ecke. Go round the corner.

Indefinite article: In English, the indefinite articles are 'a' and 'an'. The German equivalents are **ein** and **eine**.

Indirect object: The noun, pronoun, or phrase indirectly affected by the action of the verb. See *Dative case*.

Sie kauft **ihm** einen Ball. She buys a ball for him.

Infinitive: The basic form of a verb which does not indicate a particular tense or number or person.

arbeiten to work   **sein** to be

Intonation: The pattern of sounds made in a sentence as the speaker's voice rises and falls.

Irregular verb: A verb that does not follow one of the set patterns and has its own individual forms.

Masculine: One of the three genders in German.

Modal verb: These are the verbs **können** ('to be able to'), **wollen** ('to want to'), **müssen** ('to have to'), **sollen** ('to be supposed to'), **mögen** ('to like'), and **dürfen** ('to be allowed to'), and the verb form **möchte** ('would like'). They are usually followed by an infinitive.

Ich **kann** heute nicht **kommen**. I can't come today.

Neuter: One of the three genders in German.

Nominative case: The case used for the subject of a sentence.

Der Mann ist alt. The man is old.

Non-separable prefix: A prefix that cannot be separated from the verb (ver-, ent-, emp-, er-, be-, ge-, zer-).

Noun: A word that identifies a person, animal, thing, place, idea, event, or activity.

Peter, der Mann Peter, the man
die Katze cat
der Tisch table
Spanien Spain
der Frieden peace
das Fest fete
das Segeln sailing

Number: Indicating whether a noun or pronoun is singular or plural. Number is one of the factors determining the form of accompanying words such as adjectives and possessive forms.

singular:	plural:
das Kind	**die Kinder**
the child	the children
der Mann	**die Männer**
the man	the men
eine Flasche	**die Flaschen**
a bottle	the bottles

Object: The noun, pronoun, or phrase affected by the action of the verb. See *Direct object; Indirect object*.

Past participle: The form of a verb used in combination with **haben** or **sein** to form the perfect tense.

Ich habe eine Jacke **gekauft**. I bought a jacket.
Er ist **abgefahren**. He left.

Perfect tense: The form of a verb used to talk about completed actions in the past. It is mostly used in spoken and informal written German.

Mein Bruder **ist** gestern nach Deutschland **gefahren**.
Yesterday my brother went to Germany.

Person: A category used to distinguish between the 'I'/'we' (first person), 'you' (second person), and 'he'/'she'/'it'/'they' (third person) forms of the verb. The person is reflected in the verb ending and/or in the pronoun accompanying it.

Ich arbeite. I work. (first person singular)
Du arbeitest. You work. (second person singular)
Sie arbeiten. They work. (third person plural)

Plural: Denoting more than one.

Possessive forms: Possessive adjectives are used with a noun to show belonging.

Das ist **meine Mutter**. This is my mother.
Kennen Sie **meinen Bruder**? Do you know my brother?

Prefix: One or two syllables in front of a verb which change its meaning. See also *Non-separable prefix; Separable prefix*.

halten to hold   **behalten** to keep
gehen to go   **untergehen** to sink

Preposition: A word (e.g. **an, bei, nach, unter, zwischen**, etc.) used before a noun or pronoun to relate it to another part of the sentence. Prepositions determine the case of the noun or pronoun to which they are linked.

Ich gehe morgen **ins** Kino. I am going to the cinema tomorrow.
Heiner kommt gerade **aus** dem Kino. Heiner is just coming out of the cinema.
Das Glas steht **auf** dem Tisch. The glass is on the table.

Present tense: The form of a verb used to express something happening or in existence now, or as a habitual occurrence.

Hanne **trinkt** ihren Kaffee. Hanne is drinking her coffee.
Meine Mutter **hat** braune Haare. My mother has brown hair.
Montags **gehe** ich immer tanzen. On Mondays I always go dancing.

Pronoun: A word used to stand for a noun. Pronouns may refer to things or concepts ('it', 'them'), or people ('she', 'him').

Kaufen **Sie** die grüne Jacke? Nein, **ich** kaufe **sie** nicht.
Are you buying the green jacket? No, I'm not buying it.
Er wohnt in Hamburg. He lives in Hamburg.

Regular verb: A verb that follows a common set pattern.

Separable prefix: A prefix that in the present tense and simple past is separated from the verb.

auf/stehen Ich **stehe** immer spät **auf**.
I always get up late.
Er **stand** spät **auf**. He got up late.

Simple past tense: A verb tense used mostly in written language in German as the equivalent of the simple past tense in English ('I went', 'I saw').

Er **bezahlte** den Wein und **ging**. He paid for the wine and left.

Singular: Denoting only one.

Stem: The part of a verb to which endings showing tense, number, and person are added.

arbeiten: ich **arbeite**, du **arbeitest**, ihr **arbeitet**

Subject: The noun, pronoun, or phrase that performs the action indicated by the verb.

Die Kinder spielen auf der Straße. The children play in the street.
Sie kommt morgen nach Hause. She is coming home tomorrow.

Superlative: The form of an adjective or adverb used to express the highest or lowest degree. See also *Comparative*.

Ich spiele **am liebsten** Fußball. I like to play football most of all.

Syllable: A unit of pronunciation which forms either the whole or part of a word.

die Zeit (one syllable) **die Kin/der** (two syllables) **das Re/stau/rant** (three syllables)

Tense: The form of a verb which indicates when the action takes place, i.e. in the past, present, or future.

Verb: A word or phrase used to express what is being done or what is happening. It can also be used to express a state.

Wir **gehen** in das Café. We are going into the café.
Es **regnet**. It's raining.
Er **hat** lange **geschlafen**. He had a lie-in.

Index

In addition to the Language Building pages listed below, see also the relevant section of the Grammar Summary.